BHUTTO

TRIAL AND EXECUTION

BHUTTO

TRIAL AND EXECUTION

Victoria Schofield

CASSELL

LONDON

CASSELL LTD.
35 Red Lion Square, London WC1R 4SG
and at Sydney, Auckland, Toronto, Johannesburg,
an affiliate of
Macmillan Publishing Co., Inc.,
New York.

First published 1979

ISBN 0 304 30539 1

Typeset by Inforum Ltd., Portsmouth
Printed and bound in Great Britain by
Billing & Sons Ltd,
London, Guildford and Worcester

'I did not kill that man. My God is aware of it. I am big enough to admit if I had done it. That admission would have been less of an ordeal and humiliation than this barbarous trial. I am a Moslem. A Moslem's fate is in the hands of God Almighty. I can face him with a clear conscience and tell him that I rebuilt his Islamic state of Pakistan from ashes into a respectable nation.'

ZULFIKAR ALI BHUTTO

CONTENTS

ILLUSTRATIONS

PREFACE

No one is going to find it easy to write about the life of Zulfikar Ali Bhutto. To get at the truth a historian will have to steer his way between the views of enemies and friends alike. In Pakistan, as in many other countries, there is a tendency to create a cult around a political figure which hides his faults. But there is also the tendency, once the figure is no longer in the ascendancy, to erase the cult, by fair means or foul. With Zulfikar Ali Bhutto the two processes were going on at the same time and no doubt will continue to do so. The historian will have to distance himself and take a middle path with the man as he was, in the circumstances which prevailed. Undoubtedly he will go down in history as a controversial figure and a great leader.

The basic controversy lies between whether he was a dictator, as his enemies like to portray him, who ruined the country, caused the break-up of Pakistan in 1971 and brought the remaining half to the verge of economic disaster, and whose arrogance was surpassed by none; or whether he was a brilliant politician from a rich land-owning family who was inspired by socialist ideals and who determined against all odds to create a modern industrial society, a man who had ambitions with which he wished to inspire his countrymen in order to restore the morale and dignity of Pakistan after defeat in war. There are many who believe this latter view to be the correct one. But they add a few important riders: they admit but excuse the arrogance of a talented man; they also concede there was a degree of autocracy but regard this as acceptable in a country unused to the democratic process; but they see the biggest failure in his régime which brought Bhutto himself to his death, in the people who surrounded him: sycophants and fortune-seekers whose loyalty to him was only skin deep, particularly in the Army and the bureaucracy. As with other popular leaders who have fallen, the people who genuinely did support him were helpless against the might of military régime which took over.

Bhutto was highly intelligent, astute, energetic, hardworking and, above all, one of the most effective leaders of Pakistan, whose success was undoubtedly envied by many. At all times his opponents sought to prove that he had a motive to destroy one of his political opponents but very few carefully examined the obvious motives which people had to do away with him: personal dislike combined with jealousy, religious fanaticism, abhorrence of socialist policies which affected them adversely provided a sufficiently strong incentive for those who hated him to want to destroy him. The sycophants looked on as the wind changed direction. Every unrelated action of his subordinates was given a suspicious interpretation and alleged to have come from the Prime Minister. No effort was made to assume that he might in fact, have been innocent.

Putting events into perspective, his death was inevitable. Those who were blinded by hope, optimism and trust in the judicial institutions of the country only saw at the end that from the beginning the minds of the military authorities were already made up. The judicial process merely prolonged the agony and uncertainty. No one could honestly say that Zulfikar Ali Bhutto was sent to death for his alleged part in a murder; he was sent to death because in the political climate of Pakistan at the time, the people who had the power wanted him out of the way. Otherwise mercy could easily have been shown by the executive authorities. What deliberations they did have must have been over whether or not they would be able to get away with it. They scorned Bhutto's own claim that Pakistan would fragment if he, as the unifying spirit, were to be executed. But only if there is a long period of calm in a free society, unpolluted and unrestrained by the force of martial law, can he be said to have been proved wrong. At present the military authorities, keeping a tight hold on the country, do not show themselves the least bit anxious to put this claim to the test.

Such an obvious political motive makes the whole campaign against Bhutto appear as the product of those who detested him. Pakistan was angered by the amount of world attention focused on Bhutto's trial, pointing to the revolutionary measures adopted in neighbouring countries such as Iran and Afghanistan in comparison with its own judicial process.

When the question is put, why was there such interest in the trial of the former Prime Minister, the answer must inevitably come that more was expected from a country protesting its adherence to British common law traditions than that they would contemplate hanging their former Prime Minister on a split verdict where three out of seven judges said he should be acquitted.

I should like to thank Benazir Bhutto for her hospitality and kindness and generosity at a time when her life took a tragic and dramatic turn from her carefree days as a student at Oxford, to those of political turbulence and the death of her father in Pakistan. I should also like to pay my respects to Mr Bhutto's team of lawyers whose exhausting struggle I observed from close quarters — Mr Yahya Bakhtiar, the late Ghulam Ali Memon, Mr D.M. Awan, Mr Hafeez Lakho, Mr Mohammed Sharif and Mr Saleem Khan. I should like to thank Mr Awan in particular, for his help and advice over the legal aspects. My thanks also go to the friends I had in Islamabad who assisted me emotionally during this time: in particular the family of Mr Bhutto's dentist, Dr Niazi, and Gustavo Toro of the United Nations for their kindness. I am also grateful to the journalists I met who gave advice and encouragement to an aspirant member of their profession. However, all views and conclusions in this book are mine alone and I take sole responsibility for them.

Finally I should like to thank my parents who bore with the emotional uncertainty of my absence in a country ruled by martial law when my own activities, as a friend of Benazir, were under surveillance twenty-four hours a day. I am also grateful to my mother who, receiving chapter by chapter in the post, typed this manuscript. All views contained in this book are my own.

Victoria Schofield
Islamabad, Pakistan
April 1979

INTRODUCTION

Before the dawn of a warm, sunny day in April 1979 Zulfikar Ali Bhutto was hanged. Of Pakistan's line of rulers since its painful birth in 1947 one died prematurely, one was assassinated, another exiled, one died of old age. But only one has ever been hanged. No one could have predicted that the end of Zulfikar Ali Bhutto would come with the hangman's noose. In proceedings lasting a year and a half Bhutto was tried, found guilty of conspiracy to murder and sentenced to death. Throughout, the former Prime Minister maintained his innocence in such a manner as to cast eternal doubt on the verdict given.

At the height of his power Zulfikar Ali Bhutto was a well respected and internationally esteemed leader. He was polished, articulate and had a brilliant mind, with enough *savoir-faire* to tackle any political situation. He was heralded both inside and outside Pakistan as the man the country needed to keep it together. Most people assumed that he would rule Pakistan for a long time to come. 'I think I'll last longer than anyone else who's governed Pakistan,' he said, soon after he became President in 1971. But he did not; before the decade was over, he was dead. The circumstances surrounding his downfall are unique. It appeared to be more than just part of the game. According to those who supported the former Prime Minister, there was a political conspiracy against the undisputed leader of the people to overthrow him; moreover, the fight for his life became an event of world-wide importance to such an extent that people continually asked just what was so special about Bhutto.

*

Zulfikar Ali Bhutto was born into politics on 5 January 1928 in Larkana, a small village in the province of Sind. He had a politician for a father and a mother who was deeply concerned about the poverty of the masses. Almost, as it were, he developed his theory of the 'politics of poverty' from his parents. He was also born rich, of a wealthy land-owning family which gave him the opportunities and advantages, combined with his own talents, to reach his goal. As a leader he had charisma. He emerged on the political scene in Pakistan when the morale of the people was low. He could fire the people's imagination with his magnetic dynamism and his enthusiasm. He made his ambitions appear like their own. Although an aristocrat, he set out to show that he was one of the people. It was not an easy task — ridiculed by his friends, even the poor doubted his sincerity to start with. But he persevered. He promised a better life for the people, wearing a cap resembling that of Mao Tse-Tung as a symbol of socialism. Divesting himself of his well-tailored suit, he donned shalwar kameez — the baggy trousers and long shirt, the traditional dress of Pakistanis — and went to campaign in the bazaars and remote areas of Pakistan, previously shunned by politicians. At the age of forty-three he attained his goal — leadership of his country with the power to 'level mountains, make deserts bloom and build a society where people don't die of hunger and humiliation'.

'By and large the people understand,' he said, 'they know that I believe passionately in them and that if I am given the opportunity and the time I will make the country viable and strong.'

Bhutto's opponents said that he did not avail himself of the opportunity; his supporters, however, believed that he was not given enough time and by his premature removal from the political scene he was deprived of the opportunity.

Bhutto's early life set him on the road to success. His father — Sir Shah Nawaz Bhutto — as an influential politician knighted by the British had served on the Imperial Council. He was a close friend of Mohammed Ali Jinnah, the founder and Quaid-e-Azam of Pakistan. Bhutto himself wrote that politics is like a romance and at an early age he became involved, getting into trouble as a young boy for political activities during the 'Quit India' movement and 'Direct Action Day'. He continued his anti-colonial activities on the campus of Berkeley University, California, from where he graduated with honours in Political Science in 1950. Two years later he obtained an M.A. Honours degree in Jurisprudence with distinction at Christ Church, Oxford. He did not come from a mediocre background and he did not receive a mediocre education. He became a Barrister at Law at Lincoln's Inn — the hallowed Inn of Court of the Pakistanis ever since Jinnah was there. Bhutto lectured briefly in international law at the University of Southampton, the first Asian to do so. On his return to Pakistan in 1953 he started legal practice in Karachi. It was not, however, as a lawyer that he intended to make his mark, but as a politician. Bhutto was noticed and favoured by President Iskander Mirza and was sent as a member of the Pakistani delegation to the twelfth session of the United Nations in New York. The following year, in 1958, he once more returned to the U.S.A. to lead the Pakistani delegation at the U.N. Conference on the Law of the Sea, where he combined his legal knowledge and political expertise to make a memorable speech revered in the archives of the U.N. The name of Zulfikar Ali Bhutto was beginning to have a familiar ring both in Pakistan and in the outside world.

Political change did not prevent Bhutto from rising still further. A new phenomenon in Pakistan's unstable politics arose — the advent of military dictatorship. General (later Field Marshal) Ayub Khan swept Iskander Mirza out of power and out of the country, leaving him to be dumped in exile in London. But Bhutto's fortunes were still favoured. Ayub Khan made him a minister in his Cabinet. At the age of thirty he achieved his entrée into active political life with the portfolio for Commerce and was the youngest federal minister to be appointed in the Asian sub-continent.

Two years later he was put in charge of the newly created Ministry of Fuel, Power and Natural Resources. As Minister in charge of Atomic Energy he claimed to have laid the groundwork for Pakistan's bid to become a nuclear power. 'With granite determination,' he later wrote, 'I put my entire vitality behind the task of acquiring nuclear capability for my country.' He was sent to Russia to negotiate an oil agreement in 1960. Soon Zulfikar Ali Bhutto was directed into the realm of international politics, a field in which he blossomed. With the opportunity to become known to the world as Pakistani spokesman to the U.N. General Assembly in 1959 and 1960, he moved into a more prominent position as Foreign Minister in 1963. He continued to lead the Pakistani delegation at the U.N. and gained a reputation as an outstanding orator, making the most of his role as spokesman to make thundering attacks not so much on the U.N.'s role in Kashmir, as about India. These speeches were balm to the ears of Pakistanis, who felt that in the world forum the prospect of Pakistan ever getting Kashmir within its accepted boundaries was rapidly fading. When, after the dismal war of 1965 with India over Kashmir, Pakistan emerged once more the loser, Bhutto showed his disgust with the Tashkent Agreement negotiated under the auspices of the Russians, which was considered a sell-out to the Indians.

Bhutto was also getting restless under the constraints imposed upon him by the military dictator. He had new ideas for the country, better ones than those of Ayub Khan, he believed. Soon after Tashkent in 1966 he resigned as Foreign Minister: his opponents said that he was forced to do so. But ill-health was given as the official reason for his departure and he had a lavish send-off.

As it was, Bhutto had outgrown Ayub Khan. A year later he returned to political life to campaign against his former leader and make virulent attacks on him and his anti-people policies. The people themselves were weary of the military dictator and his four sons who they believed were despoiling the country. There was a political vacuum which was waiting to be filled by a new leader who could captivate the imagination of the masses and generate political consciousness. A party which was attractive to the people was bound to gain support; there were millions of poor voters who were anxious to entrust their mandate to a leader who had their interests at heart. Bhutto's own People's Party of Pakistan — called PPP — filled this void. Formed on 1 December 1967, its ideology of socialism and egalitarianism marked a radical change from the elitist politics of Ayub Khan's era. With Bhutto and his supporters campaigning all over the country it gained rapid support. Ayub Khan felt threatened by his former Foreign Minister and imprisoned him for anti-government speeches in 1968, putting him on trial in a military camp in Lahore. But this act virtually made Bhutto a hero overnight. Students, liberals and intellectuals were all looking for a spokesman for their grievances and Zulfikar Ali Bhutto was the man.

With turmoil in the country, Ayub Khan saw the writing on the wall and relinquished power. Bhutto was released in 1969; many came to him, eager to join his party since they could see the way the wind was blowing. But such was the instability that the chief of the Army, General Yahya Khan, had imposed martial law once again, becoming Pakistan's second military dictator. Bhutto remained in the limelight.

Unlike his predecessor, who had only held elections for the Presidency and was sure he himself would win against Jinnah's sister, Miss Fatima Jinnah, Yahya Khan took steps — slow ones — to hold elections for the transfer of power to elected representatives of the people. But the results of these elections led to more disaster for Pakistan. The leader of the Awami League in the eastern half of Pakistan — Sheikh Mujib ur Rehman — won an overwhelming victory, gaining 151 seats in the National Assembly. Bhutto's party gained the second largest majority with 81 seats. Disagreement arose over the Constitution. There had always been tension between the two halves of the country — West Pakistan was almost six times as large as East Pakistan but its population was only two-thirds that of the East. The East continually complained of domination by the West, where the administrative centre lay; with the recent election result, many West Pakistanis feared that the reverse would now be the case. Mujib ur Rehman appeared determined to institute his 'Six Points' on the whole of Pakistan, which amounted to virtual regional autonomy. Bhutto found this proposed framework of government unacceptable. Neither party could agree. The military, under Yahya Khan, hovering on the side-lines during the negotiations, pushing for an agreement to be reached, intervened unexpectedly and with great brutality to crush the Bengalis. With the intervention of India on the side of the Bengalis, who by this time were putting forward the idea of a completely independent country — Bangladesh, land of the Bengalis — the Pakistan Army was itself humiliated and defeated. It had to surrender ignominiously to the Indians at the Race Course at Dacca on 16 December 1971. Pakistan lost more than 5,000 square miles of territory in the west and the Indians captured more than 90,000 prisoners of war in the east.

Bhutto emerged as leader of truncated Pakistan. His enemies blamed him for the break-up of Pakistan, regardless of the impasse on both sides. They felt that Mujib's six points should at least have been tried. They thought that Bhutto, anxious for a compromise favourable for the west, perhaps did not show enough foresight and did not envisage the uncalled-for intervention of the Army. But when it came to the crunch it was felt that few in the west would have favoured Mujib's proposals. Undoubtedly, after the war, Bhutto was the undisputed leader of the western half which, although vanquished, still had great potential. The restoration of this discredited half of Pakistan was, therefore, in his hands. Still preaching socialism, he set about to build it into a strong and vibrant country. The 70 millions in Pakistan looked towards Bhutto to restore their honour and dignity in the eyes of the world. While instability remained, Bhutto became President and Chief Martial Law Administrator and an interim Constitution was signed on 12 April 1972. But he took the office of Prime Minister once the four provinces had agreed on a permanent Constitution which suited all their aspirations. It was signed on 14 August 1973, the twenty-sixth anniversary of Pakistan's independence.

People had high hopes when Bhutto came to power. In an interview with the Deputy Editor of the *Spectator*, he outlined his dream for the country: 'My vision is that of a Pakistan whose social standards are comparable to those in parts of Europe. This means a war against illiteracy and ignorance. It means fighting prejudice and obscurantism. It involves the equality of men and women. It demands the mobilisation of the people's collective energies. It dictates the restoration to the human person, the citizen of Pakistan, of the dignity which is his due. It requires a check on the growth of population and easy access to education and medical care throughout the country. It contemplates better towns and cities and cleaner villages. It poses a hundred challenges. It is a long haul. We have braced ourselves for it.' He clearly intended to show that he was the leader of a progressive, industrialised and democratic country, a country whose existence had been scorned from the start.

Pakistan was carved out of British India to be a pure land — 'pak' meaning pure — for the Moslems of the Asian sub-continent, but cynics believed that unity of faith was not enough to keep Pakistan together. The name Pakistan was formed from the names of the provinces which comprised it, though they had little else in common. P was for the Punjabis, A for the Afghanis in Frontier Province, K for Kashmir (an ever-fading dream), S for Sind and Tan for Baluchistan, a large sprawling province bordering Iran. The other half of the country, however, lay in the east on the other side of India, and was that part of the province of Bengal where the Moslems predominated. The fact that the vital link, the K for Kashmir, with its lush valleys, had never been incorporated into Pakistan, in spite of its Moslem masses, because its Hindu ruler had opted to join India, was an unending cause of instability and conflict with India. War had broken out in both 1948 and 1965.

The provinces of Pakistan differed ethnically, culturally and linguistically, each having its separate dialect. With the recent example of East Pakistan before them, many felt that Pakistan was doomed. Its creation by the iron will of Mohammed Ali Jinnah, who alone would not give way in spite of pressure from all sides to keep India united, was itself an agonising process. Millions in the Punjab and Bengal were slaughtered when these two provinces were partitioned — Moslems turned on Hindus, Hindus turned on Moslems — the Sikhs slaughtered both — there was no place for them. Separated by 1,000 miles of Indian territory many people believed it was only a matter of time before the two halves fell apart. And they were right. Now, without firm leadership, there was always the possibility that what happened in East Pakistan might recur in one of the other provinces if one felt dominated by the other. In order to avoid this, Bhutto sought to form the provinces into a federation. Ever since its inception, after the death of Jinnah in 1948, Pakistan had lurched from one lack-lustre civilian government to the next; then came the rule of the military, first under Ayub Khan, followed by Yahya Khan. Constitutions were imposed rather than unanimously agreed upon. In view of the recent loss of East Pakistan it was essential to have a *modus vivendi* amongst the remaining provinces, rather than relying solely upon the Islamic faith to bind the provinces together and prevent secessionism. No longer balanced by the weight of the eastern half, Punjab was the most populous province, with nearly two-thirds of the total population. The other provinces were liable to feel dominated and overpowered by the Punjab, especially since most of the Army was made up of Punjabis. It was a delicate situation which had to be handled carefully.

The 1973 Constitution was the first to be unanimously agreed upon by all the provinces and provided for a comparatively small but necessary degree of autonomy to be surrendered to a centralised government. In view of the regional and provincial feeling, people felt the adoption of the 1973 Constitution was an achievement. Moreover, all the political parties agreed to stand by it. Bhutto had this much headstart on the road to democracy compared with his predecessors.

For some this was not enough and insurrections both in Frontier Province and Baluchistan showed that the threads holding together the rest of Pakistan were still fragile. Under Abdul Wali Khan, a powerful Frontier leader, who headed the National Awami Party (NAP), there was a call for an independent Pakhtoonistan incorporating the Pakhtoon tribes on both sides of the Afghan border. The insurgency in Baluchistan meant that the Army, numbering 30,000 troops, was sent to prevent secessionism taking hold. Bhutto was criticised for what was considered to be the merciless crushing of the rebels, but it was felt that it was a case either of strong action or of disunity amongst the provinces, and the Army itself advised the Prime Minister that its continued presence was necessary.

Bhutto's primary concern was with the poor people. He intended to wrest the monopoly of Pakistan's wealth from the so-called twenty-two 'robber baron' industrial families who to date had controlled Pakistan's economy. He surprised the feudal landlords, to which class he belonged, by instituting more land reforms, which meant that both he and they had to surrender part of their lands. Industries were nationalised; so too were the banks. His socialist policies were opposed by many of the élite but Bhutto saw no other way. He also realised that by gaining the support of the masses he would have the majority of the people behind him. He took time and trouble to visit the more far-flung parts of Pakistan and the tribal areas to make sure that the basic amenities of life, such as water and electricity, reached them. Programmes which appealed to the people were adopted, cities were beautified; social reforms were undertaken. Women were to be recognised as individuals as opposed to being treated as chattels of men; jobs in the civil and foreign services were opened to them. Bhutto's opponents criticised him for excessive spending on lavish projects but he felt it was necessary for the morale of the people to create the image of a modern Islamic republic both at home and abroad. Even cosmetic changes, such as making Friday the day of rest according to Islam instead of Sunday, the day observed by Christians, or changing the Red Cross organisation to the Red Crescent, made Pakistanis feel that they were gaining the identity for which they had been searching for so long. It gave them dignity and restored their confidence.

Industrial projects like the Karachi steel mill, financed and built by the Soviet Union, gave more in terms of political prestige because the cost of its maintenance was vast compared with its as yet unapparent contribution to industry. But it was a method of keeping channels of communication and furthering development. Likewise, the rebuilding of the Karakoram Highway with the help of the Chinese was an immense boost to Pakistan's prestige, later to be completed by the military authorities who took all the credit for concluding a project initiated by Bhutto. But policies which required large deficit financing caused economic difficulties for Pakistan. Inflation was high for most of his tenure of power. His opponents on the side-lines, oblivious of the benefits of his policies, murmured that he was heading straight for an economic crisis. It was just one more aspect of his government for his critics to take hold of and use against him.

Pakistan formed a bridge with the Moslem Arab world. Bhutto strengthened this link by championing the cause of the Arabs and especially the Palestinians. It also served to show Pakistanis that their identity lay with the Moslems and partially cured their inferiority complex with regard to the preponderant number of Hindus on the other side of her border. Bhutto even attributed his downfall to the fact that he made no secret of his willingness to share nuclear technology with the Arabs, which gesture was frowned upon by the U.S.A. In February 1974 the Pakistani Prime Minister was chosen to be Chairman of the Second Islamic Summit Conference, an honour bestowed upon him by the late King Faisal of Saudi Arabia. The Conference was held at Lahore and it was a great boost to the prestige of Pakistan to act as host to so many Moslem monarchs, presidents, prime ministers and foreign ministers at a time when the Middle East and the Arabs began calling the tune regarding oil prices and everyone wanted to be their friend.

Bhutto also looked towards relations with his neighbour Afghanistan. The border line — along the Durrand Line, a name bestowed by the British in the nineteenth century — had never been amicably agreed upon since it cut across tribal frontiers. It would have been a great achievement to settle this and would have silenced altogether the cries of secessionism voiced by Wali Khan until he was finally tried and imprisoned for high treason. Bhutto was on the verge of exchanging Wali Khan's freedom for the recognition of the border line by the Afghan authorities with the late President Daoud when Bhutto himself was removed from power by military *coup d'état* in July 1977.

But the most important aspect of foreign affairs was the relationship with India — one of the reasons why Bhutto nurtured the shattered Army and negotiated for modern arms and equipment. To him, as to any Pakistani, to have been defeated in war not once but three times by the Indians, each time losing sight still further of the hope of ever getting Kashmir, was a great humiliation. Ever conscious of the dominance of India, Bhutto intended to divest Pakistan of its perpetual fear of once more being engulfed as part of undivided India, with other neighbours grabbing the outlying provinces of Pakistan. The agreement reached at Simla in 1972 with Mrs Indira Gandhi, then Prime Minister of India, maintaining the *status quo* over Kashmir, was designed to show that the two powers were on an equal footing and was supposed to restore relations after the Pakistani defeat by the Indian Army the previous year. Bhutto obtained the release of the 90,000 prisoners of war and the return of the 5,000 square miles of territory taken by the Indians in the war over Bangladesh. Much later, on the eve of Bhutto's death — betrayed as he believed by these same prisoners of war, most of whom had returned to active duty in the Army — two of them wrote a letter to the press imploring mercy for the former Prime Minister and recalling with gratitude that they had been amongst those 90,000 soldiers whose release

Bhutto secured.

The Prime Minister of Pakistan did not want to see his country left behind in any race, especially if it involved India. The negotiation of the Nuclear Re-processing Plant Agreement with France in August 1976 was undoubtedly influenced by the fact that India already had nuclear capability as the result of an agreement with Canada. It was not only a matter of prestige but, Bhutto believed, of political survival in the sub-continent. Pakistan felt it was all very well for the U.S.A. and countries who had nuclear power to talk of non-proliferation but they could hardly expect Pakistan to be happy with a state of affairs where her lifelong rival India had the capability and Pakistan did not. The Nuclear Re-processing Plant with its device for separating plutonium would not only enable Pakistan to use nuclear energy for peaceful purposes — her avowed intention also maintained by the military régime — but would obviously also permit her to make nuclear weapons should she so desire.

Bhutto was always aware of Pakistan's precarious position with its neighbours, much like a sailing boat outflanked by battleships. He knew that any sign of weakness or instability within Pakistan's borders might cause one or other power to take advantage of this. One of the best ways of preventing this, he believed, was to have strong and independent relations with all the powers. Contrary to Pakistan's western-orientated policy of the past, Bhutto wanted to put Pakistan back where he believed the country belonged: in proper perspective with its neighbours. To do so he wished to move out of the American camp and establish his own relations with the other great powers, which was part of the reasoning behind the building of the Karachi steel mill and the Karakoram Highway. He also had firm relations with the now deposed Shah of Iran. Bhutto promoted the idea that Pakistan should be non-aligned and should make bilateral agreements. Again this was something which he believed would give self-respect to Pakistanis all over the world. He withdrew from the Commonwealth, which many people regarded as a publicity stunt, because he wanted to draw Pakistan away from multilateral obligations which would result in her becoming a pawn or a cat's paw in the interests of other countries. For similar reasons he advocated leaving CENTO, again a policy which the military régime took over.

With his own ambitions grafted onto the policies of his country it appeared that here at last was one leader of Pakistan who was going to make something out of Mohammed Ali Jinnah's dream of a strong, independent Moslem state. Many of his opponents believed that Bhutto made a mistake in thinking that whatever he considered was good for Pakistan must inevitably be so. They thought that, like many other politicians, he had fallen prey to a leader's belief in his own indispensability. They levelled their criticism, however, without realising that a country without direction needed firm and at times autocratic government. Whatever his faults, Bhutto was a man with mass appeal, a flair for foreign affairs and a belief in his own mission to lead his people. Pakistan expected a great deal of Zulfikar Ali Bhutto. When he took over the government of the country he said, 'I'm healthy and full of energy, I can work, as I do, even eighteen hours a day.' And he certainly gave a great deal of his energies to Pakistan.

But the enemies which Bhutto and his government inevitably made did not intend to remain silent. Those undoubtedly envious of his success, alienated by policies of which they did not approve, were supplemented by the ultra-conservatives who criticised Bhutto and his ministers for what they termed an un-Islamic life-style. Bhutto himself was attacked for his expensive taste in clothes, some of which he imported from abroad, along with quantities of valuable books. For a socialist they thought he lived lavishly, and the industrialists and middle-class shopkeepers — capitalists at heart — frowned upon the policies of nationalisation. Bhutto's introduction of prohibition did little to win over the extremists of the Islamic faith who belonged mainly to groupings such as the Moslem League and the Jamaat-i-Islami. It was even considered that one of his mistakes was to attempt to appease those who would always remain hostile to him. But busy with foreign policy or the interests of the people at large, surrounded by a vast bureaucracy, it appeared to some that he was not paying enough attention to the opposition he did have— small in numbers, but influential.

Bhutto's own personality— complex and at times contradictory with his 'western mind' and 'eastern soul' — also came under attack. People found him cool and collected, intensely emotional and at times totally unapproachable, which made some people believe that he was haughty and arrogant with supporters and opponents alike. The corrupt and sycophantic people who had crept into the Government remained there. It appeared that the party was gravitating from true socialism back into the hands of feudal tenure, not because Bhutto wanted it to do so, but because some of his ministers and supporters were not in reality as concerned about the masses as was Bhutto himself, and Bhutto did not oust them. Events in Chile in 1973 provided an example of what might happen to a leader who tried to introduce socialist reforms democratically. After the death of Chile's left-wing leader Salvador Allende it appeared that some members of Bhutto's Government, not anxious to suffer the same fate, moved more towards the right. But it did not please anyone. The left wing felt betrayed and scorned a timid socialism; the rightists could not be won over.

It appeared that the People's Party was tightening its hold on the government machinery. Opponents talked of a police state and considered that Bhutto was making himself into a tyrannical dictator. Not being in the seat of government themselves irked them; those who spoke up in opposition often found themselves in jail — terrorised, they said, and forced to drink the urine of their gaolers. Surveillance and tapped telephones added to the picture of the police state. But even so, if there was an element of autocracy, most people shrugged their shoulders. It was certainly nothing new; in general, the Prime Minister was not considered to be at fault, and many of the accusations of cruelty were attributed to his underlings, making the most of their power.

But for his enemies, hatred of Bhutto's rule and those who surrounded him, prompted them — when the tables were turned on the Prime Minister and they were in power — to castigate and denigrate every achievement of the Bhutto Government with a total lack of rationality and balanced appraisal. From their actions it appeared that they never wanted to see Bhutto back in power again and they went to extreme limits to ensure this, without any shred of mercy.

*

After five years in power Zulfikar Ali Bhutto decided to seek a new mandate from his people. In January 1977 he announced that elections would be held on 7 March of that year. With the Pakistan People's Party still retaining the support of the masses it did not come as any surprise that the PPP claimed to have won a massive victory when the election results were announced. They had swept the polls, leaving the opposition party — the Pakistan National Alliance, a combination of nine political groupings fused together for the occasion — with a paltry 36 seats out of a total of over 200 in the National Assembly. But the majority was suspiciously large and members of the Opposition stated that it was not credible.

People came out on the street to agitate against the election result; they burnt buses, causing disorder and unrest in the cities. The PNA alleged wholesale rigging of the polls by Bhutto's party; they complained of stuffed ballots, kidnapped candidates to prevent nomination papers being filed and all manner of illegalities. Bhutto's party made similar allegations. The disputed election result caused chaos in the country to the extent that Bhutto was forced to enter into negotiations with the PNA to try to resolve the differences. In fact, so organised was the protest that Bhutto's party believed some outside influence had funded the agitators. The finger was pointed at the U.S.A. and the C.I.A., mindful of events in Chile. Bhutto himself hinted at this in the National Assembly on 28 April. He made a fiery speech. 'The bloodhounds are after my blood,' he cried. He believed that the U.S.A. had an interest in dislodging him from power; when he went, it was believed, the Nuclear Re-processing Plant Agreement would also go. According to Bhutto, in October 1976 Dr Henry Kissinger — then U.S.A. Secretary of State — had warned him that if Pakistan did not abandon the Re-processing Plant Agreement a horrible example would be made of Mr Bhutto. Bhutto long harboured the idea that the U.S.A. must have been instrumental in the de-stabilisation of his régime but he also conceded that the 'betrayal' must have come from within.

'I would not have suffered the fate I am suffering had it not been for internal betrayal. I do not blame any outside power,' he wrote later from jail.

Negotiations between the two parties went on for four

months. Bhutto's main adversaries were the religious right-wing members of the Jamaat-i-Islami and the Moslem League, who not only opposed his socialism but considered him far too 'western' in his ways. They had only comparatively little allegiance amongst Pakistanis but still disorder and protests continued, with people anxious to benefit from a changing situation. In order to keep the peace Bhutto imposed partial martial law in big cities such as Karachi, Hyderabad and Lahore. However, opposition to Bhutto was mounting. Violence continued. The imposition of partial martial law was challenged in the courts as being 'unconstitutional'. Bhutto, who had maintained that all his actions were in accordance with the Constitution, was obliged to accept the verdict at the end of June 1977 that partial martial law was not acceptable under the Constitution. This gave the opportunity for total martial law — many wrongly believed, under Bhutto's instructions. Martial law came on 5 July 1977, imposed by the Chief of Army Staff, General Mohammed Zia ul Haq, who introduced 'Operation Fairplay' — a period of ninety days for the purpose of holding fresh elections under the supervision of the Armed Forces. This was Pakistan's third military *coup d'état* in less than twenty years. The Government was once more back in the hands of the generals. The question of course was, how long they would in fact retain it.

*

From the time of the *coup d'état* events moved in a direction which ultimately led the former Prime Minister of Pakistan to the gallows. The turning-point appeared to come with the *coup*. If that had not taken place the unsolved murder of Raza Kasuri's father would not have been resurrected after nearly three years and registered against the former Prime Minister himself. Bhutto would not have been arrested; he would not have been put on trial for murder. The trial court at Lahore would not have been set up; it would not have concluded its proceedings in camera, with the result that no one could scrutinise the final stages of the trial. Bhutto would not have been put in a death cell, which was to erode his health for the best part of a year. There would have been no necessity for an appeal in the Supreme Court of Pakistan which confirmed the sentence. Finally, if there had been no *coup d'état* led by the Chief of Army Staff, the former Prime Minister of Pakistan would not have been hanged as a common criminal before the ink was barely dry on the rejection of hundreds of mercy petitions on his behalf.

Other factors contributed to the chain of events: if Bhutto had not held the elections in March 1977, a year earlier than the date prescribed by the Constitution, his Government might not have been overthrown. After the elections Bhutto intended to weed out some of his less reliable ministers and some of the sycophants who had wheedled their way into the bureaucracy and who were to testify against him in free abandon. Perhaps he should have done so long before. Or perhaps, regardless of the stigma of the alleged rigging and in spite of advice from those around him, he should have taken the initiative to hold fresh elections immediately, after complaints and disorder showed that the PNA was not going to accept the results, before the military took it upon itself to impose martial law.

Bhutto's appointment of General Zia ul Haq as Chief of Army Staff, reportedly because he had shown himself as a 'simple soldier', uninterested in the realm of the politicians, added another dimension. Zia, one-time ardent supporter of Bhutto, became his implacable enemy. But he need never have become Chief of Staff. His appointment was over the heads of seven other generals who took precedence. One of the characteristics of Bhutto's tenure of power which people disliked was his tendency to advance people out of line. But Bhutto did so because often he spotted people whose talents appeared to surpass those in seniority. If Zia, with his religious fervour which turned into fanaticism, had not been appointed, the process of accountability might not have been started against Bhutto and his ministers. He might either have been shot on the spot in a revolutionary *coup*, which in comparison with the suffering Bhutto underwent in the ensuing months might have been preferable, or a general with different priorities might have held elections as promised and Bhutto would have been quickly reinstated. This ill-fated appointment, resulting in his own personal tragedy, was undoubtedly one of Bhutto's biggest regrets. Yet even this need not have been crucial if only Bhutto had never left himself open to the possibility of martial law. With fresh elections held whilst he was still the Prime Minister, Zia ul Haq would have had no pretext to emerge from his barracks. Even so, with the Opposition calling for Bhutto's resignation and fresh elections under the Army and the judiciary, he had very little freedom of action once the election result was contested; and his options closed rapidly.

Curiously the charge of conspiracy to murder which was brought against the former Prime Minister was one where the intended victim, Ahmed Raza Kasuri, was not shot, but instead his father, Nawab Mohammed Khan, was killed. If his would-be assassins had killed Kasuri himself, there might not have been the same urge to resurrect the murder case. Or, if the murder had not been filed as untraced and the real culprits had been caught, there would have been no way for Kasuri to have the case reopened.

The downfall of such a man as Zulfikar Ali Bhutto was a matter of concern not just to his people but to the whole world because of his eminence and the manner in which he was hounded. No one could rid the trial of its political overtones. Bhutto's opponents were glad to see him incarcerated and were little concerned whether or not the means were ethical. After all, had he not done the same to his enemies? they asked. It seemed to escape them that whatever the alleged wrongs of Bhutto's régime, they did not justify any injustice towards the former Prime Minister, especially when the military régime which they now supported could be weighed in the balance and found wanting. And whatever anyone had suffered during Bhutto's tenure of power, most were fairly confident, as the drama reached its concluding stages, that no one had undergone victimisation to the same extent as Bhutto.

In the coming months it was significant for Bhutto which of his friends would stand by him and which of his enemies would seek to make capital out of his downfall and jump on the bandwagon of the new military régime. Bhutto himself never lost his spirit, pledging himself eternally to the victory of the people, of whom he knew he was the undisputed leader.

1
MILITARY RULE

The *coup d'état* which abruptly terminated Zulfikar Ali Bhutto's tenure of office was a bloodless one. It was after midnight on 5 July 1977. At the time, Mr Bhutto was with his family at the Prime Minister's house at Rawalpindi. He had just been with his Education Minister, Abdul Hafeez Pirzada, and his cousin Mumtaz Ali Bhutto, his Minister for Communications. In addition to their political association they were close friends. They had been discussing the present political situation. Pirzada remarked that the steam had gone out of the opposition. Bhutto laughed and asked his cousin to wash off some of Pirzada's perennial optimism. To do so, said his cousin, he would have to take him to Sukkur Barrage Dam. They all laughed. They were more relaxed than they had been in the preceding months of agitation and protest.

But after their departure Bhutto was uneasy. As he prepared to go to bed he had a feeling something was about to happen. 'Within thirty minutes we heard the other laughter,' Bhutto later said. When therefore, his Military Secretary came to inform him of the military *coup* he was not altogether surprised.

As the deposed Prime Minister, Bhutto was treated courteously. He was given time to dress; he was then allowed to have a discussion with the family on the lawn of the Prime Minister's house, smoking his last cigar in these surroundings. At about 4 a.m. he was taken into protective custody and driven to a rest-house in Murree, a hill station and pleasant resort 2,000 ft above sea level. It was on the route used by the British in the hot summer months to reach the coolness of Simla, about forty miles from the twin cities of Rawalpindi and Islamabad.

Initially, Bhutto had no cause for undue alarm. Relations between the former Prime Minister and the man who ordered the *coup* as Chief of Army Staff — General Mohammed Zia ul Haq — had been good. There was close contact between the Prime Minister and the armed forces. Bhutto had done everything he could to restore the morale of the dejected army after the defeat in East Pakistan. He had even increased its divisions from eleven to thirteen. Just over a year before, in April 1976, General Zia had said that he hoped the Pakistani Army would be able to show that the attention and affection which it had received from the Prime Minister 'did not go to waste'. He lavished praise on Mr Bhutto. There was no reason for Bhutto to doubt his sincerity or loyalty.

Zia had strong reasons for being loyal to Bhutto because of his promotion to Chief of Army Staff above the heads of seven other generals. This should have rendered him grateful and contented. It added to the speculation after the *coup* that Bhutto had engineered the military takeover himself as a stop-gap measure to diffuse the agitation. Given the close association between the military and the civilians, this theory could have been feasible. But Zia looked as if he was listening to the religious extremists who had always opposed Bhutto. A particular grievance was that they said Bhutto's declaration of partial martial law in the main cities of Lahore, Karachi and Hyderabad was contrary to the Constitution, which document Bhutto maintained he observed in letter and spirit. This appeared grounds enough to institute complete martial law in the whole country. However, the Prime Minister trusted his Chief of Army Staff and went abroad at the end of June; in so doing he left the generals to plan the *coup* behind his back.

Bhutto said that there was, in fact, no necessity for the *coup d'état*. Ostensibly martial law was declared because of the failure of negotiations between the PPP and the PNA following the disputed election results. But both sides later said that they had reached agreement earlier the night before at 10.30 p.m. even though this has been denied by the military régime which took over. Nonetheless, it appeared that this martial law would not last long. General Zia made the announcement that its sole *raison d'être* was in order to hold fresh elections which, he said, would be 'free and fair'. These would be held within ninety days: the announcement was made all the more credible to the people of Pakistan by Zia's pledge on the Holy Koran that he would stick to his word. Both parties were to be allowed to campaign in what he called his 'Operation Fairplay'. Bhutto was exonerated by Zia for whatever misdemeanours might have occurred in the last elections. Zia also made it clear that in his opinion, anyway, rigging or no rigging, the People's Party would have won the elections. There was evidence, he said, that whatever rigging might have taken place in some of the constituencies, Bhutto was not to blame. Zia's statements were completely in keeping with what would be expected from a loyal army officer. He called Bhutto a 'very tenacious fighter and a great politician' — a man with a great sense of history. There was every reason to believe that Zulfikar Ali Bhutto would be back in power in no time.

Thus, from having been the elected Prime Minister of the country, Bhutto found himself in the position of having to contest elections once more, this time under martial law direction. He was, of course, confident that he would win. He was freed from protective custody on 28 July and early in August he went to Lahore. Huge receptions assured him that he still had the support of the masses. At Lahore he was met at the airport by a sea of people. In spite of the restrictions of martial law the PPP took over the airport and from the airport building hoisted the party flag, the colours of which — red, green and black — showed prominently against the blue sky. The police could not control the people, such was their enthusiasm.

Nonetheless, below the surface there was a certain amount of anxiety. It was unfortunate for Bhutto that the *coup* had not permitted the negotiations between the opposing parties to come to fruition. Yet he was sure that once the promised elections were held he would again be in control of his fate. Initially, Zia performed the role of the 'honest broker' who had merely intervened to bring stability to the country. But despite the promise that there would be no victimisation, a series of arrests took place after the *coup*. It seemed that some sort of clean-up operation was going to take place. Attention was focused on the Federal Security Force — FSF — the national police force designed to assist the local provincial police in keeping law and order. Called the grey-shirted FSF, it was considered to be Bhutto's personal police force and as a federal force it inevitably came under the jurisdiction of the central government. Many stated that the Army felt threatened by the FSF as it challenged its own power as a parallel nucleus of armed power. It was immediately disbanded and Zia ordered an enquiry into its affairs.

On the day of the *coup* the military régime arrested Masood Mahmud, the Director-General of the Federal Security Force. But Mahmud was arrested for his own alleged misdemeanours and no one was particularly worried. Yet he was never charged. Rao Rashid Khan, Bhutto's Intelligence Bureau Chief, was also arrested on 5 July. Later, on 6 August, one of the directors of the FSF at headquarters in Rawalpindi, Mian Mohammed Abbas, was taken in. Other arrests of members of the FSF also took place; throughout the hot summer months statements were recorded. A murder case which had been filed untraced was re-opened.

There were also a number of changes in personnel. Those who had not been favoured in Bhutto's rule with government service could now hope to gain from his downfall and fulfil thwarted ambitions. Once it was clear which way the wind was blowing some of those who felt they had grievances against Bhutto took the opportunity to air them. Eleven top leaders in Bhutto's Government were also arrested on various charges, mainly corruption while in office. Zia claimed that he was astounded to discover the misdeeds of the previous government. A puritanical régime with horrifying overtones seemed to be replacing that of Bhutto. Emphasis was laid on the more outdated aspects of Islam. Criminal and, as it turned out, political offences were made punishable by flogging. Those who stole were liable to have their hands cut off. Hangings could occur in public and three public hangings took place soon after the *coup*. Floggings too were often carried out in public and crowds flocked to see them out of a combination of curiosity and horror. These crude punishments marked a big change from the sophistication of Bhutto's régime. Although his tenure of power had been the target of criticism, many believed that whatever had gone on then bore no relation to what appeared like a return to barbarism. Yet what went on under Bhutto's régime was precisely what the military régime said it was going to investigate.

Finally, in the early hours of 3 September the military came to arrest Bhutto. This time it was not to take him into protective custody but to charge him with conspiracy to murder a political opponent. The arrest at his home in Karachi showed that the tune of martial law had changed considerably. The house, with its bronze plaque on the outside gatepost stating modestly 'Zulfikar Ali Bhutto — Barrister at Law', was raided. About fifty commandos and personnel of the Federal Investigating Agency (FIA) approached the house from all sides. Bhutto was arrested at the point of sten guns and other automatic weapons. Army commandos also entered the bedrooms of his daughters, the servants were beaten up, the house was ransacked. Later Bhutto described the whole operation as 'quite unnecessary'. 'I was not in hiding,' he said. 'The door-bell could have been rung, I would have gone out.'

Bhutto was flown from Karachi to Lahore and taken to an army bungalow which was fully guarded and barricaded. He hardly slept that first night of his imprisonment, listening to the ceaseless sound of the goose-steps of the army troops parading around the compound. Each room had a small blue light bulb in it, otherwise the place was dark. He was not allowed to contact anyone, not even his lawyers. He was plunged into virtual physical and mental darkness, ignorant of what might be in store for him.

Later in the night he was taken to be issued with a remand, but he was not permitted to see his lawyers for two days. Abdul Khaliq, the deputy-director of the FIA, came to him. He warned his former Prime Minister that if he did not 'co-operate' he should be prepared to face the painful consequences. Bhutto lost his temper, which brought forth an apology from Khaliq. This man was later a witness for the prosecution in the trial.

Having seen his lawyers on 5 September, the next day Bhutto was transferred under heavy army and police escort to Kot Lakhpat jail, about ten miles from the centre of Lahore. He was brought to court before Mr Justice Samdani on 13 September and granted bail. The charge was one of conspiracy to murder, but the judge said there was 'contradictory' evidence in the case, which meant he could not be re-arrested without the permission of the court. But this was nullified three days later on 16 September when he was seized under a martial law order. The regulation — No. 12 — which detained him was character-ised by its sweeping powers. It had unlimited power to arrest for three months (renewable on expiry) any persons 'To prevent them acting in any manner prejudicial to the purpose for which martial law was proclaimed or to the security of Pakistan'. This covered just about anything the martial law authorities cared to consider prejudicial. It did not need to furnish any grounds for the arrest.

At the time Bhutto was celebrating the festival of Eid, mark-ing the end of the month of fasting — Ramzan — at his ancestral home in the interior of Sind at Larkana. Surrounded by por-traits of his ancestors Bhutto appeared not only as a Prime Minister according to a democratically elected parliamentary system, but also as a powerful landowner whose wealth came from his ancestors and who was already well established as the leader of his people. The military surrounded the house of 'Al Murtaza' in Larkana in a similarly hostile fashion as they had in Karachi, army boots tramping over marble, their sten guns spotlit by the light coming from the chandeliers. Under heavy escort Bhutto was taken to Sukkur jail, about 65 km from Larkana, driving for the last time through his ancestral lands. He spent the night at Sukkur and then was flown to Karachi Central Prison. His final destination was Kot Lakhpat in Lahore. He was to be tried in the Punjab, in the province where the crime with which he was charged was committed. But instead of being heard in the lower sessions court where the case was registered, it was transferred to the High Court at Lahore. Bhutto was thus deprived of one right of appeal. The prelimi-nary hearing was fixed for 24 September. Many witnesses had already made their statements before the magistrate.

But even in spite of the arrest of the former Prime Minister, General Zia still maintained that elections would proceed as announced. The election campaign began on 18 September, only two days after Bhutto's arrest on the 16th. And in the elections lay Bhutto's hopes. He was totally convinced that there was no case against him, but surmised that the intention was to eliminate him politically from the scene by trying to discredit him in the eyes of the people with such a horrendous charge and thereby keep him in jail. He was still sure, however, that elections would be held and that his party would win. His belief was confirmed by the Pakistani spokesman's announcement at the U.N. General Assembly on 28 September. Before the world forum Mr Agha Shahi said that elections would be held in Pakistan on 18 October. But two days later Zia made a very different announcement, saying that elections were postponed indefinitely. Henceforward the promise of elections became a mirage. The breaking of Zia's oath sworn on the Holy Koran aroused suspicions as to the true motives of the 'simple soldier' who said he was anxious to return to the barracks as soon as possible. With Bhutto in jail charged with conspiracy to murder, and elections postponed indefinitely, there was little need for him to hurry his exit from the political scene. For Bhutto, it was a clear indication that quite possibly the result would be to eliminate him not only politically, but physically as well.

There was, of course, a way out of what was happening and that was to get rid of martial law. On 20 September Begum Nusrat Bhutto, wife of the former Prime Minister, challenged the validity of martial law in a petition in the Supreme Court of Pakistan. A day after the petition was accepted for hearing in the Supreme Court, all judges of the superior courts were requested to swear allegiance to the martial law régime over and above the oath they had already sworn to respect the Constitution of 1973. The Chief Justice of the Supreme Court, Mr Justice Yaqub Ali, refused to take the oath. He was replaced by a new Chief Justice, Mr Justice Anwarul Haq. Under his Chief Justiceship it was ruled that martial law should be validated according to the 'doctrine of necessity'. However, it was stipulated that its validation was for the purpose of holding free and fair elections. It further stated that the Constitution remained the supreme law of the land. But the nebulous 'doctrine of necessity' left loopholes. It was a matter for speculation just how long 'necessity' would demand the rule of martial law. Would the maxim 'Necessity makes the law' rule the day? Apart from everything else, it was feared that if the period were too long, although in theory the Constitution might be the supreme law of the land, in practice it would be indefinitely suspended. When, therefore, the time came to reimpose it, the provinces which with difficulty had surrendered a degree of their autonomy to a centralised government might not be prepared to accept it any longer. Thus the failure of Begum Nusrat Bhutto's petition to put a time limit on martial law meant too that no time limit could be put for the holding of elections.

As well as having to prepare his defence for the murder charge, the former Prime Minister was also arraigned for his political career. Following his arrest by martial law, he was obliged to appear in the Lahore High Court to answer political charges relating to the break-up of Pakistan in 1971. He defended himself in a 100-page affidavit the publication of which was banned. In it he castigated the military régime and his political opponents. 'My status is written in the stars,' he said. 'Your time will pass, my time will pass.'* Characteristic of the military régime's attack on the former Prime Minister, staggering publicity was given to the charges against Bhutto, but scant attention was granted to his replies, which he had to make from jail without the necessary facilities.

Bhutto also had to answer accusations in the Supreme Court regarding alleged rigging, bribery and corruption whilst he was in office. These charges amounted to more than sixty accusations with regard to the alleged misuse of government funds, in institutions and the country in general. The responses were later printed in pamphlet form and circulated as 'Chairman Bhutto's Rejoinder in the Supreme Court', which foreshadowed a greater document he would write and followed another response to yet more charges. From his cell, Bhutto took pains to show that certain luxury items which he had been accused of purchasing through embassies abroad out of official funds had been bought out of the family's personal account. He was accused of distributing motor-cycles and bicycles to party workers. To refute this, photocopies of invoices were reproduced in the rejoinder to show that they had been bought out of party funds. Other charges were vague and sweeping. 'I am not a walking encyclopaedia to retain all the information in my head,' he said, 'especially when detailed information is sought for almost every decision and every action covering the last five and a half years.' He felt bombarded by the questions levelled against him. 'Case on top of case has been instituted. We have to

---

* This was later printed by the Bhutto Memorial Trust and entitled *My Pakistan*

fill in forms galore virtually every day,' he said. 'How is it humanly possible to simultaneously attend to a host of vital matters in a period of a few days from the four walls of this jail? I do not have my books or files or papers with me in jail to do justice to all these mounting demands.'

In fact they soon faded into the background and attention was focused on the main charge against Bhutto — the one of conspiracy to murder. By the time the verdict in the constitutional petition in the Supreme Court validating martial law was reached on 10 November 1977 Bhutto was already on trial; the elections had already been postponed.

Once Zia had had his tenure of power legally approved, the process of accountability began in earnest. Henceforward his perpetual excuse for not holding elections was that accountability had to be accomplished before free and fair elections could take place. Such was the instability and, to a certain extent, sheer tedium caused by the prolonged process of accountability instigated against the former Prime Minister and many of his ministers, that people said that General Zia regretted not having turned, or on the other hand that he should have turned his *coup* into a bloody one. Keeping a rival for the leadership always poses problems. But at the time it was reasonable to assume that with charges of conspiracy to murder, corruption and rigging of elections against him, the popularity of the former Prime Minister would wane. It looked as though at first this was all Zia wanted. It seemed incongruous that the man who owed his own career and advancement to Bhutto would be prepared to see him obliterated altogether. In the early days Bhutto's supporters thought Zia was sincere, later they thought he was a hypocrite and a fanatic.

Although Bhutto believed the plot was hatched soon after the March elections, most people believed that Zia, possibly prompted into taking power by the U.S.A. and definitely by the religious right wing, groped his way into the role he was to assume. If he had not been interested in politics at the outset, it did not take him very long to enjoy the taste of power and seek to cling onto it on the pretext of accountability before elections. Behind the scenes, Bhutto's enemies were rejoicing at the prospect of seeing him done away with once and for all. They were convinced he was best out of the way, but in order for the whole operation to go through the legal process they did not mind the seemingly interminable court proceedings. Having the ear of the Chief Martial Law Administrator, they could sit out the bid to save Bhutto's life, mindful that power was in their hands.

Nonetheless, during the time of Bhutto's confinement, even after the sentence of death imposed on him, his popularity grew to such an extent that people believed even his death would not remove him from the hearts of the masses. Like it or not, he was becoming a legend, and the military authorities had to take the risk that in his execution he would become a martyr.

2
THE TRIAL

Almost every aspect of the murder case has been bitterly contested by both sides. But at least the time and place of the occurrence are accepted. On the night of 10 November 1974 some men armed with sub-machine guns were waiting, hidden by a shoulder-high hedge, at a roundabout called Shadman Shah Jamal in Lahore. Nearby a wedding ceremony was taking place. One of the guests was Ahmed Raza Kasuri, a member of Pakistan's National Assembly. He left the wedding ceremony after midnight, and drove off. His father, Nawab Mohammed Khan, was in the front passenger seat, his mother and aunt were in the back. As they reached the roundabout the car was moving slowly. The gunmen opened fire, hitting the car and damaging the dynamo. The car's lights went out. Firing continued as Kasuri accelerated away, believing that he had escaped the attack. No one was following; but soon Kasuri noticed that his father was resting on his shoulder. Blood was at his mother's feet.

Nawab Mohammed Khan was taken to the United Christian Hospital but died just before 3 a.m. The death of Kasuri's 72-year-old father, a man whom Kasuri described as being 'very kind' and 'my patron', was clearly accidental. Kasuri believed, rightly so, that he, not his father, was the target of the assassins. Before the ambush at Lahore there had been other attacks on him — in particular one in the town of Kasur in January 1972; another only a few months before the Lahore attack, in August of that year at Islamabad. Clearly, someone wanted to kill Kasuri.

Kasuri spent the best part of the night of the murder filling out the First Investigation Report (FIR). He was too disturbed to write it himself and so dictated it to a neighbour and friend, and signed it; in it he said that most probably the attack was political. He felt compelled to mention the name of the Prime Minister, Zulfikar Ali Bhutto, since he had in mind recent altercations in the National Assembly and their own political differences.

In a Privilege Motion in the National Assembly on 29 November 1974 which was, however, ruled out of order because it *was* out of order, Kasuri enumerated fifteen attacks made on his life from May 1971 to November 1974. During the investigation which took place to enquire into the murder, Kasuri moved away from the categorical accusation against the Prime Minister. In a statement made in February 1975 before the enquiry bench under Mr Justice Shafi ur Rehman, a prominent judge of the Lahore High Court, he said that there were four possible motives for the attack. He pointed to his political opponents in Kasur — a man called Yaqub Mann and others whom he believed had been responsible for the attack in Kasur; he also considered that since he had been criticising the Quaidiani sect in the National Assembly stating that they should be declared as non-Moslems, it was possible that some members of this sect had attacked him. Alternatively, any 'trigger-happy' individual, as he put it, in or out of government, belonging to the ruling party or not, could have attacked him. Finally, he stated that the Quaidianis living in Kasur city were opposed to him and could have made such an assault.

The investigation which took place did not turn up sufficient evidence to trace the assassins. Notably, the enquiry did not extend to the Federal Security Force — the national police force, which co-ordinated the activities of the local provincial police — the reason being that there was not considered to be sufficient evidence to take the investigation in that direction: the fact that the ammunition used was discovered to be of 7.62 mm calibre — a type used by the FSF — was not believed to be sufficient grounds since this calibre was also known to be used by the Civil Armed Forces as well as by private individuals. Ultimately, the case was filed as untraced; it was not the first murder case where the assassins had not been caught. The incident appeared to have been forgotten.

Kasuri accepted the condolences for his father's death from the Prime Minister and Begum Bhutto as well as from many others. He even appeared apologetic for having mentioned the name of the Prime Minister in the First Intelligence Report. Whereas previously he had criticised the Prime Minister in the National Assembly, he now turned to praise. He rejoined the People's Party and requested a ticket for the elections: this was refused. At the time of the July 1977 *coup* his political career was not progressing.

With fortunes rapidly changing after the military *coup* the murder case was immediately re-opened by Kasuri. This time the former Prime Minister became the principal target of the accusations. Bhutto was accordingly charged with having conspired to murder Ahmed Raza Kasuri with his Director-General of the FSF, Masood Mahmud. Already under arrest since the day of the *coup* for his own offences and corruption in office Masood Mahmud had decided on 14 August to make a 'clean breast', as he said, of all the misdeeds of the FSF. Amongst these misdeeds was the allegation that the FSF was used for the attack against Kasuri in November 1974 and more important that the direction came from the Prime Minister himself. But Mahmud was not charged with co-conspiracy; instead he was granted a pardon after submitting his statement before the magistrate and becoming an approver, i.e. turning State's evidence. So too, was the second approver — Ghulam Hussain — an Inspector in the FSF, who confessed to having organised the assassination attempt. Like Mahmud he had been arrested and kept in detention; two days after making his statement he applied for a pardon, which was granted.

Four others were alleged to be involved in the murder. They were put on trial with the former Prime Minister. But the case was known as the trial of 'Z.A. Bhutto and others'. Bhutto was referred to as the 'principal accused', wrongly, his defence lawyers maintained, since he was not directly involved in the crime, if he were involved at all. The case was not a private one, but instead the State was the prosecutor. Its case was that the FSF, in its capacity as the Prime Minister's police force, was used to carry out Bhutto's personal vendetta against Kasuri. Arshad Iqbal, an assistant sub-inspector in the FSF, and Rana Iftikar, a sub-inspector — both small fry in the force — were the 'assassins'. They were the men who fired the shots from behind the shoulder-high hedge. Another sub-inspector, Ghulam Mustafa, was said to have been involved in the supply of arms. The whole operation was supervised by Mian Mohammed Abbas, a director of operations and intelligence in the FSF, who had been deputed by Masood Mahmud to carry out the task. So ran the prosecution case. It stated that the order came from above — they were to kill or be exterminated themselves.

It was a great shock for the former Prime Minister to find himself on trial for conspiracy to murder but now, in the hands of the military authorities, he had to subject himself to justice in the ordinary manner. Many said that he was lucky not to be tried by a military court and done away with at once. But the court in which he found himself had its drawbacks. To start with, the judge who was trying him — the Acting Chief Justice, Maulvi Mushtaq Hussain — was his personal enemy. This caused Bhutto to have little faith in the proceedings from the beginning.

Their hostility dated back many years. In 1963 Bhutto was Foreign Minister and Mushtaq was Law Secretary. A misunderstanding arose between them during the debate on the fundamental rights bill in the National Assembly in Dacca. Later, Maulvi Mushtaq was the one who presided over Bhutto's trial in Lahore camp trial when he was imprisoned under Ayub Khan in 1968. Then too, there was hard feeling and a sharp altercation. Although released from jail, Bhutto was always anxious to point out that this was not because Maulvi Mushtaq had released him but because the government of Ayub Khan had withdrawn the detention order on account of the changing political situation. In the course of the trial Bhutto objected to Mushtaq's statement that he had given him a 'very fair trial' in Lahore camp jail, as though a fair trial were a favour rather than a right.

However, more important in the history of their relations was the supersession of Maulvi Mushtaq in the appointment of Chief Justice of Lahore High Court, an office which he deemed his by seniority. The issue of supersession was one which affected many judges in Bhutto's time; they took their ascendancy to positions in the Supreme and High courts as a matter of right according to seniority; however Bhutto, if he believed another judge to be more meritorious, was not beyond advancing him 'out of turn'. Bhutto's opponents believed that in this manner he put his 'own men' in the coveted places in the judiciary. Maulvi Mushtaq had been superseded not once but twice under Bhutto; clearly he had not forgotten this and even took it as a hypothetical case in a discussion during the course of the proceedings. Only after the *coup* did he achieve what he termed his rightful post as Chief Justice of Lahore High Court, shortly before he pronounced the death sentence on the former Prime Minister.

From Bhutto's point of view Maulvi Mushtaq — now an irascible lawyer in his fifties — was unsuitable on other grounds. Along with his office of Acting Chief Justice he was given the position of Chief Election Commissioner, an office which Bhutto believed had executive overtones and fused judicial and executive functions. Bhutto's party, the PPP, with himself as Chairman, were not above pointing this out at a meeting of the Central Executive Committee held in early August in Karachi. They felt that as an appointee of the military régime he had shown himself biased against Bhutto and the PPP, stating that they had rigged the elections. They did not believe he would be impartial in the coming October elections. When it came to being tried for conspiracy to murder, therefore, Bhutto did not feel at all confident.

Before the trial began, Bhutto realised how he was to be subjugated before the Acting Chief Justice. The bail he had been granted by Mr Justice Samdani was inevitably cancelled by his arrest under M.L.O. 12 — the martial law regulation. He was accordingly confined in Karachi central jail. However, soon afterwards he was ordered to appear at once in the court at Lahore. Bhutto believed the duplicity of the court, with Maulvi Mushtaq as its Acting Chief Justice, emerged almost at once. Because Mushtaq was his personal enemy Bhutto believed that he would not get a fair trial. He had made several petitions against Mushtaq hearing his case — on the grounds that he held an executive and a judicial post as Chief Election Commissioner and Acting Chief Justice; and that he was biased. Bhutto also argued against his cancellation of bail. Anxious to supplement the remarks of his counsel, he was told that he would be given the opportunity to do so after his counsel had finished his submissions. 'For hours and hours' he was told he might speak. But when the time came, he was informed that he could make his submissions in writing — a poor substitute, Bhutto believed. His complaint that he had no confidence in the Acting Chief Justice was merely filed on record. At the same time as Bhutto was preparing to make his defence in the murder charge, he was also involved in defending himself in the political charges. He felt himself the object of a barrage of attack.

Just before the trial, a dock was constructed to seclude the former Prime Minister from contact with others. Instead of being permitted to sit with his counsel, as was customary procedure, he was confined behind the dock. Bhutto considered that this was especially designed to cage and humiliate him, since it was an entirely novel practice in the Lahore High Court. At one time Bhutto showed his discomfort; seeing this Maulvi Mushtaq reportedly said: 'We all know that you are used to a very comfortable life. I am providing you with a chair behind the dock instead of a bench.' The sarcasm in his voice was unmistakable.

The trial commenced on 11 October 1977. The court room was packed; Bhutto's wife and daughter were present. The former Prime Minister, dressed elegantly, was composed and calm. Maulvi Mushtaq looked down at him from his high-backed chair, flanked by two judges on either side. Out of the twenty-five judges who sat on the bench of the Lahore High Court it was Maulvi Mushtaq who had the right to select four others who would hear the case. Aftab Hussain was a strict Jamaat-i-Islami with notions of extreme piety and sanctity; another, Zaki-ud-Din Pal, was at one time opposed to Bhutto politically; the other two were Gulbaz Khan and M.S.H. Quereshi, a former bureaucrat. It was considered to be a privilege to be tried by five judges as opposed to two, which constituted the quorum, but Bhutto believed the will of the Chief Justice reigned supreme. It was contrary to normal legal practice that the two judges who had been dealing with the complaint and had heard his bail application were not included on the bench. Pakistan continually equated its legal system with that of other countries, particularly Britain from whom it had derived its practice. But people found that when it came to the trial of the former Prime Minister, there were irregularities such as this which did not fall within the accepted practice. The authorities maintained that Bhutto, as an ordinary prisoner, was having an ordinary trial. But his supporters said that if that had been the case he should first have been tried in the lower sessions court, which would have enabled him to appeal first in the High Court and then in the Supreme Court. No explanation was given for the unwarranted jump to the High Court. On account of suspicions that he would not be given a fair trial Bhutto was advised at the outset to boycott; yet, determined to show he had nothing to hide, he did not do so.

The lawyer who had acted for Mr Bhutto in his application for bail — Mr Mohammed Hayat Junejo — did not take part in the trial. Engaged to argue for the bail application, he was requested to be available for the trial. He said originally that he would assist and help Mr D.M. Awan, Bhutto's senior counsel for the trial, but his sudden disappearance meant that his services could not be called upon. It was an understandable and yet demoralising part of being on the losing side. Mr Awan had formerly been Advocate General of the Punjab under Bhutto. He was assisted by Syed Ehsan Qadir Shah, a trial lawyer from Sargodha, also Mr Awan's home town; Inayatullah Cheema, Miss Tallut Yaqub and Mohammed Ehsan made up the team. Mr Yahya Bakhtiar, former Attorney General, advised on the case although his own antipathy to the Chief Justice prevented him from being part of the defence counsel. It was a toss-up as to who had the poorer relations with Maulvi Mushtaq — Bakhtiar or Bhutto.

Bhutto felt too that the hand of the military régime was behind his trial. From the moment of his arrest for conspiracy to murder, the Chief Martial Law Administrator, General Zia ul Haq, issued statements saying that Bhutto was a murderer. He gave a press conference stating the same.

The government-controlled newspapers abounded in criticism of Bhutto as a leader and condemned his régime. The English-speaking newspapers turned from praise of the Prime Minister to criticism of Bhutto as a former Prime Minister. Ironically, the same journalist performed a different job, praising Bhutto whilst in power, criticising him when he was not. Another journalist of the *Pakistan Times* lost his job and ended up at a later stage writing for the pro-Bhutto newspaper

Musawaat. This newspaper was temporarily closed down in Karachi. Intransigent journalists were flogged and imprisoned. On occasions, papers appeared with substantial parts of their columns blocked out. When the trial began, extensive publicity was given to the prosecution's case.

On the first day of the trial the Acting Chief Justice read the charge sheet.

'We, Mushtaq Hussain, Acting Chief Justice, Zaki-ud-Din Pal, M.S.H. Quereshi, Aftab Hussain and Gulbaz Khan, Judges of the Lahore High Court, hereby charge you, Zulfikar Ali Bhutto, as follows:'

Bhutto, asked to stand, listened patiently. It was a dramatic moment. The Chief Justice went on:

'Firstly that you, some time in the middle of 1974, conspired with Masood Mahmud Approver countenancing the murder of Ahmed Raza Kasuri then a member of the National Assembly, through the agency of the Federal Security Force.'

It took perhaps two minutes to read the charge sheet. The other two charges related to his aiding and abetment in order to carry out the conspiracy. Mr Bhutto pleaded not guilty. He was then permitted to sit.

The prosecution began confidently. The most important aspect for it to establish was that the Prime Minister was the one who had the motive to kill Raza Kasuri. The man himself appeared as the prosecution's first witness. He spent five days in the witness-box testifying vehemently against Bhutto. A tall man with black hair and flamboyantly dressed, he spoke as though he were intoxicated with the sound of his own voice. He gave a short history of their political relations. Kasuri claimed he was one of the founder members of the Pakistan People's Party in 1967 but he fell out with Bhutto over East Pakistan.

'I could read the heinous political design of Mr Bhutto in a rather visible term,' he said.

He blamed Bhutto for the break-up of Pakistan and the war in Bangladesh. He attributed the reason for Bhutto not co-operating with Sheikh Mujib ur Rehman, leader of the Awami League, to the fact that he was 'power hungry'. In his opinion Mujib ur Rehman had won an overwhelming victory in the 1971 elections and should have been allowed to rule an undivided Pakistan.

'I was the only member of PPP who went to Dacca to attend the Session [of the National Assembly] which was scheduled to be held on 3 March 1971, because I thought that only by attending the session of the National Assembly of Pakistan could we have kept the integrity and solidarity of Pakistan intact.'

For this reason he believed he fell from favour. He also refused to sign the 1973 Constitution because, he said, 'it had neither Islam nor democracy nor fair play in it.'

He refused to recognise Bangladesh, calling it 'an illegitimate child of Indian aggression, foreign conspiracy and power ambition of Mr Bhutto'.

Kasuri criticised Bhutto on the floor of the National Assembly. He spoke of a 'terrorised parliament' and compared conditions in Pakistan to those of Hitler's Germany, with witch-hunts, tapped telephones and police spies listening in on conversations in the lobbies and the cafeterias of the National Assembly.

But apparently one of the most crucial turning points, according to Kasuri's testimony and documents, came in June 1974 a few months before the murder. Bhutto was addressing the National Assembly. Always proud of the 1973 Constitution, he referred to the fact that it was unanimously adopted. An interruption came from the assembly. It was Kasuri. He objected because, he said, he wished to put the record straight. Nine members of the National Assembly had not signed the Constitution, he protested, himself being one of them. Bhutto found this an unnecessary irritant. The nine members who had not signed the document were considered not to have opposed the Constitution but to have abstained. But Kasuri insisted. Bhutto lost his temper. 'You keep quiet,' he said. 'I have had enough of you. Absolute poison.' They argued. 'Virtually a parliamentary scuffle took place,' stated Kasuri. Bhutto concluded this episode by exclaiming, 'I have had enough of this man. What does he think of himself?'

Kasuri and the Prime Minister were reconciled after the murder but this reconciliation was apparently only skin deep; so too had been his earlier patch-up after the Kasuri attack, for which he also blamed the Prime Minister.

'I made a temporary peace as a matter of political strategy ...

because Mr Bhutto was Chief Martial Law Administrator ...
immediately after the lifting of the martial law on 21 April 1972,
I showed my teeth against Mr Bhutto.' (Many believed that it
was because there was martial law in the country at present that
Kasuri had once more aligned himself with the military
authorities.)

Kasuri narrated in detail the facts of the murder and his
subsequent conduct.

'I joined the PPP because of an instinct of self-preservation,'
he said, 'because I knew that I was a marked man.'

Later in his testimony he stated:

'I simply maintained a posture of affiliation with the party as
a measure of expediency and self-preservation to maintain the
smoke-screen of friendship with Mr Bhutto.'

Kasuri excused his eulogising letters to the Prime Minister
saying that it was 'to keep Mr Bhutto in lull'. Later he enlarged
on this theory — a politician, he believed, was entitled to change
his strategy without altering his fundamental beliefs. Kasuri,
seeing that his offensive policies and speeches of criticism bore
little fruit, turned to praise of the former Prime Minister in
order to lull him into a false sense of security and then attack.
Obviously the time to attack had come with the change in
government.

With Kasuri's testimony on record, the special public prosecutor, M. Anwar, proceeded to the next witness — the
approver in the murder case, Masood Mahmud. Kasuri had
alleged a motive, he had pointed to conspiracy, the subsequent
conduct of Mr Bhutto after the murder which, he said, was such
that he was being prevailed upon to rejoin the party, as well as
alleging that the murder was not properly investigated. Kasuri
pointed the finger; but he had no proof. It was up to Masood
Mahmud to forge the link between himself, the Prime Minister
and the subsequent murder.

Mahmud spoke at length, spending nine days in the
witness-box. A small, clean-shaven man, he said that the murder had been committed upon the instructions of his former
Prime Minister and boss. He described in detail his early career
and how he was threatened to accept the position of Director-
General of the Federal Security Force, a high-grade job.
Further, he and his family were threatened if he did not instruct

Mian Abbas, the Director, Intelligence and Operations in the FSF, to carry out the murder of Kasuri.

'He said to me that he would hold me personally responsible for the execution of this order,' Mahmud pleaded. 'I was naturally shaken on hearing these orders and pleaded with him that the execution of these orders would be against my conscience and against the dictates of God ... The Prime Minister lost his temper and shouted saying that he would have no nonsense from me or from Mian Mohammed Abbas.'

According to his testimony, Mian Abbas was not 'the least disturbed,' although Abbas had testified that he had performed the task under the coercion of Masood Mahmud. The witness also introduced Saeed Ahmed Khan, Bhutto's Chief Security Officer, and his assistant, Abdul Hamid Bajwa, into the picture, saying that they also kept on reminding him and goading him to perform the execution.

Mahmud also described the functions of the FSF, saying that the Prime Minister had told him that it was to be a deterrent force. From his testimony his job meant that he had a close relationship with the Prime Minister.

'The Prime Minister would call me frequently,' he testified. It was also clear that he had been well treated whilst holding the post of Director-General of the FSF. He had stayed in five-star hotels at government expense and been permitted to go abroad for medical treatment.

Mahmud absolved himself from the incident at Islamabad when Kasuri was attacked, saying he only had a 'hunch' about it. But he and the prosecution placed significance on Kasuri's visit to Quetta in Baluchistan for a political meeting in September 1974. According to his testimony, he gave directions to a man called M.R. Welch, the Director of the FSF in Quetta, to 'take care of' Kasuri whilst he was in Quetta. The words 'take care of him' were interpreted by Welch when it was his turn to testify to mean 'eliminate'.

'What do you mean by "elimination"?' the court asked.

'It meant his assassination,' Welch replied.

Welch however said that he 'had no intention of committing heinous murder' and therefore Kasuri returned from his visit to Quetta unharmed.

This left only the Lahore attack. As the man who had merely

been told to instruct another who, in turn, instructed another, Mahmud had little to do with the actual performance of the crime. But it was he who received the brunt of the Prime Minister's anger when the operation failed, according to Mahmud. He said that the Prime Minister telephoned him early in the morning of 11 November saying that 'your Mian Abbas has made a complete balls up' of the operation and summoning him later to his presence. Both were at Multan at the time. Thus ended the conspiracy. With the murder of Kasuri's father no further attack was made on Kasuri. Yet, although Mahmud never executed the murder which he said he had been pressurised into doing, it was remarkable, the defence later said, that he remained in favour and in office until the military *coup* of July 1977.

Mahmud stepped down from the witness-box. He was replaced by Saeed Ahmed Khan, Bhutto's Chief Security Officer. Short, fat and dark, he took the stand. During the recording of his testimony the loud-voiced Public Prosecutor — M. Anwar — died of a heart attack. Into his shoes stepped his assistant, Ejaz Hussain Batalvi, a man with an even louder voice and a pride in his advocacy.

The prosecution was anxious to show by the testimony of other witnesses that the investigation was not conducted properly after the murder; that efforts were made at the instigation of the Prime Minister to bring Kasuri back into the People's Party to keep him quiet; according to its case, Saeed Ahmed Khan, once Bhutto's Chief Security Officer and prosecution witness No. 3, and his assistant Abdul Hamid Bajwa, prevailed upon Kasuri to return to the party. The prosecution also regarded the personal file kept on Kasuri as an indication that in Kasuri's own words he was 'a marked man'.

In order to exonerate himself somewhat, Saeed Ahmed Khan pointed to the independent behaviour of his assistant, stating that Bajwa acted with the Prime Minister 'directly over my head'. But it was only in January 1975 when the special tribunal under Shafi ur Rehman had already been constituted that Saeed Ahmed Khan was ordered by the Prime Minister to 'look into the case'.

'I found to my dismay that nothing had been done worth the while in the investigation of this case, although over one and a half months had passed since the time of murder,' he said.

'I could also notice the helplessness of the local police who were deliberately avoiding to make investigation towards this line [of the FSF],' he testified, stating that when he mentioned the fact to both the Prime Minister and Mahmud that the FSF used the same ammunition, he had been told in so many words to 'Keep the FSF' out. The defence believed it was only too easy to insert the name of the Prime Minister to make an inefficient investigation appear to be at his behest.

Saeed Ahmed Khan sang like a kettle. Everything the prosecution wanted to hear from him he said in order to corroborate the evidence of Masood Mahmud. Yes, he had helped to channel the investigation away from the FSF: yes, he had kept a file on Kasuri, albeit routine: yes, he had interceded with Kasuri to rejoin the PPP. He and his assistant Abdul Hamid Bajwa had been the jacks-of-all-trades. At times he appeared pitiful, not of course wanting to seem to be too involved as otherwise he might end up being charged himself.

'I had therefore, only a very limited role to play,' he testified, 'and could not do anything further because I was taken away from the case and it was not so much out of fear of losing the job as the fear of my life, which had already been threatened by Mr Zulfikar Ali Bhutto in so many words. In short, I lived and worked in fear and suspense,' he whined.

Another of Saeed Ahmed Khan's misdemeanours, it emerged, was his interest in the course of the Shafi ur Rehman tribunal which produced the report in which Kasuri had mentioned that there might be four groups of people with a motive to murder him. Ironically, one of the complaints of the prosecution was that Bhutto did not have the report published. In fact, on account of Kasuri's admission that there were four possible motives, the report, if it had been published, would have been seen to exonerate Mr Bhutto. For their various reasons both defence and prosecution wanted to have this report put on record, but the Acting Chief Justice refused.

The fourth witness was Welch, the tall Anglo-Pakistani with a British name whose testimony took less than a day to record. He said he had received instructions from Masood Mahmud both orally and on the telephone. In one such conversation Welch said that with regard to Kasuri he had been obnoxious in his speeches against Mr Bhutto, the then Prime Minister, and what he understood from Mahmud was that he should be eliminated. Welch also testified that in Quetta he was responsible for keeping an eye on the political leaders and their activities and also anti-government elements. 'I also used to submit intelligence reports,' he said, 'on the activities of the aforementioned persons', one of whom was, of course, Kasuri.

With the evidence of these four witnesses on record the threads of the prosecution case were woven. It merely had to be supplemented by the statements of the remaining thirty-seven witnesses to strengthen the story. Witnesses were introduced testifying with regard to ammunition; the guns supplied; the jeep used; those involved in the investigation past and present belonging to the Federal Investigating Agency (FIA): all testified in a manner which worked to establish the prosecution's case. Several policemen gave their accounts of the occurrence; often it was factual and did not involve the Prime Minister. P.W. 12, Mohammed Asghar, Senior Superintendent of Police on duty in Lahore, had a great deal to say. In court he made particular reference to a meeting held in the house of the then Inspector General of Police— Rao Rashid Khan— when he was allegedly told to remove the dead body of Kasuri's father and bury it. Yet although Mohammed Asghar clearly remembered the details of the occurrence, he did not remember whether he had mentioned this supposedly important meeting in his previous statements. (He had not.) He emphasised that he did not have a free hand in the investigation because of Saeed Ahmed Khan and Bajwa. But he also stated that 'there were no specific directions to stop the investigation'. Nor could Mohammed Asghar remember whether or not he had said if he had a free hand in the investigation when he appeared before the tribunal of Mr Justice Shafi ur Rehman.

However, he was quite adamant that the police were not in a position to interrogate the Prime Minister, from where he believed the investigation should begin because, he said, with a 'blind murder' it was necessary to start with motive.

His statement was supplemented by that of Abdul Vakil Khan, Deputy Inspector General (DIG) of police— P.W. 14— who corroborated Asghar and complained of the interference of Saeed Ahmed Khan and his assistant Bajwa. He appeared to attribute a suspicious interpretation to the fact that Bajwa asked why the name of the Prime Minister had been included in the First Intelligence Report and his suggestion that this could have been avoided. He did not give the spent cartridges to Bajwa, he said, because he 'suspected' that Bajwa, with his close association with the FSF, might tamper with them. Later, however, the prosecution made out that the only link between Saeed Ahmed Khan, Bajwa and the FSF was in the person of the Prime Minister; but Asghar's statement showed that without the Prime Minister there was 'close association' anyway.

A great deal of what Vakil Khan had to say was hearsay, based on what others told him — Abdul Ahad, a Deputy Superintendent of Police, was also involved in supervising the investigation of the case, he said. But Ahad was a 'dead' witness and much of Vakil Khan's testimony was full of what Abdul Ahad said Abdul Hamid Bajwa — another dead witness — should do regarding the spent cartridges.

Vakil Khan also mentioned the meeting in Rao Rashid's house, although contrary to the statement of Asghar he said he himself was not present. There were many points Vakil Khan did not remember. He did not remember where he was on 11 November and when asked about certain conversations, replied somewhat curtly, 'I do not keep a running diary.' Nonetheless his statement served to corroborate what Asghar and other police officers said and was considered adequate for the prosecution's case.

The fifteenth witness — Mohammed Waris, who took over the investigation as an assistant Director of the Intelligence Bureau — also complained that 'Saeed Ahmed Khan used to control the entire investigation'. But some of his remarks were less incriminating. According to his statement Saeed Ahmed Khan and Bajwa had 'told us that the name of the Prime Minister had appeared in the FIR and that we should proceed with caution'. He described meetings held by Saeed Ahmed Khan and said he gave directions regarding the investigation of this case. Waris said he was kept busy looking into the disputes of the Kasuri family. On 1 October 1975, he said, the case was filed as untraced. He said he was not satisfied with the investigation of the case because it did not travel in the direction of the FSF — from the prosecution's point of view, one of the

strongest indications it could have had that the FSF had something to hide; yet again its association with the Prime Minister
was merely conjecture. It looked as though the former Prime
Minister was going to be blamed for the inefficiency of his
subordinates, and perhaps the guilt of others.

Three more policemen were examined whose testimony
mainly concerned the time at which the parcel of spent cartridges was handed over and to whom. The delay in sealing the
package of spent cartridges was, according to the prosecution
case, one reason to infer that they were substituted.

P.W. 19 was the driver of Ghulam Hussain. He was illiterate
and therefore could not read the entries made in the log-book
when the jeep which Ghulam Hussain used was taken out. Nor
did he have any clear recollection precisely when he drove the
jeep which the prosecution maintained was used to carry out the
murder. From the defence's point of view, the log-book entries
showed a contradiction in the prosecution's case.

The prosecution was halfway through its list of witnesses by
the time the statement of Amir Badshah — its twentieth witness
— had been recorded. It was early December. Bhutto himself
had been ill and had only just returned to the court room,
having been confined to his cell in Kot Lakhpat ever since the
conclusion of the testimony of Saeed Ahmed Khan — the third
witness. Amir Badshah, an inspector in the FSF, testified that
he supplied weapons to Ghulam Mustafa, a co-accused, whose
sole function in the attack appeared to be his receipt of the
weapons. According to Badshah's testimony he had received a
telephone call from Mian Abbas in September 1974 and had
been ordered to deliver weapons and ammunition without making any entry in the register. He testified that he 'did not ask
Ghulam Mustafa the reason for his taking away those weapons
but in those days they were deployed in public meetings and
they required weapons for their own protection,' he said.
According to his statement Ghulam Mustafa came twice, on the
second occasion with Ghulam Hussain.

The prosecution's twenty-fourth witness — Fazal Ali — who
was in charge of the FSF armoury, according to his statement
supplied weapons and ammunition in August 1974 to Ghulam
Hussain on the authorisation of Mian Abbas. Again it was
issued without the proper registration — merely a receipt —

according to the instructions of Mian Abbas who, Fazal Ali said, 'shouted at me' when he appeared not anxious to issue the ammunition without following the procedure of the standing order with regard to issuance of ammunition. Prior to that, on 9 May 1974 he had also issued 1,500 rounds to Ghulam Hussain. He concluded his statement by saying:

'Had I known that the ammunition was being drawn and the weapons were being taken away for a surreptitious purpose, I would certainly have kept the photostat of the receipt that was taken away from me. I was under the impression that these things had been taken for special duty.'

In the meantime, Masood Mahmud's driver — a man called Manzoor Hussain — had given his statement as the prosecution's twenty-first witness. His remembrance of the day's events differed from that of his Director-General of the FSF — a point later to be used by the defence.

These witnesses hopped in and out of the witness-box, taking less than a morning's session. When it came to the prosecution's thirty-first witness — Ghulam Hussain, the second approver in the murder case — he remained testifying in court for seven days, four of which were before the Christmas break. According to Ghulam Hussain's testimony, he acted upon instructions from Mian Abbas to perform the murder of Kasuri. Ghulam Hussain said he was unwilling to become involved in the murder but, he testified, his life was in jeopardy if he did not do so. 'I had joined the FSF to provide for my family and was not prepared to commit the crime,' he testified, but he was unable to escape the assignment.

Ghulam Hussain tried once at Islamabad and then at Lahore, failing both times. According to his statement, at Islamabad his courage failed him and he fired in the air.

'I took a decision on the spot not to murder Mr Ahmed Raza Kasuri,' he testified. But reprimands from Mian Abbas that he had allowed the quarry to escape 'although it was broad daylight' meant that he was kept on the job but told to be 'cautious'. He also testified that he believed his life was in jeopardy because he was aware from his 'private sources' that Mian Abbas had instructed another team to do away with him if he did not perform the task. He added to what Fazal Ali had said about the ammunition. It appeared that out of the 1,500 rounds supplied to him on 9 May 1974, 30 rounds were fired at Lahore and 7 at Islamabad. In all they were short of 51 spent cartridges, the rest being lost in practice, he said.

Ghulam Hussain gave his version of the Lahore incident. He said that he himself was pacing up and down a by-lane although the co-accused said at the outset that the first shot was fired with his pistol. Ghulam Hussain also mentioned two other people — Liaquat and Zaheer — who, as members of his group, were assigned the task of killing Kasuri. Liaquat was also there on the night of the occurrence.

Ghulam Hussain's testimony only involved the Prime Minister by assumption on the part of the prosecution. All his instructions came from Mian Abbas and he admitted, 'I had no knowledge that Mian Mohammed Abbas had thick relations with the then Prime Minister. Whatever orders were given to me were by Mian Mohammed Abbas', a man who also seemed to be in two minds about the murder. Despite his strict reprimands to Ghulam Hussain after the failure of the first attack, his comments according to Ghulam Hussain after the Lahore attempts were quite mild.

'If God was saving him, we cannot kill him,' he announced.

Ghulam Hussain gave far more information than had been recorded before the magistrate — Zulfikar Ali Toor, P.W. 10. He concluded his statement to the prosecution by stating:

'I had no animosity of my own with Mr Ahmed Raza Kasuri. I did not even know him ... The firing at Islamabad and at Lahore at Ahmed Raza Kasuri had been made due to pressure and coercion.'

His plea was echoed by all those allegedly involved who pointed the finger at Masood Mahmud, via Mian Abbas and indirectly to the Prime Minister.

Ghulam Hussain's statement contained many contradictions and facts which were not corroborated by the other witnesses. He appeared to be aware that his statements might be slanted. He made the following excuse:

'When Mian Mohammed Abbas came to know about it [his application to become an approver] he sent me a message through a convict. He said that if my application was accepted and I was made an approver, I should *adopt a method by which I could get pardon* and *also at the same time try to save him also*. Since he had begged of me, I made my statement in a way that he should not be implicated to a very large extent.' (*Author's italics*)

The defence lawyers put in their word to try and upset the prosecution case; often the words 'I do not remember' could be seen to conceal contradictions in previous statements. This applied especially to Ghulam Hussain. At the time too, the defence had its suspicions that the evidence was not being recorded correctly, an allegation denied by the court. According to normal procedure even interchanges which are uttered in court and then deleted should appear on the record, said the defence. But not everything which was said appeared on the record.

The defence lawyers of Mr Bhutto complained that 'very often the evidence of the prosecution witnesses is tailored, polished, tightened and improved upon'. They tried to highlight this in cross-examination. A British lawyer, John Mathews, Q.C., who came to attend the trial for a few days in November, made the following remarks regarding this aspect: 'Particularly, I was concerned at the way a witness's favourable answer would be the subject of immediate interruption from the Bench, who would take over the witness, and cause him to whittle down or change his answer. None of this would be recorded by the typist contemporaneously, but ultimately the court would dictate to the typist the original question and the final answer, which frequently bore no resemblance to that which the witness had first said.' He also said he noticed the antagonism of the Bench and the 'outbursts' of the Chief Justice. So exasperated had Bhutto himself become with the conduct of his trial that he decided to submit an application for the trial to be transferred to another bench; when this did not succeed, he boycotted the proceedings altogether.

The long application to transfer the trial to another bench was filed in court on 18 December just before the Christmas break. It contained many complaints both in the conduct of the trial and the conduct of the bench. Mr Bhutto stated:

> To fill in gaps in the prosecution story, to remove inconsistencies in each other's former statements and to cure other crucial defects of the prosecution case, most of these witnesses have changed their testimony in some material particulars.

The application also made the following objection:

Some have introduced complete new versions of certain aspects of the case. They were duly confronted with their previous statements ... but not a single confrontation has been permitted to be brought on record.

Quite apart from the legal aspects, Bhutto believed that the attitude of the Chief Justice was patently inimical. As Mushtaq came from the same district as the Chief Martial Law Administrator — that of Jullundur in East Punjab — Bhutto was sure that there was close association between the two, and that for their various reasons, neither would be displeased if Bhutto were found guilty. With the postponement of elections in September just before the trial began, the former Prime Minister became more and more convinced that the trial was being used for political purposes to get rid of him. His supporters fervently believed that if the case had been registered against an ordinary citizen it would have been dropped at once. But they thought that because he was a powerful political figure, the case had taken on an unprecedented importance. In his report, Mathews implied that such a weak case should not even have been brought to court and that the evidence would be inadmissible in British law. But so complicated and confused was the case itself, with numerous witnesses and incidents, that it was not difficult for the layman to become confused and lost in the proceedings, and therefore leave the untangling of the case to the hands of the legal experts — the judges.

As Mathews said, there was animosity from the Bench towards Bhutto. The Chief Justice also appeared to become infuriated with the defence counsel. Early on in the trial when already the proceedings had not gone smoothly, Bhutto's counsel, D.M. Awan, was anxious to interject a point.

'My Lords ...' he began.

'Sit down,' cried the Acting Chief Justice.

Awan, impervious to the judge's remark, stated audibly, 'My Lords, we know all the restrictions are for the defence counsel.'

This served the purpose of aggravating the Chief Justice, who sternly reprimanded Mr Awan. Awan having nothing better to do than observe the Chief Justice in his fury, suddenly heard Maulvi Mushtaq Hussain shriek at him, '*Why* are you

staring at me?' The Acting Chief Justice forbade this incident to
be publicised in the press. Later Awan was himself formally
criticised for his conduct in the court.

The defence complained that whereas ample time appeared
to be allowed to the prosecution to put questions, those of the
defence were often termed 'irrelevant'.

Bhutto's illnesses in Kot Lakhpat Jail had a bearing on the
conduct of the trial. His malaria and influenza attacks, when
combined with colonic trouble, made him a very sick man. In
the middle of November he became ill when the evidence of
Saeed Ahmed Khan was being recorded. Only two days'
adjournment was granted. But Bhutto did not recover and the
court was obliged to adjourn for another day; when he was still
not well enough to come to court, however, the proceedings
continued without him. At this time the evidence of the next
fifteen witnesses was recorded. This was totally against common law practice, under which the accused is meant to be
present throughout his trial.

Ironically, earlier, at the beginning of November Maulvi
Mushtaq had given a press conference to foreign journalists
stating just this — that the trial was being conducted in the full
light of day and according to common law traditions, no doubt
for the benefit of the British journalists who were interviewing
him. But even this was objectionable to Bhutto and his lawyers,
who considered that Mushtaq had no right to discuss the manner in which the trial was being conducted, more especially
since they disagreed with his analysis. But their petition outlining their client's lack of confidence in the Chief Justice on
account of this incident was ordered to be heard after the trial.
Bhutto did not realise how soon his 'full light of day' would
vanish.

So, absent for the best part of three weeks, Bhutto returned
to court on 7 December. He was still looking ill and pale. More
altercations followed when the Chief Justice tried to make the
court sit from 8 a.m. to 4 p.m. — as opposed to the regular
hours from 8.30 a.m. to 1 p.m. — to make up for lost time. It
was asking a great deal of client and lawyer. As it was, Kot
Lakhpat was not in the centre of Lahore and it would mean an
exhausting day. After much protest the order was dropped.

Maulvi Mushtaq had shown little sympathy for Bhutto's

obvious desire to see his wife and daughter, who attended the trial. At the outset they were allowed to take tea with him during the interval and after the proceedings with the lawyers. But after a week they were forbidden even this right. When an incident took place involving both of them, the Acting Chief Justice was not sympathetic. On 16 December mother and daughter went to attend the Test cricket match at Gaddafi stadium in Lahore. Spectators, anxious to show their support for the jailed former Prime Minister, shouted enthusiastically 'Long Live Bhutto'. There was general confusion and pandemonium, during which both Begum Bhutto and Benazir were wounded by the lathi blows of the police. Benazir's shoulder was hurt; Begum Bhutto was hit on the head, with the result that she had to go to hospital and undergo surgery. Upon hearing of this incident Bhutto was, not unnaturally, disturbed. He was anxious for the latest news and gave instructions for this to be obtained during the break for tea at 11 a.m. However, on that particular day the Chief Justice stated that the court would rise at 10.30 and return before 11 a.m. Bhutto's patience was short. During the course of the morning's proceedings, separated from his counsel by the dock, he requested the court to continue sitting so that he might receive the necessary news at 11 a.m. or for permission for the tea break to be continued until after 11 a.m. Mr Awan had not grasped what Mr Bhutto wanted and did not make the request. As the court was about to rise Bhutto swore at his counsel, saying 'Damn it, make it clear to the court.' These words were uttered in tones audible enough for the Chief Justice to hear. Thereupon Maulvi Mushtaq made strong objection to the use of swear-words in court. Bhutto apologised and said that he was 'in a very disturbed state of mind' on account of the incident the day before. The Acting Chief Justice retorted, 'We don't care.' The altercation did not end there. Bhutto expostulated at the humiliations and insults to which he felt he had been subjected.

'I've had enough,' he exclaimed.

'Enough of what?' questioned the Chief Justice.

'Of your insults and humiliations.'

This was provocation enough for the Chief Justice to order the police officers to 'take this man away until he regains his senses', at which one of the other judges remarked,

'He has not behaved well. We cannot tolerate this. He thinks he is the former Prime Minister, but we do not care for him.'

For the rest of the day's hearings Bhutto was not allowed to attend the court. The Chief Justice passed an order deeming that he was not 'capable' of so doing.

All these incidents were recounted in his 18 December application for the trial to be transferred to another bench, which was not taken up until after the Christmas recess on 9 January. Perhaps, angered by the fact that the application had been released to the press over Christmas, before the justices themselves had time to pass judgment on it, or anyway because to them the allegations were not plausible and were embarrassing, the Acting Chief Justice and the other judges did not take much interest in it. Bhutto was handed the application and told to argue it himself, in chambers, as opposed to the open court. Surprised at being requested to argue the application himself, he insisted on the presence of his lawyers. They were allowed in after some more sarcastic remarks as to why could Mr Bhutto not make up his mind — sometimes he himself wanted to speak; at others he wanted his lawyers. Mr Awan argued on law; Bhutto then began to make a submission on merits and facts, after reluctant agreement by the court that he might do so. But he was stopped in mid-stream because, allegedly, his submissions were political. The petition was accordingly dismissed without further consideration.

But anticipating its dismissal, Awan declared that he could no longer represent his client and asked permission to withdraw from the case. Infuriated by this new tactic, the Chief Justice refused. He gave an hour-and-a-half recess for a decision to be taken. But the discussions which ensued between client and counsel merely capped the decision to boycott.

Awan got to his feet. 'My client,' he said, 'has cancelled his power of attorney and disassociated himself from the proceedings.'

Obviously irritated by this new drama and anxious to thwart it, the Chief Justice thereupon appointed D.M. Awan and Eshasan Qadir Shah to act as Bhutto's lawyers at the State's expense. But, said Awan, they had not had instructions from their client and were unable to cross-examine the witness at present in the witness-box — Ghulam Hussain. The Chief

Justice gave in, stating that he had wanted to throw pearls to them but they did not accept and so it could not be helped. The implication of the biblical reference was clear — he wished to imply that he had wanted to cast pearls before swine. The transition to the boycott did not bode well for Bhutto.

Once the decision was taken to boycott there would obviously be no chance of Bhutto's counsel calling defence witnesses who would be able to throw a different light on the testimony of the prosecution witnesses, whose statements alone would be on record. This might ultimately prove crucial since the judges maintained that they would not consider any material other than that on record, which they accepted entirely.

By the time Ghulam Hussain's testimony was concluded the boycott was taking effect. When it came to Bhutto's turn to cross-examine the remaining witnesses 'Nil' was the reply because he had disassociated himself from the proceedings. In all, the statements of ten more witnesses were recorded in the boycott, which from Bhutto's point of view meant their testimony went down on record virtually unchallenged.

P.W. 34 — Abdul Hayee Niazi, a sub-inspector in the police on duty on the night of the occurrence — once more bore out the testimony of those who had said they did not have a free hand in the investigation.

'The circumstances were such,' he said, 'that neither could I investigate the case nor could I make any statement with my free consent.'

He, along with other policemen, Mohammed Bashir (P.W. 8) and Abdul Aziz (P.W. 11) were involved in the investigation in its initial stages. Bajwa and Abdul Ahad, a Deputy Superintendent Police, he said, had instructed him. Abdul Bajwa 'intimidated and put pressure on me,' he pleaded.

Niazi also referred to the meeting in Rao Rashid's house on the night of 11 November which, like Asghar, he had not mentioned in his previous statement. Again because of the boycott, Rao Rashid was never summoned as a defence witness to testify whether this meeting, at which he allegedly took uncalled-for interest in the murder case on behalf of the Prime Minister, was real or not.

Most of the remaining witnesses to be examined belonged to the FIA and were involved in the re-investigation of the case after the military takeover. As P.W. 39 — Mohammed Boota, an inspector in the FIA — said, 'the entire investigation was being conducted under the control and supervision of the DD [Deputy Director of the FIA]' Abdul Khaliq, who himself appeared as the last witness. In later stages of the proceedings the defence was to recall the role of Abdul Khaliq in the investigation. All these witnesses vehemently denied any suggestion of torture and inducement given to the accused when their statements were recorded before the magistrate, Zulfikar Ali Toor (P.W. 10). But the magistrate admitted that he had not asked whether there was any pressure on the accused, whether their statements were voluntary, nor for that matter, why they were making them. He merely recorded what they had to say.

Bhutto's boycott did not, however, prevent him from wanting to speak when the time came for his statement to be recorded. During the course of the trial he had been told by the Chief Justice that he would have ample opportunity to make his defence which was, it appeared, designed to make up for the Chief Justice's orders to Bhutto to 'shut up' and 'sit down' when he wanted to interject a point during the course of the witnesses' testimony. After the evidence of the remaining ten witnesses during the boycott, the time finally came for Bhutto to speak. On account of his boycott he chose to answer only those questions put to him which had no relevance to his actual defence. When the court adjourned on the first day of the recording of his statement — 24 January — they were at question No. 53 out of 67. Bhutto was therefore astounded to find on the following day an empty court room. He was informed that henceforward the trial would be conducted in camera. The hearing in the 'full light of day' promised to him by the Acting Chief Justice when he gave his press interview in early November had vanished. Once he saw that the rest of the proceedings were to be conducted in camera, he refrained from dealing with two points which he had previously intended to talk about: (a) the reasons why the case had been 'fabricated' against him and (b) the reasons for his lack of confidence in getting a fair trial. He protested at the further injustice of a secret trial: 'It is said that justice must not only be done, but must be seen to be done,' he said. He believed that insofar as his trial was concerned, there was one law for him, one law for the prosecution. 'There is a limit to everything,' he declared. 'I have borne this torture and agony for the sake of my country', and therefore, he said, he expected to have the right and opportunity to speak in public to defend himself. He was sure that it was because of his importance as a political figure that he was being treated in such a way. He made the plea:

'You call this justice? You call this a trial? Forget the fact that I have been the President and Prime Minister of Pakistan. Forget the fact that I am the leader of the premier party of this country. Forget all these things. But I am a citizen of this country and I am facing a murder trial. Even the ordinary citizen — and I consider myself one — is not denied justice.'

But from now on, his words fell on stony ground. No one other than the judges was there to hear him and they appeared to be unmoved by his discourse. In answer to the remaining questions put to him, he merely shook his head. When the last question was asked: 'Will you produce evidence in your defence?' he did not answer. 'I am not participating in the proceedings,' he said, such was his disgust with the way he was being treated. As it was he complained that, as with the recording of the testimony of the witnesses, his own statement was not correctly and accurately recorded by the stenographer in the court room. Bhutto's supporters also were angry that, whereas the case of the prosecution and the statements of the confessing co-accused were accorded full publicity in the press, no coverage was given to what Mr Bhutto had to say.

What with Bhutto's boycott and the in camera proceedings, the trial concluded in virtual silence. It was over by 2 March; and its conclusion in secret finally convinced those who supported the former Prime Minister that their leader had not in any way been given a fair trial. At the end of the trial he was whisked back to Kot Lakhpat to await the judgment.

With the testimony of forty-one witnesses, including two approvers, four accused and only the Prime Minister maintaining his innocence, the prosecution case, complicated as it was, at a glance emerged as almost plausible. The judges appeared to have their minds made up already. 'The dice was loaded against me,' Bhutto later said. 'The Chief Justice was kindness itself to the confessing accused. He smiled at them ... the taunts and frowns and shouts were reserved only for me.' But behind the scenes the case was not as watertight as it seemed. One of the co-accused — none other than Mian Mohammed Abbas, the man who had apparently assuaged Masood Mahmud's fears when entrusted with the task of taking care of everything — had himself retracted his confession on the first day of the hearing and he stood by this retraction, stating that his confession had been given under duress. He said he and the others were coerced, threatened and offered the promise of pardon to make their statements. If he admitted to lying under pressure, might not others have done the same, Bhutto's supporters asked? The question of pressure and duress was of course difficult to gauge. Later, another lawyer, Mr John Melville-Williams, attended the proceedings and when asked about pressure in a BBC interview, he replied: 'The witnesses were almost entirely accomplices, which means they would be very susceptible to pressure in the sense that they would be looking to save themselves.' He said that the political background was such that the witnesses could well feel themselves under pressure.

Initially, the trial of Mr Bhutto did not stir up very much world interest. Notwithstanding the fact that the trial of a former Prime Minister is not a common occurrence, in many western circles it was considered that murdering a political opponent was not unusual, especially in the third world countries where the price of life was supposedly cheap. If people believed that Bhutto ordered the murder, they did not blame him for so doing. It was all part of the game and he was one politician who had got caught. Some people believed that even if he did not order the murder of Kasuri it had been done by the FSF, an organisation which came under Bhutto's jurisdiction and now he had to take the blame. Comparisons were even drawn with the English King Henry II's fateful remark about Thomas Becket when he cried, 'Who will rid me of this turbulent priest?' People outside Pakistan were prepared to see justice take its course. They were fairly certain that anyway the penalty would merely be a few years' imprisonment, especially since Bhutto was only indirectly involved, if involved at all.

On 18 March the sentence was announced — at 8.30 in the morning before huge crowds could assemble. As it was, crowds gathered outside the court house daily, waiting for judgment to come. Before the sentence was announced many party workers of the PPP were arrested. Reserves of police were stationed in the principal cities. They expected trouble once the people knew what the verdict was. Not one of the five judges dissented from the judgment. All five voted unanimously in favour of the death sentence for Bhutto and the four other 'confessing' co-accused. The fact that five Punjabi judges condemned a Sindhi to 'hang by the neck until he die' weighed heavily on the hearts of the Sindhis, ever mindful of the dominant position of the Punjab in Pakistan. Whereas many believed that such a severe penalty could not be inflicted on a man who not only had been the former Prime Minister, but also on a man whose trial was questionable and who had boycotted it, it did not come as a surprise to those who had been close to the proceedings. Bhutto had been forewarned of the verdict by his advocate. But the world was shocked. 'Bhutto to hang' was plastered over the billboards in London on a crisp Saturday afternoon. Clemency appeals flooded in from Heads of State all over the world as well as the United Nations and Amnesty International. Seven days only (as opposed to the normal thirty) were permitted for Bhutto to appeal against the sentence. There was panic when Bhutto, a proud man, said he would not appeal to save his life. Begum Nusrat Bhutto had already been under house arrest in Lahore almost continuously since December. (Trouble being anticipated on 5 January, Bhutto's fiftieth birthday, in view of the already publicised application of 18 December for the transfer of Bhutto's case to another bench, Begum Bhutto had been arrested at the end of December.) On the eve of the announcement of judgment Benazir, already detained for her 'political' activities was placed under house arrest in Karachi. The family, unable to communicate with each other or with the outside world, faced the prospect of finding that Bhutto had already been hanged if the appeal were not lodged within the prescribed seven days. This fear was confirmed by his immediate removal to the death cell in Kot Lakhpat jail in Lahore. Initially, Bhutto was not willing to file an appeal but finally, with the advice of his family and counsel, he accepted that due to the boycott he had not defended himself properly, and he consented to lodge an appeal in the Supreme Court, hoping that he would get better justice than he believed had been meted out to him in Lahore. Unrest after the sentence in the cities was spasmodic and disorganised. A few protest marches were organised; several buses were burnt. But because the military authorities had arrested most loyal supporters in one of the 'sweep operations' there was generally little outcry on behalf of a man who was leader of the premier political party. Possibly the fear of the lash — Zia's new method of instilling fear into the people — or else general incredulity at the harshness of the sentence, rendered Pakistan comparatively immobile. It did not mean, however, that it condoned the sentence and the judgment imposed upon the former Prime Minister.

The judgment itself had unique features: it was drafted by the ardent member of the Jamaat-i-Islami — Aftab Hussain — and had high religious overtones. It delivered a moral lecture to the accused, calling him a compulsive liar and the arch-culprit. Bhutto was called 'a Moslem only in name' and told that 'such a person in all probability would destroy the very basis of the Constitution and the law which he is sworn to uphold'. It accepted in its entirety the prosecution's case.

'All the offences with which the accused are charged are thus proved to the hilt,' said the judgment. Bhutto's complaints against the court were 'imaginary and false'.

Bhutto was sentenced to death for conspiracy to murder Kasuri, resulting in the death of his father; seven years' imprisonment for the attempt to murder Kasuri; five years' imprisonment for the conspiracy to kill Kasuri, since although he had not been killed, the conspiracy was still there. A fine of 25,000 rupees was imposed automatically with the death sentence as compensation to the family of the deceased (failure to pay being punishable by a further six months' rigorous imprisonment). Finally the judges regretted the lack of sufficiently strong laws to deal with 'a recalcitrant party like the principal accused'. They considered that the law of contempt with a penalty of six months' imprisonment was not enough of a deterrent when the accused was already in jail. The whole judgment was steeped in religious piety.

After announcing this judgment in camera in the High Court of Lahore, Bhutto was driven back to what he described as the black hole of Kot Lakhpat. Policemen in the van encircled him with automatic weapons with the barrels of the guns touching his temples and chest. Helicopters flew overhead. On the way, the vehicle passed the site where three hangings had recently taken place. It was reported that Bhutto remarked, 'Well, if they hang me they had better make the rope good and strong for twenty-two generals will hang after me.'

When the gates of the jail were opened to let the van pass, Bhutto saw that the place was full of troops. Sub-machine guns were placed strategically at all corners of the jail. The gallows had been inspected and, as Bhutto said, given a 'spring cleaning'.

Bhutto's hanging appeared imminent at this time; but over a year was to elapse before he knew what was ultimately in store for him.

3

SOLITARY CONFINEMENT

A High Court judge has estimated that one month in solitary confinement is equivalent to a year's ordinary hard labour or rigorous imprisonment. Zulfikar Ali Bhutto spent a total of nearly nineteen months in solitary confinement: eight in the prison at Kot Lakhpat in Lahore during the trial, ten and a half in Rawalpindi District Jail during the hearing of the appeal. Comparisons with what others had suffered under his régime or were suffering under the present one did not make his confinement any easier to bear. Whereas his opponents pointed gleefully to his distress, his supporters bemoaned the humiliation meted out to a man they revered as their former Prime Minister. Other people had obviously suffered for longer periods, but for Bhutto, a man accustomed to being surrounded by people, it was hardship enough. Considering that his task was outside with those people, together with his belief in his own innocence, the whole period must have seemed like a never-ending nightmare.

Whereas the other accused and even Bhutto's former ministers who had been jailed on various charges did not appear to be having too bad a time in confinement and managed to find ways to bend the rules, or at any rate get substantial concessions, Bhutto complained bitterly about the humiliating conditions under which he was kept. As well as the jail authorities, there was an army colonel on duty at the jail, perhaps to make sure that the jail authorities did not weaken and grant concessions to their former Prime Minister.

The conditions under which Bhutto was kept were not conducive to good health, nor did he ever receive the medical

attention he badly needed. Torn between retaining his dignity
and keeping himself alive, he generally refrained from seeking
assistance. Others were left to protest on his behalf to the
authorities in order to secure him better conditions. At the
insistence of his lawyer after his arrival in Kot Lakhpat, a few
concessions were made. The ventilator window and door of the
cell were covered only by wire gauze and the inevitable iron
bars. As winter approached in Pakistan, the temperature in the
cell dropped at night to zero. Eventually, curtains affording
some protection were hung. There was no flush on the toilet —
something to which the former Prime Minister had to accustom
himself in Rawalpindi — but after a couple of weeks one was
installed at Kot Lakhpat.

In addition to these conditions at Kot Lakhpat, for three
months Bhutto was subjected to a peculiar kind of harassment,
which he thought was especially for his benefit. His cell, separated from a barrack area by a 10-foot-high wall, did not
prevent him from hearing horrific shrieks and screams at night
from the other side of the wall. One of Mr Bhutto's lawyers
made enquiries amongst the jail staff and ascertained that they
were in fact Indian prisoners-of-war who had been rendered
delinquent and mental during the course of the 1971 war. When
the time came to exchange prisoners, the Indian Government
would not accept these lunatics, who had no recollection of
their place of origin, and so they were retained as prisoners to
eke out their existence in Kot Lakhpat. Bhutto, discovering the
precise temperament of the inmates, wrote to the jail superintendent with a copy of the letter addressed to his lawyer (which
was released to the press), requesting that they be moved —
finally they were. Obviously the authorities would not accept
that Mr Bhutto's sleep was being disturbed on purpose, but
Bhutto did not forget the sleepless nights he spent and referred
often to the lunatics in other letters of complaint. 'Fifty odd
lunatics were lodged in the ward next to mine. Their screams
and shrieks in the dead of night are something I will not forget,'
he wrote.

Allegations were also made that there was a plot afoot to kill
Bhutto by slow food poisoning. Although he had permission to
receive food from outside, this passed through the hands of the
jail authorities, as did breakfast, tea, coffee and biscuits, which

came direct from the jail. In March just after the death sentence, Bhutto's wife wrote a letter to the jail superintendent alleging food poisoning. The story was picked up by the international press and the London *Times* wrote that according to Begum Bhutto, 'the idea was to make it appear that her husband, who had been sentenced to death, committed suicide rather than face execution.' The authorities called this 'claim 'preposterous and baseless' but nonetheless the Bhutto family always considered it was a possibility.

As soon as the sentence of death was given, Bhutto was moved the same evening at 7 p.m. to a death cell, leaving a reasonable-sized cell for a 10 ft by 7 ft one. Many other prisoners, once condemned, had been allowed to stay in their cells and have them deemed death cells once convicted, but this was not so in the case of Bhutto. At first told he might remain in his cell, he was then speedily shifted to a death cell — a taste of what was to come when he would spend more than ten months in a death cell at Rawalpindi district jail.

He remained in Kot Lakhpat until 17 May. His appeal in the Supreme Court was due to begin on 20 May. As the Supreme Court of Pakistan was situated in Rawalpindi, he accordingly had to be moved. This was done unceremoniously; no effort was made to reduce his discomfort in the sweltering May heat of Pakistan. Dressed in one of his best suits, Bhutto was made to wait in uncertainty for over three hours before the move was accomplished. Travelling in a small twin-engined Cessna plane the 170 miles from Lahore to Rawalpindi, he was then conveyed from the airport to the district jail in a dirty police truck like a condemned prisoner rather than a former Prime Minister. He had already learnt, and the lesson was about to be impressed on him even more deeply, that he was not to be accorded any preferential treatment. What special treatment there was, was more in the nature of excessive guards and bars and bolts than would have been used to confine an ordinary prisoner.

The District Jail was at one end of Rawalpindi, on the way to the airport. Plaster was falling off the parched walls on the outside, which had at some point been painted white. Police and a huge bolted door indicated the use to which this building was put. Outside the walls, people gathered in groups — some waiting to visit the inmates, others just looking. Bhutto was whisked into the jail and installed in his new cell. If he had had a view to look out onto, it would have been the gardens of the Prime Minister's house, which was situated nearby. Perhaps he would even have been able to glimpse the house where he had spent five years as Prime Minister. It was as though fate were playing a cruel joke on him.

The months he was to spend in Rawalpindi were to be even more solitary than those in Kot Lakhpat. Whereas he had been present for some of his trial and, therefore, had the motivation to get up and dress each day, it was not customary procedure for an appellant to be present at his appeal. The hours which he had to himself therefore dragged endlessly. Although during the appeal a request was made for Mr Bhutto to attend, this was quietly dropped, as the Chief Justice stated that he was not anxious for the proceedings to turn into a second trial. The request was repeated towards the end of the appeal. But it did not seem likely that Bhutto would emerge from his cell quarters throughout his stay in jail. Since March, therefore, no one other than the jail authorities, his lawyers, his family and a random sample of doctors were permitted to set eyes on him. Requests for permission to visit him from any outsider were turned down by the highest authority in the land. Since the 'in camera' proceedings at Lahore, he was virtually in camera from the world. No impartial observer was permitted to give an unbiased picture of what his conditions of detention in the death cell were like. People had to choose between what the Government said and what his defence lawyers and family described. Government statements regarding the VIP treatment of the former Prime Minister in jail were consistently and emphatically denied by his lawyers and family. Bhutto's own method of protest at the conditions was to go on hunger strike.

According to the Government the former Prime Minister had the use of four cells which were neat, clean, spacious and well ventilated, with 'ample daylight and fresh air'. The fact that he could receive food from outside (including ice cream from the Intercontinental Hotel) was considered a luxury. According to Bhutto and his lawyers he was permitted to emerge for one hour per day out of his small cell. Once, when two prisoners escaped from another part of the jail, even this right was curtailed. At times too, when he was protesting against his conditions, he would use his non-emergence as a weapon of protest.

In fact, there were six cells in the quarters designated for the former Prime Minister, three facing three more, and separated by a narrow corridor. Bhutto's cell was at the end. There was no window. The door was formed of thick iron bars which permitted the entry of mosquitoes and flies. Once even a sparrow penetrated the cell. For some reason when Bhutto arrived the light switch for the one light bulb and the regulator to control the speed of the fan — by this time essential in the hot Pakistani summer — had been placed outside the ventilator in a position inaccessible to the inmate. His 'bathroom' was contained in the cell opposite — a bucket, a mug and a wooden commode were apparently considered to be sufficient. There was no curtain covering the iron bars and since Bhutto had to attract the attention of the guards to unlock his cell door to permit him to use the bathroom, there was little chance of privacy once he was inside.

To watch over him four guards remained in the corridor and slept in two of the cells. Another cell was allotted for his clothes and valuables — again opened to him only upon request. The sixth cell was used as a store room for food and cooking arrangements to supply tea and coffee. Bhutto was so disgusted with the conditions when he arrived that he went on hunger strike immediately in protest and was so weak that he could only greet his lawyer lying down when he came to visit him two days later. Protests and applications finally secured him a curtain over the iron bars of the bathroom and light and fan switches inside his cell. However, the toilet was unhygienic and never received proper attention during the hot summer months when the place was like a dust bowl.

Another annoyance was the telephone used for reporting his activities, which was placed within hearing distance. Eventually, upon supplication by the defence lawyers in the Supreme Court, this was also moved. For security, Bhutto was locked into his own cell, locked again into the complex of the six cells, and once more into the area which comprised the small court-yard where he was allowed to sit under the eyes of guards housed in three prison tents. The whole area surrounded by barbed wire was again under lock, as was, of course, the main entrance of the jail, which was manned by prison guards. As in Kot Lakhpat, an army colonel was on the premises.

Bhutto's family guarded jealously the right to send him meals. Initially, when Begum Bhutto was under house arrest in Lahore and her daughter Benazir in Karachi, the lawyers took charge of his meals. Later, however, when the family were free in Islamabad or under house arrest, they took over the supply of his meals, Begum Bhutto finding cooking for her husband therapeutic when she herself was under house arrest. The supply of food by the family was an important asset since after the episode in Kot Lakhpat, they never ruled out the possibility of food poisoning. Sometimes, as a kind of harassment, the food would be forbidden entry by a servant, and a lawyer would have to be transported to accompany it. At other times it was refused entry altogether. There seemed to be little reason or rationale to the vagaries of the jail authorities.

Bhutto lost about 40 lb. in weight in jail. His consumption of food home-cooked or otherwise was undoubtedly very small. This was mainly on account of his ill-health. He was troubled constantly by his teeth, with sore and infected gums, and this affected his general health. During the later stages of the appeal he made the pronouncement not so much that he was on hunger strike, but that he simply could not eat. He often became giddy and faint with exhaustion.

The bouts of influenza and malaria, as well as the colonic trouble he suffered from in Kot Lakhpat he believed were never properly treated, with the result that he did not completely recover. Throughout his confinement he was constantly pleading to be taken to a hospital for a proper medical examination. He was medically examined in jail in early August 1978 but the recommendations were never followed up. The sole achievement of the examination seemed to be the securing of a mattress to alleviate the back pain from which he suffered, according to the report. Even the supply of this took several weeks as it remained for a fortnight or so in the office of the jail superintendent. Bhutto had initially slept on a bed with iron springs which protruded and scarred his back but this was replaced by the bed without a mattress. A mattress, although necessary, was not, however, all he wanted. Again his critics said that these conditions were no worse than he had made others undergo. In their opinion the mighty had fallen and must be treated like the masses. The amount of compassion shown to Bhutto was minimal. No other man of his standing and reputation had been subjected to such conditions. Political leaders condemned for high treason and imprisoned under Bhutto's régime never suffered as he did. As Prime Minister he also had in his power the fate of Sheikh Mujib ur Rehman, who was condemned to death for high treason and yet was freed by him. No opponent was subjected to anything like the same degree of humiliation. Bhutto himself, the once powerful, arrogant autocrat that he is alleged to have been, bore the conditions of his confinement with dignity.

Because of his long history of teeth trouble he had been allowed treatment by Dr Zafar Niazi, who had been his dentist for twelve years. However, Niazi, appalled by the conditions under which Bhutto was kept in the Lahore jail, wrote what he termed non-political letters purely on humanitarian grounds to Members of Parliament in the United Kingdom and members of the U.S. Government, drawing attention to the treatment meted out to a former Prime Minister and Head of State. Then at the beginning of May, Niazi himself was arrested on charges of alleged political activities. One such charge related to the possession of anti-government propaganda in an envelope addressed to his office which was still unopened; another was that two empty whisky bottles were found lying in his house. (In fact these belonged to his colleague, an American, who, not being a Moslem, was permitted to have alcohol.) Niazi accordingly spent several months in Jhelum Jail about a hundred miles from Islamabad. Most people suspected that the reasons for his detention were not to be found in the charges brought against him, but in the letters he had written. Niazi protested that he was not a political man, but the government believed otherwise. Reputed to be the best dentist in Islamabad, his cause was championed passively by the diplomats. Released briefly on bail in July, for medical reasons, although no complaint was made, Niazi remained in jail until 10 November. From then onwards he consistently took pains to secure both medical and dental treatment for Mr Bhutto. While in jail himself he said he had been requested to incriminate Bhutto in some charge or other but had refused to do so.

Therefore, especially when Dr Niazi was in jail, Mr Bhutto's medical treatment was virtually non-existent. He himself was not anxious to be treated by any doctor, particularly one coming from the military authorities. He knew that the military régime would have a great deal to gain by his sudden death and believed that, as an alternative to food poisoning, it was possible for oxygen to be injected into his blood, which would make him die as it were of a heart attack. Once he was visited by a friendly army dentist who, in fact, recommended that he should receive proper treatment in a dental clinic. But the dentist did not reappear nor was the treatment forthcoming. His personal physician requested not to be summoned because pressure was being put on him by the military authorities, he said. There were those who believed that Bhutto's ailments were greatly exaggerated; others that he did not make enough complaints. As a proud man he did not like his health to be a constant matter of discussion. He was more concerned with his reputation than his life.

Permission to visit Bhutto for one hour per day was given to two of the lawyers. They took it in turns and the hour had to be rigidly observed. At one time the superintendent of the jail complained that the defence were overstaying the prescribed time and Bakhtiar was instructed by the Chief Justice to keep within the time limit. In Rawalpindi district jail in the hot summer months visiting time was from 7 to 8 p.m. In the winter this was changed from 4 to 5 p.m. Bhutto normally spent this hour of fresh air and daylight in the courtyard with the lawyers, taking tea. They discussed the case, talked about the past and often told jokes. Bhutto was allowed to wear his own clothes. If he were going anywhere, such as to Lahore High Court, he wore a suit; but these days in Rawalpindi district jail he was not going anywhere at all and so he wore shalwar kameez, comfortable, loose and for those who had criticised his western dress, totally Pakistani.

Bhutto's family — his wife and daughter, since his three other children were abroad — were allowed to visit him separately for two hours per week. Generally Begum Nusrat Bhutto went on Tuesday, Benazir on Saturday. Sometimes the hours were stretched to three but normally two was the limit, which the family believed was far less often than the visiting rights given to the other confessing co-accused. Bhutto complained that he could hear them making merry with a constant stream of visitors while he stagnated in his cell with little distraction to pass the time of day. Bhutto was also visited on occasion by his first wife, Amir, who was also his cousin and ten years his senior. She lived in the village of Naudero near Larkana and it was understood that the marriage had been one of convenience. He was thirteen, she was twenty-three when they were married. She had not however, been divorced when Bhutto married the attractive Iranian Begum Nusrat, since under Moslem law a man may have as many as four wives. His first wife spoke Sindhi rather than the 'national' language of Urdu.

Meetings with Begum Bhutto and Benazir did a great deal to re-charge their emotional batteries. Begum Bhutto often expressed her astonishment and admiration at Bhutto's strength in such adverse and patently hopeless circumstances. As they all believed the cell was heavily bugged it was prudent for both lawyers and family to whisper close up to the ear of Bhutto or write messages from one to another during the meetings.

The Begum and Benazir did not always pass through the jail gates without a certain degree of harassment. On her first visit after the death sentence, Begum Bhutto was ordered to subject herself to a body search. The Bhuttos considered this humiliating when searches were carried out at the airports for security reasons. On this occasion outside the jail Begum Bhutto refused to subject herself to the treatment. Finally the authorities had to make do with searching her handbag and packages. On another occasion Begum Bhutto felt that she had been so gravely insulted as to refuse her visit altogether. Once Benazir took some new plates for her father to replace those impregnated with grime. But these were refused entry. The intended humiliation could not be ignored.

Bhutto could also be visited by other members of his family. His two brothers were dead, as was one sister. The sole surviving full sister, Begum Munawarul Islam, lived in Karachi and

she came at times to visit her brother. He had one half sister in
Hyderabad. Bhutto's cousin, Mumtaz Ali Bhutto, was arrested
at Larkana on 16 September at the same time as Bhutto. Visits
from him were obviously precluded and his father, Bhutto's
uncle, was old. Both Bhutto's parents were dead.

Every day the lawyers brought him the newspapers — four or
five Urdu dailies, some which supported him, others which
clearly opposed him in their columns — as well as the English
language government-controlled press, the *Pakistan Times* and
Dawn. These were supplemented by magazines such as *Newsweek*, *Asia Week*, the *Far Eastern Economic Review* and the
Guardian weekly. The family brought flowers: the graceful
tuberoses with their unmistakable fragrance appeared to be his
favourite. Often Benazir would buy them in Karachi if she had
been there for the weekend and bring them on the plane for her
Saturday morning visit. Bhutto also smoked a number of cigars
— Romeo y Juliettas — which seemed to make up for his lack of
food intake. His family were in constant search for new books
for him to read. He enjoyed reading the memoirs of Richard
Nixon, a man with whom, however, he felt he had little affinity.
Nixon had gone down in history as a man who had fooled the
people; Bhutto would go down as one who had always been
supported by them. He also liked reading other political books
and up-to-date biographies. He read Sanjay Gandhi's story; a
book called *Oil* by Jonathan Black, *The Life of Eva Perón* by
John Barnes, *Sir Richard Burton* by Michael Hastings, *The
Great Mutiny* by Christopher Hibbert, the book on Nehru by
his private secretary, and the fictitious *Crash of 79* depicting
CIA involvement in Iran. He read late into the night; he also
wrote.

He was allowed pens and paper. He had a special preference
for felt pens and large writing-pads; stocks of these were bought
in order to have them on hand when he requested them. Many
believed that he might be sitting in jail writing a book — his own
memoirs, perhaps. There was a belief that all Bhutto's activities
were monitored, to the extent that television cameras had even
been installed in the ceiling of his cell, casting an unwinking eye
on whatever he might be writing. But he was allowed writing
material exclusively for giving instructions to his counsel with
regard to the appeal proceedings. Any letter he wrote had to go

via the jail superintendent. When the Annual Session of the
United Nations General Assembly was meeting on 21 September, he sent a telegram to the Secretary-General, Dr Kurt
Waldheim, complaining about his conditions of confinement
and about those of Pakistanis in general under the martial law
régime. The text of the telegram was released to the Pakistan
press but prompt censorship meant that only a large picture of
Bhutto and the Secretary-General appeared on the front page,
thus making it clear that a communication from Bhutto to the
Secretary-General was the object of the censorship. If the pictures had been censored as well, no one would have been any
the wiser.

As no reply to the telegram from the Secretary-General was
forthcoming, Bhutto assumed that it had not been despatched
by the jail superintendent. He therefore wrote a cutting letter to
the jail superintendent outlining the humiliations which he had
undergone since his arrest in September 1977.

It would be time-consuming to reproduce all the physical and
mental tortures I had to endure in solitary confinement from
3 September 1977 to 18 March 1978. The same afternoon (of
18 March) I was taken to the Death Cell and kept chained for
twenty-three hours out of the twenty-four. I still carry the
marks on my ankles of those happy days.

In this letter he talked about his ailments.

I had two serious attacks of malaria and influenza during the
winter. I was frequently troubled by stomach upsets and
acute headaches. In addition, I developed severe pains in the
chest. On three occasions I vomited blood and also bled from
the nose.

But no one seemed to care; some thought Bhutto was making
a fuss for publicity's sake; others that he might die and still the
authorities would not care. He concluded the letter by stating
that 'The aim is that I should wither away in this Death Cell.'
He named the régime and 'its collaborators' as being solely
responsible for the 'dire consequences' if he were not given
proper medical treatment.

As Bhutto was not permitted to communicate with the outside world in any other manner than through the jail superin-

tendent, information on his state of mind and/or state of health therefore came by word of mouth from his family or his lawyers. Since the authorities would not permit an impartial observer to see the conditions, it was only too easy for them to deny allegations of maltreatment on his behalf made by those who were obviously interested parties. Sometimes the lawyers reported that he was in a 'good mood', at others, he was annoyed at the slowness of the appeal, angered at the ma-noeuvres of the military régime after, for instance, some new measure for changing the Government was announced; frustrated at the lack of medical attention accorded to him. At no time did he appear to be dejected — 'My morale is high,' he said, 'because I am not made of the wood which burns easily.'

4

LINE-UP FOR
THE APPEAL

In order at least to try to win his case in the last court of appeal, Zulfikar Ali Bhutto needed the best defence he could get.

He relied upon some of those who had served him in government — two former Advocate-Generals and the former Attorney-General — later joined by his former Education Minister. These were supplemented by others who were proficient in the legal profession. A combination of outstanding qualities — hard work, brilliance, tolerance and perception — was necessary. In the group of lawyers who ran Bhutto's defence from a series of hotel rooms first in Lahore, then in Rawalpindi, these qualities were not lacking. Bhutto could not afford to have anything less than complete loyalty. Nor could those who became involved afford to be in two minds about it because inevitably they would feel the pinch of being on what was at present the losing side. It was not opportunism to support a fallen leader, but conviction and devotion. There was no surety of satisfaction, material or even emotional, when the man they were defending was condemned in a death cell and looked perilously close to execution.

The name which people associated most with Bhutto's appeal in the Supreme Court was that of Yahya Bakhtiar. As Bhutto's senior counsel he received quantities of fan mail and letters of encouragement from all over the country and all over the world. To Bhutto's supporters his legal battle became almost a spiritual fight to save their fallen leader. Bakhtiar also retained the prestige of having been Bhutto's Attorney-General. A tall Baluchi from Quetta in his late fifties, he was an imposing figure, often having to stoop to hear the remarks of his smaller colleagues and compatriots. The dark glasses he put on when emerging from the court gave him a semi-gangster look. At times, after a bad day in court, he looked like a harassed bear, with soft, slightly watering eyes peering through the haze of smoke which filled the tea-room after each session.

But Bakhtiar was in the mould of a true Baluchi warrior. He fought hard for his points and, raising his voice, was often not far from losing his temper. When this happened he excused it light-heartedly by saying that he had not taken his tranquilliser and had become irritated by the Chief Justice. 'He won't let me speak,' he pleaded (which was true — often it was hard to get a word in edgeways). Bakhtiar did have a series of ailments and from time to time swallowed various pills. When particularly tired, his hand trembled holding his tea-cup. At times in court he failed to speak clearly and had difficulty reading the small print of law books. He relied heavily upon the 'brain' of the team, a Sindhi lawyer called Ghulam Ali Memon.

Bakhtiar's own integrity had been questioned by the military régime: he, like his client, faced a charge of rigging in the March 1977 elections in Baluchistan. During the appeal he was on bail, which was liable to be cancelled once the appeal was over. Whenever the appeal looked like ending he would state mournfully, 'I think they will arrest me in a few days' ... and added, 'so I had better travel light.' Yahya Bakhtiar had a sense of humour — he kept the rest of the team in good spirits and settled the occasional inter-team rift; his best diversion was telling jokes, and he kept his listeners amused. He had studied at University College, London. There he met and married an Englishwoman who had converted to Islam and was almost more Moslem than Bakhtiar himself, since he used to enjoy his tipple of whisky before prohibition and lashing made it less attractive.

Ghulam Ali Memon — second in line — lived throughout the entire struggle only to die of a heart attack on the eve of its conclusion. It was a tragic and traumatic death for all concerned. Under Bhutto he had been Advocate-General of Sind High Court. A dark, medium-sized Sindhi, he had trained under A.K. Brohi, the Minister for Law and Parliamentary affairs under Zia ul Haq, who in the present clash was 'on the other side'. Memon admired Brohi's brand of brilliance. Once

asked why he had 'changed sides' he replied wisely that it was
not the business of the lawyer to have 'sides', which was characteristic of his own magnanimity in such agonising times. He did
concede, however, that it was very difficult not to. Memon too
had his own brand of brilliance; with a sharp, penetrating
mind, he was complimented by one of the judges during the
course of the appeal on being an 'encyclopaedia of law'. This
praise received resounding publicity in the local press. Memon
put exceptional efforts into the defence of Bhutto: he was
always at Bakhtiar's side, assisting him with the legal points
which were well within his knowledge and of which Bakhtiar
might not be sure. Behind the scenes Memon showed his
humanity. He had a sense of humour and chuckled at Bakhtiar's jokes. Respected and esteemed by all, his untimely death
came when he was only fifty-three.

Bhutto's senior counsel during the trial at Lahore, D.M.
Awan, was also one of the team of lawyers. With an excellent
memory and an eye for detail, he knew the evidence and statements of the witnesses by heart and could quote page numbers,
dates and events on the instant. He was a man of extraordinary
tolerance. He spoke in slow, measured tones, weighing his
words, for which he was sometimes teased by his colleagues. He
had been subjected to extreme pressure at Lahore, the Chief
Justice showing hostility to him and reminding him that as a
practising lawyer at Lahore he would have to appear in the High
Court before Maulvi Mushtaq again and so he had better watch
his conduct. He was making efforts to have the criticism that he
had aligned himself with his client expunged from the judgment of the Lahore High Court. At forty-six only a few years
younger than Bhutto himself, Awan both as senior advocate for
the trial and advocate for the appeal, had spent a great deal of
time with Bhutto. Often, during the course of the appeal, but
when the court was in recess and the lawyers returned to their
families in Quetta or Karachi, Awan, living not far away in
Lahore, remained to hold the fort and meet Bhutto for the daily
hour allotted to him. Awan was a Punjabi from the hilly area of
Sargodha, near Lahore. Like most Pakistanis he had his 'village' as well as his city life. He had travelled widely in Pakistan
but had never set foot out of the country.

Coming from entirely different areas and each with his

seniority in his own sphere, all the lawyers were on friendly terms. Only the pressures of work made one impatient with another on comparatively rare occasions. There was no time for energy to be wasted. They were assisted by two other lawyers from Karachi— Mr Hafeez Lakho and Mr Mohammed Sharif. Like Memon they had been taken on at the appeal stage and had to familiarise themselves with the weighty evidence in the few weeks which preceded the appeal after the judgment. Sharif adopted nephews and nieces wherever he went and was known as 'uncle' by all. Small, dark and fat, he was the only lawyer to bring out his prayer mat like a true Moslem and say his prayers five times a day— for them all, it seemed— and to compensate for the friendly curses and abuses he had given to all and sundry throughout the day. This was his light relief; for Mr Lakho it was his pipe— he had come with thirteen for the duration of the hearing. Only a little taller than Sharif, he was half the size of him in circumference. These lawyers did a great deal of research work behind the scenes in the Supreme Court library. Saleem Khan, in his late twenties, educated in England and known as the Pakistani who did not speak Urdu, completed the team. He and Sharif worked closely under the direction of Memon and complemented each other. They also provided a sharp contrast in features: small dark Sharif at the typewriter, tall, slender, pale Saleem Khan nearby, both composing notes which Bakhtiar would vet, have re-typed by one of the two typists and then use in court. The secretaries had to work to all hours; they also had to be prepared to do odd jobs, run errands, buy air tickets, medicines and quantities of stationery. Haroon Pervez, a young Pakistani, left his job in Lahore as well as his newly married wife; Peter Jilani closed down his stationery shop. The latter ended up in jail, as did another secretary-cum-assistant who worked for the lawyers in the initial stages. Atta ur Rehman disappeared from the scene in August when in a sudden police swoop on Flashmans Hotel, he was arrested. Dissemination of propaganda material appeared to be the charge for both of them although the charges were never substantiated.

The office was sited in Mr Sharif's room which was strewn with books, papers and a typewriter or two. Everyone drank innumerable cups of tea and smoked quantities of cigarettes.

Mr Noori, the Advocate on Record, remained only for the duration of the defence's arguments. He then returned to Karachi. While he was there he took pride in pouring the tea at the Supreme Court during the tea interval. He always left the court a few minutes early to prepare the cups and supervise the sandwiches. Later, for the concluding stages of the appeal Afzal Siddiqi, a lawyer from Rawalpindi, replaced Mr Noori as the Advocate on Record. He joined the team at the same time as Bhutto's former Education Minister and earlier Law Minister, Abdul Hafeez Pirzada, and Yasin Wattoo. The latter was acting Secretary-General of the PPP; Pirzada — a close friend of Bhutto — had been arrested after the *coup* and therefore petitioned to join the counsel as soon as he was released. Dynamic and active, he added a new dimension to Bhutto's defence.

There were only two hotels in Rawalpindi of any real standing — the Intercontinental and Flashmans. Whereas the Intercontinental was Europeanised, catering for foreign businessmen and tourists, Flashmans was entirely Pakistani and marginally less expensive. The lawyers were, accordingly, housed in the bungalow hotel of Flashmans at their client's expense. And with such a lengthy appeal it did prove expensive. But since none of the lawyers came from Rawalpindi or Islamabad it was the most convenient way of running the defence, although if it had been known how long the appeal would last a house could have been rented for one-tenth of the price. It was generally assumed that Bhutto was very rich and could easily meet the costs of his legal defence, without realising the heavy financial burden such protracted proceedings would make. As an economy, however, the lawyers did not order food from the hotel; instead they organised a system of bringing food from the nearby Rawalpindi club. This was accomplished by two young brothers, which necessitated an internal system of book-keeping and accounting. If Mr Bakhtiar were taking lunch, his room became the dining-room — a white tablecloth appeared and places were set. If he was not there Mr Memon's room was used, and so on down the line. But companions were flexible; sometimes they all ate together, at others, in their own rooms. The whole process required organisation and co-ordination. Domestic details and preoccupations were in general given the least consideration.

Flashmans was on the direct route to the Supreme Court on the Mall; it marked a halfway mark between the court and Rawalpindi district jail. In the morning they went in one direction, in the evening in the other. They commuted daily from one place to the other, followed in their wake by volumes of law books and notes and a secretary or two. The driver — Iqbal — who had been a foot-soldier in the British army and retained a magnificent moustache, alone could reduce the length of any journey by two-thirds of the customary time. If he was not to be seen and yet the car was standing there, he was most likely to be found asleep inside it, pulling himself to attention at the first thud on the window.

The lawyers worked late into the night, sleeping in the hot afternoons, taking dinner late, to be followed by a seven-minute walk in the cool of the summer evening outside the rooms which gave directly onto a convenient walking space. It was an all-consuming existence. While the court was in session there was no such thing as a holiday, a break or even an evening out.

The prosecution lived in the Government Guest House at State expense. It appeared that they were just as tired of the sort of hotel existence as were Bhutto's lawyers. As lawyers, they too had their case to win and they were equally concerned to exert their legal expertise. As well, they had to undergo the insults and black looks given to them by Bhutto's supporters, who believed their legal efforts were merely a manifestation of the state's machinations to get rid of Bhutto. They too were human; they just had a different job from the defence lawyers which to the public eye appeared less pleasant. Pleading for a man to be hanged does not afford the same attraction as pleading for his innocence.

There were three lawyers for the prosecution — they were nicknamed 'father, mother and child' by the other side. In addition there were suspicions that others behind the scenes lent a helping hand. The learned Public Prosecutor, Ejaz Hussain Batalvi, who had taken over at the trial when the Chief Prosecutor died, objected strongly when inferences were made to this effect, but calmed down when the Chief Justice himself said that there was nothing wrong with a bit of help from one's friends. Once Mr M.A. Rehman, the Advocate on Record for the State, remarked that Mr Bakhtiar had been fed by Mr Memon, insinuating that he had not done all his work, and Bakhtiar retorted, 'At least the people who feed me are sitting beside me and are not behind the scenes.'

Rehman had a significant role as Advocate on Record. Like Batalvi, he was middle-aged, medium height and medium size. He assisted his colleagues with the devotion of a wife, their opponents said, urging that the correct page numbers and exact quotations be given to add weight to their case. When, for instance, 'Lahore' was once mentioned by mistake, a distinct whisper 'Peshawar' was heard in correction, much like a prompt off stage. (In fairness Memon did the same for Bakhtiar.) As it was, Batalvi had a very loud, theatrical voice which made his delivery much clearer than that of Bakhtiar. It was said that he had once been on the stage, but now practised law in Lahore. At one time when he was making his submissions he spoke in such thundering tones that one of the judges asked if the learned Public Prosecutor would kindly repeat what he had said but in a much quieter tone of voice — obviously he had been deafened to the extent that he had not grasped the vital point. A young lawyer — Mahmud A. Shaikh — in his twenties, completed the group. Upon request he had interrupted his commitments at Lincoln's Inn to act for the State and said that he would be returning there once the appeal was over.

As State Prosecutor, these lawyers were putting forward a case to reject the appeal of the former Prime Minister against his conviction for conspiracy to murder. They had this much headstart on their counterparts. One set of judges had already believed their story.

Both Batalvi and Rehman clearly seemed to think that Bhutto was guilty and that the trial at Lahore had been conducted in a proper manner without the bias alleged by the defence team. They further believed that the judiciary was totally independent of political influence and were horrified when a suggestion was made to the contrary. Batalvi was far more jovial than his colleague, who at times could not hide his antipathy to Bhutto.

From a legal point of view relations between the two sides were generally cordial, although strained at times. It was not the first time they were facing each other in the Supreme Court. Winner or loser, they had both won and lost cases before. At times there was also the impression that the whole appeal was a charade, and that they were merely acting out the roles which they had been called upon to play. Many believed that the decision was already a foregone conclusion. Below the surface the two ideologies lurked — the political divisions which split them into supporters and opponents of Bhutto could not be hidden. Prevalent among onlookers was the view that both sides were arguing not just about the fate of one man, but the fate of the country and perhaps their own fates as well.

Theoretically, of course, and many people hoped in practice, the decision rested with the judges. This onerous task would weigh heavily upon these men until the conclusion of the appeal and the announcement of judgment. It would be their signatures which would validate the death sentence of the former Prime Minister or reject it in favour of a lesser penalty, retrial or acquittal. It would be upon their consciences if anything other than judicial considerations came into play. The independence of the judiciary was an issue at all times during the hearing of the appeal. Many people asked how independent from the arm of martial law were the judges and what sort of metal would they be made of? At all times they protested impartiality, even, it seemed, at the expense of rejecting the verdict of their brother justices in Lahore. They took umbrage whenever it was suggested that they might be prejudiced by propaganda.

Bhutto was to be tried by a full bench of nine judges which, people said, would give him the maximum chance of securing justice. He himself never had much faith in the Supreme Court. His experience with the Lahore Court left him unmoved and sceptical. Whereas his supporters might show enthusiasm and hope in the proceedings when, for instance, some departure was made from the procedure at Lahore, Bhutto remained aloof. For most of the time he was expecting an upheld verdict. He had not been declared innocent at Lahore and he did not expect to be now. It was, after all, after Anwarul Haq had just been appointed Chief Justice that martial law had been validated. Furthermore, Anwarul Haq had agreed to hear the appeal, which he could have rejected out of hand if he had given credence to Bhutto's protestations that the trial had been unfair.

The row of judges was fit for an art gallery. Tall, short, fat, thin: they were all sorts. They moved in procession solemnly into the court and sat on high-backed chairs which were ceremoniously moved in and out for them by costumed bearers. These attendants were clad in white tunics with gold sashes across their chests and wore white turbans or puggarees with a fanned piece of material resembling a large feather sticking out of the top. In winter they changed into green and the judges donned black gowns over their suits which rendered their appearance even more sombre. Once they were seated behind a pile of law books the atmosphere relaxed. There was often conversation and interjections which made the court room seem like a forum for discussion when several spoke altogether. At times there was banter and repartee which the Chief Justice, in particular, seemed to enjoy. The personalities of the judges themselves emerged. Mr Justice Anwarul Haq was a small, portly man, white-haired but balding. He had an astonishingly unwrinkled face for his age and the amount of strain he must have had to undergo to reach the exalted position of Chief Justice of the Supreme Court of the land. He had a habit of moving his neck from one side to the other of his starched white collar like a bulldog. He also had the rather irritating habit of interjecting 'yes' and 'quite' every second sentence in the course of a submission before the point was made, thus interrupting the flow of discourse. At times too, he interrupted altogether, which had the effect of annoying Bakhtiar immensely.

Next in line of seniority was Mr Justice Mohammed Akram, a tall man who looked like a corpse; his face lacked lustre and his features never moved. He rarely spoke but when he did he sounded like the ghost in *Hamlet*, his voice rattling deep in his throat. Both he and Anwarul Haq were Punjabis. Like Maulvi Mushtaq both had been superseded when Bhutto was in power and vehemently opposed any system whereby judges were not automatically appointed according to seniority.

Mr Justice Waheeduddin Ahmed was portlier still than Anwarul Haq and likewise balding, his lined and wrinkled face indicating the stress and strain of the life of a justice. He appeared to sleep for most of the proceedings and yawned frequently. But suddenly he would come up with a pertinent and relevant remark which showed that he was not sleeping but merely had his eyes shut. Unfortunately, in the later stages of the appeal he fell ill. This illness marked a crucial stage in the appeal and in the morale of Bhutto's supporters. Coming from Delhi in 1947 at the time of partition, he had settled in Karachi.

Mr Justice Dorab Patel, a small, almost wizened man, was a Parsee. He lived in Karachi but came from Quetta in Baluchistan. Unmarried at over fifty, he was immensely wealthy. Often he could be seen strolling around Islamabad in the evening, undoubtedly pondering on the events of the day. Mr Justice Safdar Shah was tall and dignified. Married to a German, he looked almost European himself and was nicknamed 'Abe Lincoln' by the foreigners. One wondered whether he was ever aware of this comparison made to him by association of features. He had been Chief Justice of Peshawar High Court in Frontier Province whence he came. It had been considered that he would not favour Bhutto because he had been retired from his position earlier than anticipated on account of an amendment to the Constitution made in Bhutto's time. Irrespective of age, judges of the High and Supreme Courts were retired after a limited tenure of Office. Although this amendment had the advantage of clearing out the dead wood and preventing judges remaining in office until they were of the accepted age for retirement, the judges could feel that their services had been dispensed with prematurely. In view of this, Safdar Shah surprised everyone by his apparent openmindedness and his aggressive questioning of the prosecution. He did not harbour the grudge against Bhutto which was expected of him.

Two more judges were similar in appearance. Mr Justice Mohammed Haleem entered and left wearing dark glasses — as if the light of the hall outside were too bright for him, although he was the only judge who rarely wore glasses for visual purposes when in the court. More often he would squint at law books rather than put glasses on. But five minutes before the court was about to rise he put on his dark glasses — which provided a clearer indication that the proceedings were over than the hurried movements of the bearers. Huddled together on the steps beside the justices' bench, they scurried to take up their positions behind the chairs of the respective judges to whom they were assigned, in order to move the chairs out as they rose.

The other judge of this pair — and they sat side by side — was

Mr Justice Karam Elahee Chauhan. He was a sympathiser of
the Jamaat-i-Islami religious sect, as was Aftab Hussain in the
Lahore Court. It was considered that he would be no more
sympathetic to Bhutto's case than had been his counterpart at
Lahore. Chauhan came from the Punjab; Haleem from the
United Province in India and had now settled in Karachi. As
events were to show, their similarity ended with their appearance since they had very different views on the case. Chauhan
rarely spoke; he drank several glasses of water throughout the
morning's proceedings.

Chauhan surprised many people by waiting patiently at the
end of the proceedings to clasp hands with the smallest of the
judges, Dr Naseem Hassan Shah, who was no more than four
feet tall. This was clearly a sign of friendship but it looked very
odd. Dr Naseem Hassan Shah, however, appeared even odder
when, emerging in procession, he was side by side with the very
tall, thin Safdar Shah, himself not only very small but round
and fat. He was also characterised by his squeaky, high-pitched
voice; yet these traits did not detract from his sharp mind. He
had received a doctorate in France and he too, came from the
Punjab. It was said that when the judges were showing themselves for and against the prosecution story, he sat on the fence.

The ninth judge, Mr Justice Qaiser Khan, from Frontier
Province, was a sore subject amongst Bhutto supporters, who
were initially relatively relaxed at the prospect of having a full
bench — three being the requirement for a quorum. Qaiser
Khan was due to retire as a judge from the bench of the
Supreme Court on 30 July. It was hoped that should the appeal
continue beyond that date he would be appointed on an ad hoc
basis for the duration. But the farewell ceremony took place and
off he went into retirement. He was the only judge who had
criminal trial court experience, having worked his way up
through the judiciary. Bhutto supporters bemoaned his loss;
they believed he had shown himself in favour of Bhutto's case
and would not uphold the death sentence. But once gone he
could not be brought back.

At times, even at the outset, there was speculation as to the
way the voting would go and many predicted that, in accordance with the death sentence given by five Punjabi justices, the
Punjabis would uphold the verdict, the non-Punjabis would not

— resulting in five for Bhutto, four against. The provincial association might be considered coincidental but it worked its way into the thoughts of Bhutto's supporters. It was of course impossible to tell what would happen. Much attention was focused on the Chief Justice, who not only came from Punjab but from Jullundur in East Punjab, now part of India. The two other men in positions of power who also came from Jullundur were, of course, the Chief Martial Law Administrator, General Zia ul Haq, and the Chief Justice of the Lahore High Court, Maulvi Mushtaq Hussain; these were supplemented by another general in a high position— General Chisti. They were all called the 'jullundurites' by Bhutto supporters. Bhutto was very sensitive about the close association between the 'coterie', as he called it. They all moved from East Punjab at the time of partition and were considered as intruders, indeed usurpers, by the old-established families, more especially as this particular group appeared to be intent on hanging the Sindhi Prime Minister. Throughout the appeal Bhutto's supporters kept a close watch on the activities of the Chief Justice for any hint of partiality. More subtle than the Chief Justice of the Lahore High Court, people suspected that his comments could not be taken at face value, when, for instance, he remarked, 'We are going through the evidence with an open mind.'

Even before the appeal began Bhutto lodged a complaint. He had only been given seven days in which to appeal instead of the customary thirty, which did not afford time to collect the proper documents and only a preliminary appeal could be filed, to be supplemented by a more detailed one. But when the time came for the appeal to commence it was postponed for one week. This was because the Chief Justice assumed the Acting Presidency in the absence abroad of the President of Pakistan, which precluded him from acting as Chief Justice for the duration of his acting presidentship. In Bhutto's opinion this was a clear indication on which side of the fence Anwarul Haq sat. If he had been so anxious to begin the appeal early there was no need for him to afford himself the luxury of becoming Acting President, Bhutto's supporters believed. Bhutto thought not only that Anwarul Haq was biased, but that he had fused his judicial functions with those of the executive and that therefore he should not hear his appeal. Anwarul Haq defended himself by saying that his assumption of the presidency was perfectly normal and in keeping with the Constitution. He also proferred that if he had not taken the office it might have gone to another military man in a régime already run by the military. But Bhutto never became reconciled to this and objected when it occurred again later in the course of the appeal. However, it was generally agreed that compared with the atmosphere in the Lahore High Court, that in the Supreme Court was calm and cordial.

With Bhutto locked away in his cell, these men — the judges, lawyers for defence and prosecution — kept each other company in the wood-panelled court room for what seemed like an interminable time, arguing their way through the weight of evidence in the case of their former Prime Minister 'Z.A. Bhutto and others'.

*

The Supreme Court of Pakistan, situated about half a mile from Rawalpindi's main bazaar, was a white marble building with attractive gardens. It had formerly been East Pakistan House and was only serving the purpose of Supreme Court while the new Supreme Court in Islamabad was being built. It would, however, do so for quite some time to come since the only advance made in constructing the new Supreme Court so far was a sign saying 'site for Supreme Court', Bhutto himself having laid the foundation stone.

The court met from 9 a.m. to 1 p.m. each day from Saturday to Wednesday since Pakistan observed the Islamic weekend of Thursday and Friday. Passes were issued by the Registrar for attendance. This was a novelty in procedure; they had only been required once before when Begum Nusrat Bhutto challenged the validity of martial law. The court room in which the appeal was heard had a seating capacity of 80 to 100 persons. Attendance was spasmodic. At times, only a handful of spectators turned up to hear the proceedings; at others the court room was crowded. Comparatively few of Bhutto's supporters attended regularly. The former Foreign Minister, Mr Aziz Ahmed, who came virtually every day, was one of the few members of Bhutto's old guard who had not found himself in jail. Bhutto's Chief Minister from Sind — Ghulam Mustafa Jatoi — also put in an appearance from time to time. The Urdu journalists came frequently; the foreign journalists less so. They dropped in on the off-chance that something other than the appeal might be discussed — for instance, a complaint from Bhutto himself about the conditions in the jail, or if they had had a tip-off that some mini-climax was about to be reached. At the end, however, virtually more foreign journalists and television teams came than spectators when judgment was announced. They were an indication to the Chief Justice and his brother justices that the eyes of the world were on the outcome of the appeal.

The tea break between 11 and 11.30 provided a convenient meeting-place when odd snatches of information could be exchanged and photographs of the lawyers were taken. They appeared in the local press the next day. The lawyers for the prosecution, though available for questions in the tea break, went to their own hide-out. They were not such an attraction for photographers. Moreover, whereas the defence lawyers were only too willing to talk to journalists and give information, the lawyers for the prosecution appeared to scorn informal contact with the press. At times the atmosphere after the proceedings was tense; at others it was one of sheer fatigue. Regardless of the fact that the lives of five men — Bhutto and the four confessing co-accused — were at stake, a great deal of the appeal was tedious. It did not have the action and movement of a trial. The accused were not present and the mere reading of the evidence, plus the fact that at times Bakhtiar read in rather a monotonous tone of voice, had nothing of the colour of the question and answer format.

At the outset however, the feeling was one of urgency. People really did believe the appeal would be over in about six weeks. In the end it took more than ten months. As the appeal stumbled from month to month, with intermittent breaks, the military régime dug its toes in, making one pronouncement after another. It became inpossible to separate the hearing in the Supreme Court from the political situation in Pakistan. Zia had committed himself to holding elections but it was clear that no such elections would take place until after it was concluded. Whatever people might say to the contrary, most believed that what was decided in the Supreme Court about Zulfikar Ali Bhutto would have important consequences for the political future of Pakistan.

5

IN DEFENCE
OF BHUTTO

The defence counsel for Zulfikar Ali Bhutto took fifty-seven days to present its case. Yahya Bakhtiar began on 20 May. What the judges were to go over again and again by the time the appeal concluded, on the first day surprised them and they appeared taken aback. Having given a brief outline of the prosecution's case which the Lahore High Court had accepted entirely in its judgment, Yahya Bakhtiar then set out what grounds the appeal would be based on.

'I will very briefly state the main points,' he began. 'The defence case, as is apparent, of Mr Zulfikar Ali Bhutto is based on three main grounds.' The Chief Justice was expectant. 'Yes.' With this invitation, Bakhtiar struck home. 'It is a false, fabricated and politically motivated case — a case of the international conspiracy of which Mr Zulfikar Ali Bhutto is a victim. He was removed from power as elected Prime Minister of the country forcibly, with a view to eliminating him politically and physically.'

The Chief Justice wanted to make sure he had heard correctly.

'Politically and physically ...'

Bakhtiar confirmed '... so that he is politically and physically eliminated.'

One of the other judges woke up to the significance of Bakhtiar's statement: 'Politically eliminated?' he asked.

'Yes, my Lord,' replied Bakhtiar, 'and physically. My second ground of attack is that he was tried by a thoroughly hostile and biased Bench.'

Another judge did not quite grasp this. 'Pardon?'

Bakhtiar repeated his submission.

'Biased and ... ?'

'Biased and hostile,' said Bakhtiar confidently. 'That he did not get a fair trial and therefore he was compelled to boycott the proceedings of the trial, after making every effort for over two months to defend a case, but the Bench made it impossible for him to do so.' Mindful that journalists, foreign and local, were busy taking down his outline, Bakhtiar was getting into his stride. He set out to show that the prosecution had no basis in fact or in law whatsoever, on account of the inconsistencies in the statements of the witnesses, quite apart from the conduct of the trial which, the defence counsel believed, vitiated the whole proceedings. In no way had Bhutto been proved guilty beyond all reasonable doubt.

Bakhtiar's first task was to read the evidence of the forty-one witnesses. It took him thirty-five days, allowing time for frequent interjections by the judges and prosecution calling for explanations, as well as Bakhtiar's own submissions. The first testimony for him to tear apart was that of Kasuri. Claiming to be a political 'opponent' of Bhutto, he did not emerge as such in reality. There were other opponents who posed far more of a threat to Bhutto's leadership than Kasuri, like Asghar Khan, the leader of an opposition party, the Tehrick-i-Istiqlal, or Abdul Wali Khan, leader of the NAP. Motive was alleged to have arisen after the altercations in the National Assembly but criticism for a politician was part and parcel of political life, said the defence. Bhutto was used to it.

From the record of his political career Kasuri appeared to have drifted since his membership of the PPP. He had not made any real headway on the political scene. It was known that he was an admirer of Bhutto in the early days, but when confronted in court with the contents of a letter which he had written to Bhutto in the early days stating:

> You have served the cause of toiling, teeming millions of Pakistanis with your sweat, tears and blood, which I am certain will go deep in the pages of history with golden words

his reply to the question, whether or not he recalled having written it, had come 'I do not remember.' He did not appear anxious to admit the virtual reverence in which he held his 'leader whom I have loved the most'.

Although criticising Bhutto for several years he had resumed this sycophantic stance after the murder of his father and Bakhtiar showed him as an opportunist who had changed his colours to suit the occasion. Insofar as concerned his hatred of Bhutto after Bangladesh, many others believed that Bhutto's actions were questionable but most accepted that it was a difficult situation for both sides. They attributed the break-up of greater Pakistan to far more fundamental reasons than those furnished by Kasuri. The defence also indicated that Kasuri had himself agreed with the line adopted by the People's Party at the time. His pursuit of Bhutto in the guise of enemy and friend appeared dangerously close to the failing of which he accused Bhutto — hunger for power at all costs.

After the murder it was Kasuri who himself appeared anxious to rejoin the party. Whereas there was plenty of documentary evidence to this effect, there was none in the reverse direction indicating that Bhutto wanted him back as the prosecution said. All the notes indicated that the initiative came from Kasuri. He begged that he might not be kept on tenterhooks any more but be brought back into the fold of PPP without delay. He assured Bhutto of 'complete loyalty' to his Chairman.

But Bhutto was not particularly keen to have a reconciliation. He wrote in the margin of a note from his Chief Security Officer, Saeed Ahmed Khan, in July 1975, requesting that Kasuri might be given an interview ...

He must be kept on the rails, he must repent and he must crawl before he meets me. He has been a dirty dog. He has called me a madman. He has gone to the extent of accusing me of killing his father. He is a lick (boot-licker). He is ungrateful. Let him stew in his juice for some time.

Hardly the attitude to be taken, the defence maintained, if the former Prime Minister had a guilty conscience after the murder of Kasuri's father; he would have been much more likely to appease him and pander to his requests.

Known as the 'dirty dog' document, when a photostat was produced in court the prosecution took exception to it, stating that the remarks were forged. Bhutto had made an additional comment 'please file' and this appeared in a different shade of ink, indicating that a different pen was used and therefore, they maintained, it could not be proved that Bhutto wrote those remarks back in 1975. The defence, however, argued that it was perfectly possible to write the two separate comments on the same day. The change in ink was explained by the fact that the 'dirty dog' comments were much paler, but when it came to the date, Bhutto took up another pen because the one he was using was running out to conclude writing it and then to write 'please file' and the date — '29/7' — once more. The original document could not be found. Bhutto's supporters maintained that those in league with the military régime had destroyed it.

Waiting to be accepted back into the PPP, Kasuri hovered in the background. Finally he was allowed to rejoin the PPP in February 1976 but he did not keep a low profile and instead tried to curry favour. He sent an effusive report after a trip to Mexico in June 1976. His praise of the Prime Minister reached its pre-1971 pitch when the time for elections in March 1977 approached. Bakhtiar read out parts of Kasuri's speeches made in early 1977 in the National Assembly which eulogised Bhutto. On the face of it, it appeared, according to the defence, that he had readily forgotten the death of his father and his grievances against the former Prime Minister, in favour of his political career. What Kasuri in his testimony termed self-preservation looked very much like political opportunism. The defence believed that if Kasuri feared so much for his life, he should have kept his distance or retired from politics altogether, rather than try to project himself once more into the limelight. In court he had tried to explain away his frequent demands for an interview with the Prime Minister by saying that for the period in question the nomination tickets for the People's Party were going to be decided, 'and,' he said, 'I was seeking an interview in relation to that', as if that were sufficient excuse. But the tenor of a letter addressed directly to the Prime Minister was chatty and familiar:

My dear Prime Minister [he began], Earlier I have requested over half a dozen times to your MS (military secretary) for an interview with you...

He concluded:

I trust this letter finds you and Begum Bhutto in best of health, happiness and prosperity. With warm regards ...

It was far more feasible, the defence believed, that if Kasuri still harboured the hatred against Bhutto which he later claimed, when the time came for elections he should have taken the opportunity to expose and denounce Bhutto as a dictator and the murderer of his father, rather than try to gain favour and obtain a ticket in Bhutto's own party. Again, the fact that Kasuri was not given the party ticket proved that Bhutto did not have a guilty conscience. The defence also gave the instance of another member of the PPP — a man called Rao Khurshid Ali, who had been a bitter critic of the Prime Minister throughout his tenure of power and yet who still had been given a ticket for the 1977 elections. This example was an indication that a motive to kill Kasuri could not be attributed to the Prime Minister just because he had been criticised by him in Parliament.

Kasuri's criticism of Bhutto had to be put into the perspective of the criticism inevitably levelled at any politician, but it did not constitute sufficient motive. Although in Lahore Kasuri had chosen to deny the testimony he had given before Mr Shafi ur Rehman regarding the four groups of people with a possible motive, he had clearly made himself unpopular amongst many PPP workers by his constant criticism, with the result that he was subjected to the fifteen attacks. It was hardly possible for the former Prime Minister to have instigated all these attacks in different parts of the country. Nor had Kasuri named the Prime Minister in the First Intelligence Report filed after the Islamabad incident less than three months before the Lahore ambush. All aspects raised by the defence moved away from being able to attribute sole motive to Bhutto; in a departure from the Lahore trial the Shafi ur Rehman report was admitted as evidence by the Supreme Court; at least the defence felt that it was now on record that Kasuri had named four groups who might have had a possible motive to kill him. With motive in doubt, the time soon came to attack the prosecution's story of conspiracy.

With regard to Kasuri, the defence also objected to the fact that his private complaint which he lodged soon after the *coup* at the end of July had not been taken up first. In this complaint he accused not only the former Prime Minister, but also Masood Mahmud, Saeed Ahmed Khan and Rao Rashid. Kasuri's statement was already being recorded and two judges were dealing with the matter. If all four senior men had been tried a very different picture might have emerged from the one where Bhutto, as principal accused, was put on trial with four junior officers of the FSF. In the defence's opinion, it was clearly a government manoeuvre aimed at eliminating Bhutto to take up the stance of Public Prosecutor, against the former Prime Minister, rather than let Kasuri fight it out himself. Quite apart from anything else the proceedings would doubtless have crippled Kasuri financially.

Masood Mahmud's was the testimony on which the case for conspiracy rested. But circumspection had to be shown on the evidence of the man who allegedly conspired with Bhutto since he had an obvious motive in becoming an approver if it meant his life would be spared. In addition, whilst in detention throughout the trial, Mahmud drew a salary on the same grade as his former position as Director-General of the FSF as officer for special duty under the MLA. Bakhtiar said he was kept in 'cotton wool' by the military authorities. His own motive in implicating the former Prime Minister was far too apparent to make his testimony sustainable.

The defence stated that because, according to his statement, Mahmud was forced under duress to give instructions for the murder of Kasuri he could not therefore be a party to the conspiracy. According to the prosecution the conspiracy was hatched soon after the altercation in the National Assembly on 3 June 1974. But when the attention of Mahmud was drawn to the attack on Kasuri's life in Islamabad in August 1974, the fact that he said he had no knowledge of it but that he merely had a 'hunch' about it, was hardly credible. Surely, the defence asked, if he were a co-conspirator in a plot to murder Kasuri he would have had knowledge of this attack, again organised by the second approver, Ghulam Hussain? Furthermore, Mahmud was seen to improve on the precise timing of the conspiracy in his testimony. In his previous statement before the magistrate he said it was hatched 'a month or two' after he became Director-General of the FSF (which was on 23 April 1974). But in court at Lahore he said it was a day or two after the 3 June altercation, thus coinciding more precisely with the prosecution case. This was just one of the many improvements the defence were anxious to highlight and bring out on record during the course of Bakhtiar's submissions.

Certain facts made the defence describe Mahmud as having been assigned a role without a role. According to Mahmud's own testimony Bhutto had already instructed his predecessor, Haq Niwaz Tiwana, to carry out the murder of Kasuri; and Haq Niwaz Tiwana had already given the orders to Mian Abbas. Was it, therefore, logical for the former Prime Minister to engage another person in the conspiracy who, by his own admission, was unwilling to conspire? This brought out another inconsistency in the prosecution's case: on the one hand Mr Bhutto was charged with hatching the conspiracy in mid-1974: on the other hand he had allegedly already hatched it prior to that with Haq Niwaz Tiwana. The latter had died and was unable to corroborate or deny Mahmud's statement.

So much of the conspiracy had been conducted on the 'telephone' according to Mahmud as to make the whole affair common knowledge. Mahmud said that he had telephoned Welch in Quetta from Rawalpindi where there was no direct dialling and therefore the operator could easily have been listening in to Mahmud's instructions that Kasuri was to be 'taken care of' when he visited Quetta. This sort of irresponsible act on the part of a co-conspirator hardly stood the test. In his later statements he avoided using the telephone story after the defence pointed out the unlikelihood of its use. There were numerous other instances of improvements and inconsistency which made the defence believe that he was an unreliable witness.

In order to convict a man for murder on the word of an approver, the defence said that according to the demands of law, a double test should be applied to his evidence: firstly it should be believable — they said it was not — in which case the accusations did not stand; secondly, since any man who would depose against another to save his own life was considered to be a man of 'depraved character', another test had to be applied — that of corroboration. The defence also maintained that his testimony could not be matched with that of any other independent witness. To hang the former Prime Minister on the word of the approver Masood Mahmud was, to the defence, wholly untenable in law. In Islam too, many pointed out that it was strictly prohibited.

The time came for Bakhtiar to move on to one such 'independent' witness — Bhutto's chief security officer, Saeed Ahmed Khan.

*

Outside the court the temperature was very high, but inside the Supreme Court it was a little chilly, due to the air conditioning and the atmosphere. Bakhtiar launched into Saeed Ahmed Khan with as much aplomb as he could muster. This man, Bhutto's Chief Security Officer, according to his testimony, appeared at times as a conspirator, channelling the investigation, hushing up the case, persuading Kasuri to rejoin the PPP and keeping a personal file on him. Yet if his testimony were to be accepted he also had to emerge as an independent witness, otherwise he would clearly have a motive to depose against the former Prime Minister to cover up his own part in the plot. Both Saeed Ahmed Khan and Masood Mahmud declared that Bhutto was their enemy and this, the defence believed, gave them a clear motive to implicate the former Prime Minister; accordingly their testimony was questionable. Furthermore, as had been shown in cross-examination at Lahore, Saeed Ahmed Khan had said that he lived in fear of his life, but he was also confronted with letters he had written to the Prime Minister in 1972 stating in extravagant terms:

> I am devoted to you and your cause ... I can lay down my life for you, but I only need a little encouragement from you and a word of cheer in return. Kindly bear with me when I say I have burnt my boats and sink or swim with you.

The issue of the personal file, taken and blown up by the prosecution to mean that Kasuri was about to be eliminated by the former Prime Minister, appeared from Saeed Ahmed Khan's own testimony as a routine affair in political life.

'I was asked to report on a number of persons who included

practically all Opposition Leaders and PPP renegades and PPP legislators also,' he said.

Bakhtiar treated with circumspection Saeed Ahmed Khan's statement that he was told by the Prime Minister to 'remind' Mahmud about the work he had been assigned with regard to Kasuri. If, according to Mahmud's testimony, he was in frequent touch with the Prime Minister, would the Prime Minister not have been able to 'remind' Mahmud about the task himself, instead of telling Saeed Ahmed Khan to do so and involving yet another person?

The defence believed that Saeed Ahmed Khan and Abdul Hamid Bajwa were busybodies, poking their noses into everything. There was no proof that what they did was ordered by the Prime Minister. As already shown, all the notes and letters produced as evidence at the trial indicated that the initiatives came from Kasuri to rejoin the party, and that Saeed Ahmed Khan and Bajwa were acting as intermediaries on his behalf. Saeed Ahmed Khan sent a document clearly stating that Kasuri 'wishes to return to the fold and would carry out the Prime Minister's directives and can be used in any way desired by the Prime Minister'.

Nor was there any evidence from the witnesses that they were prevented from getting evidence and making enquiries after the murder; they merely said they were 'instructed'. But if, according to Saeed Ahmed Khan's testimony and that of the other witnesses such as Mohammed Asghar and Vakil Khan, he had had a hand in channelling the investigation away from the 'real culprits', then it was obvious that he was an accomplice and his testimony could not be used to corroborate that of Masood Mahmud. On the one hand he appeared tainted and involved; on the other he was an innocent party. The defence also pointed to the fact that his assistant — Bajwa — had died in early 1976 and was therefore not in a position to corroborate Saeed Ahmed Khan's testimony. On close examination Saeed Ahmed Khan was not, the defence believed, the independent witness necessary to make Masood Mahmud's testimony acceptable.

Nor could Masood Mahmud's evidence be corroborated by that of the fourth prosecution witness — M.R. Welch — the FSF chief in Quetta. He stated that the reasons for Kasuri's elimination were because he had been making 'obnoxious' speeches against the Prime Minister in Parliament. But this evidence was not furnished by Mahmud and therefore, in the legal sense, did not act as corroboration. Welch, too, appeared in the guise of an accomplice since he had known about the attempted murder which he refused to carry out. His evidence also was not helped by the disclosure in court that it had been given on solemn affirmation, when the defence had proof that he was a practising Christian and that he should therefore, have been sworn into the witness-box on the Bible. His failure to make his faith known seemed to point to the fact that he was not always telling the truth, although the prosecution remarked that it was a bit 'late in the day' to disclose this. But as it emerged, his testimony did not show that the order for Kasuri to be taken care of/eliminated in Quetta during his visit came from Bhutto, but from Masood Mahmud. Nor, when examined, did parts of his statement appear all that harmful. When asked about the duties to be covered by the FSF under the provisions of its charter, his reply came:

'Any orders which were not criminal were obeyed by us.'

The defence counsel for one of the confessing co-accused wanted confirmation.

'The subordinate officers were used for the purpose of carrying out the orders which were not covered by the charter of duties?' — as if to suggest that unorthodox activities were encompassed in these duties. But Welch replied:

'Only those orders were carried out which were *not* criminal in nature.'

Which admission did not correspond with the prosecution case that the FSF was used for precisely those criminal activities.

In relation to his own duties to report on the activities of persons under surveillance Welch stated, 'It was routine to send reports to the higher officers', much as Saeed Ahmed Khan had been obliged to admit that personal files were also routine. So, the defence submitted, Kasuri's surveillance was not unusual.

The evidence of these four witnesses, making up the bulk of the prosecution's case, took twenty days to be examined at Lahore out of the forty-eight days during which the evidence of the prosecution witnesses was heard. In the opinion of the defence they were all dubious. So too, were the remaining thirty-seven witnesses yet to be dealt with by Bakhtiar.

*

Bakhtiar was going minutely through the evidence of the witnesses, pinpointing inconsistencies and improvements between what was said before the magistrate and what was said in court. The evidence of the remaining witnesses was much shorter than that of the first four. Some of them had testified for only a day or two. Their statements were brief but equally tendentious, the defence believed. There was often a great deal of argument in court, with the result that not infrequently Bakhtiar protested. 'There's so much noise, I can't even make my submissions.'

One of the chief grievances of the prosecution had been the alleged pressure put on those who investigated the murder in 1974. But it had already been shown that none of the witnesses could be very specific as to the precise nature of the pressure other than naming Saeed Ahmed Khan and Bajwa. It was merely conjecture on the part of the prosecution which linked their activities with the Prime Minister. And if they had purposely not properly investigated the case, they too were accomplices in covering up the murder.

One such prosecution witness, a senior Superintendent of Police, Mohammed Asghar (P.W. 12), had stated that pressure had been put on him. But when in cross-examination he had been questioned as to the nature of the pressure he had somewhat sheepishly replied:

'I have already stated that pressure was exerted on me, but I have not stated that I accepted that pressure. The only pressure on my mind was that I *was not in a position* to interrogate Mr Bhutto.' (*Author's italics*)

This admission merely made it appear that he felt too timid to interrogate the Prime Minister and that therefore, the investigation could not be carried out. Notably however, when the case was reopened in the summer of 1977, those who had investigated it had done so to the satisfaction of the prosecution without the then Prime Minister being interrogated — merely swiftly arrested in September.

Asghar's Deputy Inspector-General, Vakil Khan, and the

prosecution's fourteenth witness, although complaining of the interference of Saeed Ahmed Khan and Bajwa, ultimately testified that he himself did not 'pressurise or bring any influence to bear on any Investigating Officer for investigating the case on other than the correct lines'.

Furthermore, his information appeared to come from what Asghar told him. The prosecution, alleging interference right from the start, stated that the investigation did not travel in the direction of the FSF, but Vakil Khan himself said he did not give any direction to investigate the FSF because he could not do so until after the spent cartridges had been proven to be of the calibre of the ammunition in use by the FSF—which came after the report of the ballistics expert, by which time he was no longer investigating the case. Even then, because many other units used this ammunition, the defence maintained that the involvement of the FSF could only be an assumption.

The fifteenth witness — Mohammed Waris, Deputy Superintendent of Police who took over the investigation in its later stages — again complained of interference but with no specific description of the sort of pressure used. Nor could he give a complete account of the manner of the investigation because he only took over in its later stages: the spot had already been inspected, the post mortem carried out, the recovery of the spent cartridges carried out and the people living nearby had been examined. Therefore, he said, 'I am not in a position to say if the investigation of this case ... has been properly conducted.'

Again, asked by the defence counsel, 'What fear made you accept the pressure of Saeed Ahmed Khan?' his reply came: 'All the fears that were the order of the day in that régime.'

He could be no more specific than that and his explanation appeared to be equally applicable to present-day fears. Even if Saeed Ahmed Khan's pressure were correct there were other innocent interpretations of his actions, the defence maintained. Moreover, it was possible that the alleged pressure to keep the investigation away from the FSF came not from the then Prime Minister but, for instance, from the Director-General of the FSF himself.

Bakhtiar believed the meeting referred to by Asghar in his statement in the house of Rao Rashid Khan on the night of 11

November, to which Abdul Hayee Niazi (P.W. 34) had also referred in court, was a complete fabrication since neither of them had mentioned this important meeting in their previous statements. He believed this was done to give credence to the prosecution theory of substitution, implying that this was one occasion when spent cartridges might have been substituted. In the defence's opinion, it was suspicious that such an important witness as Rao Rashid Khan— Inspector-General of the Punjab Police — was not summoned and they had lost their own opportunity to call him as a defence witness because of the boycott. But only with his testimony could this meeting be verified. And at about the time of the reading of the evidence of these witnesses at the beginning of June, Rao Rashid was back in prison, undoubtedly being subjected to further interrogation.

*

Bhutto's former Chief of Intelligence Bureau at the time of the *coup* and Inspector-General Police in the Punjab at the time of the murder — Rao Rashid Khan — was one man whose testimony looked as though it would stand in Bhutto's favour. Just before the appeal began in the Supreme Court he had filed an affidavit which supported the defence's contention that pressure was exerted on people close to events to make them incriminate the former Prime Minister. Rao Rashid himself had been arrested on the day of the *coup* and held in detention for eight months while the trial was going on in the Lahore High Court. In the affidavit filed after his release he described the 'carrot' and 'stick' treatment he had received at the hands of the military authorities. At times he was pressurised; at others he was offered the prospect of retaining his job — if only he would provide evidence against Bhutto, he was told.

'I knew the price I would have to pay for telling the truth,' he wrote. 'I think it is my duty ... I am also aware of the consequences of submitting this affidavit' ... one of the few pieces of evidence on record in Bhutto's favour — a mild compensation for not having his testimony on record as a defence witness.

Yet his re-arrest under martial law on 5 June meant that there was the possibility that more pressure might be exerted in order to make him withdraw his affidavit. At periodic intervals, information leaked out that he was being tortured again in Attock Fort — one of Pakistan's least pleasant jails — and that his food was being poisoned. His wife was also placed under house arrest. But his affidavit remained on the record — he did not change his statement.

Other affidavits were also furnished in favour of Bhutto, one by Jam Sadiq Ali, an ex-provincial minister in Sind, the other by Ghulam Mustafa Khar, former governor and chief minister of Punjab, indicating that they had been under pressure from the military régime to incriminate Bhutto. However, these two were both safe in London, albeit in exile, escaping from charges which would be brought against them should they return. The price they had to pay was considerably less than that of Rao Rashid. Bhutto himself admitted that men like Rashid were few and far between. He remained under arrest until finally he was released towards the close of the appeal in December. At this time he wrote a letter to the Chief Justice stating that he still stood by his affidavit. The defence always hoped to call him as a witness if additional evidence were to be allowed, but it never was.

During the appeal his arrest was a talking point amongst Bhutto's supporters. It also added to the suspicions of many that interference in the case by the military authorities was still going on.

Part of the defence's case was that the evidence of the witnesses was full of contradictions, not only with their previous statements before the magistrate, but with each other. 'On the basis of this moonshine,' Bakhtiar once expostulated, 'this case is based.' It was up to him to point out some of the important contradictions in order to cast doubt on the whole story. One vital contradiction appeared in the evidence of Masood Mahmud's driver — Manzoor Hussain (P.W. 21). In Masood Mahmud's evidence he stated that the morning after the murder he was telephoned by the Prime Minister (once again the use of the infamous telephone) and being severely reprimanded that the job had been bungled, he was summoned to come and see him at the house of his friend Sadiq Hussain Qureshi in Multan. But when it came to the turn of the driver to testify he could not be sure that Masood Mahmud had gone anywhere on the morning of the 11th before leaving Multan.

'So far as I know,' he said, 'DG (Masood Mahmud) had not visited any place in Multan on the morning of 11 November 1974. I drove DG to the airport from Canal Rest House on 11 November 1974 and,' he added, 'I drove the car whenever the DG wanted to go anywhere in Multan.'

This did not corroborate Mahmud's evidence that on this very morning he was 'ushered into the presence of Mr Bhutto'. According to the driver's statement he was not ushered anywhere other than to the airport. Qureshi, a friend of Bhutto, was not summoned to testify whether or not Mahmud had come to his house.

Bakhtiar found that with regard to what the prosecution witnesses said about the supply of ammunition and weapons, there were great inconsistencies which made the case of the prosecution unbelievable, he said. He was to highlight the inconsistent findings time and again but, it appeared, to no avail. The position as it emerged from the testimony of Amir Badshah (P.W. 20) and Fazal Ali (P.W. 24) was not tenable, the defence submitted, since the spent cartridges did not match the guns allegedly used and there was no positive proof that they had been substituted — merely inference on the part of the prosecution.

So much of the prosecution's case regarding the attack relied on the evidence of the second approver — Ghulam Hussain — whom the defence had not had adequate chance to cross-examine because of the boycott. In the statements of many of the witnesses they were seen to side-step the issue by saying, 'I do not remember.' This applied in particular to the testimony of Ghulam Hussain who, in custody for fourteen days before confessing, could well have been subject to pressure. What was also significant, Bakhtiar submitted, was that whereas he could not remember what he said in his statement before the magistrate a few months ago in August, he was able to remember facts quite clearly about the incident nearly four years ago. At other times his memory failed him altogether. When asked in court whether he had fired a shot at the scene of the crime — the sort of thing one might normally recall — the reply at first came, 'I do not remember if I fired the pistol.' A few minutes later in answer to the question: 'Did you fire your pistol before you heard the burst of the sten guns and while you were pacing the street?'

'No,' came the reply. But this was contradicted by the confessions of Arshad Iqbal and Rana Iftikar who said that he was the one who fired the first shot. Whereas they made out that he was at the scene of the crime, Ghulam Hussain insisted that he was pacing a street twenty yards away, coming only occasionally to talk with them. No investigation was made to trace the two others who had been involved in the reconnaissance, Liaquat and Zaheer, despite the fact that Ghulam Hussain mentioned that Liaquat was present with him on the night of the ambush. In his earlier statements before the magistrate which turned him into an approver, Ghulam Hussain maintained that he supervised the operation in Lahore. However, during the course of the trial the defence got a tip-off that he was not in Lahore either before or after the occurrence for a period of about ten days, but instead was in Karachi, as indicated by his travel account (TA) bill submitted to his battalion of the FSF. When the defence made an application to bring this document on record during the course of the trial having received the tip-off, P.W. 31 then added the new piece of evidence which was not confirmed by Mian Abbas that he filled in his TA bill wrongly under instruction from Mian Abbas: 'to ensure that I had not indicated my presence at Lahore during the days of the occurrence.' In the defence's opinion this was an added improvement to explain the entry in the TA bill and patently not corroborated by the man alleged to have given the instructions to make a false entry. It was also a vital omission in his statement regarding his conduct which should have been made known at the time he became eligible to become an approver and was given a pardon.

In order to show that Ghulam Hussain was not a reliable witness Bakhtiar filed a series of charts with forty indications of Ghulam Hussain's 'falsehood' and nineteen indicating his omissions and improvements. The court, however, showed itself sceptical of all the grounds, considering some to be 'hair-splitting', others 'trivial'. At times some members of the bench appeared appreciative of his arguments; others were not impressed. It was an uphill task.

Again, as with so many of the witnesses, the involvement of

the Prime Minister was by innuendo. Bakhtiar highlighted Ghulam Hussain's comments: 'the only undue influence and coercion exercised upon me for the attempt on Ahmed Raza Kasuri was by Mian Mohammed Abbas', the man who according to Ghulam Hussain's testimony had begged him to make his statement in such a way that he 'should not be implicated to a very large extent'. The defence believed Ghulam Hussain after his first failure at Islamabad had illogically been kept on the job: with different accomplices he was again entrusted with a task he had clearly shown himself unwilling to carry out. It was also not credible, the defence maintained, that although Ghulam Hussain testified that he went often to the National Assembly, he did not know Kasuri by sight— a man who was considered to be a political 'opponent' of the then Prime Minister.

Nor did Ghulam Hussain's testimony clarify the position with regard to the ammunition. Ghulam Hussain was supposed to have run a Commando Camp independently of his battalion of the FSF, which would explain the fact that no register was kept of the 1,500 rounds drawn from the FSF armoury on 9 May 1974. But the defence maintained that any Commando Camp was attached to battalions of the FSF and that neither Fazal Ali (P.W. 24) nor Ghulam Hussain was telling the truth when they talked about the issuance of the ammunition, more especially since the lot number in question had not been proved to be in stock in the FSF armoury at the time Ghulam Hussain said he obtained it on 9 May 1974.

In comparison with what these witnesses said, Bakhtiar felt that no consideration was given to the testimony of Nadir Hussain Abidi, a deputy director in the FIA (P.W. 36), whose assistance was asked by Abdul Hayee Niazi regarding the spent cartridges and what type of guns they would have been fired from. It was Abidi who said that the shells did not correspond with the guns. Virtually denying the opinion given, Niazi said in fact Abidi was not able to give him an opinion. Abidi's finding was supplemented by that of the ballistics expert, who remained anonymous throughout the proceedings.

There was also confusion over the lot number of ammunition supplied. The voucher relating to the ammunition produced at the trial by Fazal Ali (P.W. 24) who was in charge of the FSF's armoury did not indicate the same lot number as that allegedly used, but it did not have any number at all. In the recovery memo filled in after the attack the designation was bbl/71 for all twenty-four cartridges but two, which were marked 31/71. The prosecution had made out the case that his memo was wrongly filled in to confuse the situation but the two public witnesses who were present when it was filled in were never summoned to give their testimony. Abidi proffered the opinion that a mistake could have been made by a person with weak eyesight. The court observed that the witness was not qualified to give this sort of opinion even though later some of the judges relied upon it to support the prosecution. The prosecution had relied on the testimony given in a letter by Lt-Col Wazir Ahmed, the head of the ammunition depot, stating that the lot number in question was supplied to the FSF. The defence maintained that this letter was, by itself, not sufficient evidence and that the colonel should himself be summoned to testify, although clearly he could not testify that this calibre was issued to the FSF alone.

The defence pointed to the fact that because the kind of ammunition used — 7.62 mm calibre — was clearly in use by other units, it was not reasonable to state that the FSF was the only party which could have been involved. Notably, it was only after the guns and spent cartridges had been sent to the ballistics expert and it was shown that they did not match, that the prosecution developed the theory that the spent cartridges had been substituted. This theme was developed by the prosecution in the Supreme Court when the time came for them to present their case.

Apart from the fact that many witnesses were not called who could have been, another feature of the case was the death of not only Saeed Ahmed Khan's assistant, Abdul Hamid Bajwa, but also of Haq Niwaz Tiwana, Masood Mahmud's predecessor and another police officer — Abdul Ahad — who, according to Niazi's testimony, instructed him in the investigation of the case. As a deputy Superintendent of Police Abdul Ahad, as well as Bajwa, allegedly gave instructions to misdirect the case. To the defence it was an important allegation to be proved and because they were both dead, the testimony of many could not be verified.

According to the plans of the murder site, of which there were two different, although similar versions, cartridges were picked up in four places: eleven were in the roundabout, five at one place, six at another, separated by a distance of about ten paces; thirteen were outside the roundabout, seven at one place, six at another, separated by a distance of about 190 ft. This, the defence believed, pointed to the conclusion that there must have been four assailants, not two. None of the accused hinted in their statements that they had moved — only one said that he turned around, which could not account for the vast distance of 190 ft. between one pile of cartridges and another. Furthermore, the accused said they fired in the air first whereas, according to Kasuri, the first burst hit his car.

In one of the 'infamous' intelligence reports on Kasuri submitted in fact by Bajwa, Kasuri himself said at the end of November (28th) that four people had been deputed to kill him and that his friends had collected some of the spent cartridges after the attack which they were going to disclose at the appropriate time; but nothing was ever heard about the cartridges and Kasuri never again referred to four assailants.

There were other discrepancies which emerged during the course of Bakhtiar's submissions; one was that the log book of the jeep allegedly used for the attack — LEJ 7084 — showed that it was being used by another officer of the FSF at the time. Again, because Ghulam Hussain's driver was illiterate and did not fill out the log book, only Ghulam Hussain's testimony could be relied on when he used the jeep.

Just as there were queries about Ghulam Hussain's whereabouts, so were there about Mian Abbas's. His travel account stated that he was in Peshawar during the occurrence and in his evidence he said that he returned to Rawalpindi by the 6 p.m. flight on the 12th. Ghulam Hussain said that he himself left Lahore for Rawalpindi on the 12th, arriving there at 2.30 p.m. and went 'straight' to see Mian Abbas, which he obviously could not have done since Abbas was still in Peshawar. These factors and others raised by the defence made the case of the prosecution appear far less plausible than it was when presented at Lahore. Doubt had been cast on much of the evidence to the extent that many believed that if there were not to be an acquittal, there would at any rate be a re-trial. With, perhaps, a little over-confidence, the defence did not feel it necessary to present full arguments on the reduction of sentence.

Finally the evidence of the forty-first witness was read: the testimony of Abdul Khaliq, the Deputy Director of the FIA and the man who had told Bhutto that he had better 'cooperate' with the martial law authorities or else he would have to face the consequences. The three previous witnesses, as subordinates of Khaliq, had testified in court that they acted upon his instructions, a fact which the defence believed was significant in view of Khaliq's own role in the investigation. Khaliq had testified that 'the whole investigation in this case was conducted by my officers under my direct supervision and control'. It was he who had arrested all the accused.

The statement of one of Khaliq's subordinates— Aslam Sahi (P.W. 40)— an inspector in the FIA since January 1976, to the effect that 'I always obeyed the instructions given to me about carrying on the investigation of the case' was as capable of a suspicious interpretation as were those of the police officers who had testified regarding the 'instructions' given to them by Saeed Ahmed Khan and Bajwa. With the exception of Kasuri, all the forty witnesses were government servants and Bhutto's supporters believed that, as with Mian Abbas, inducements could have played a significant role. It was thought that to save their jobs they could be induced to depose falsely.

Naturally, if any capital were to be made out of this assumption, it would have to be confirmed. Ironically, confirmation came later in the course of the appeal through the hand of Abdul Khaliq himself. After the *coup* he had been assigned the task of enquiring into the activities of the FSF, which inevitably involved him in the murder case. He appeared to set out to 'crack' it with all possible means.

The defence counsel had secured possession of a letter from him to his superior— the director of the FIA— requesting the appointment as a member of the FIA of a certain Riaz Ahmed. He happened to be the brother of one of the co-accused — Iftikar Ahmed. Khaliq stated the reasons why his appointment should be considered in the following terms:

'Both father and son,' he said, 'had done a commendable job in safeguarding the confessional evidence of Iftikar Ahmed ... The father sincerely helped us in this case by not only controlling his own son but also by influencing the other two accused.'

Subsequently, the appointment of Riaz Ahmed was confirmed although he was above the accepted age-limit. When confronted with this piece of evidence — a clear indication of bribery — the shameless answer came back from Abdul Khaliq that 'yes,' inducements had been offered, 'but' he said, 'fatter inducements came from the other side' — an obvious retort, the defence believed, of which there was no proof. But from their point of view they now had clear proof that the man in charge of the investigation had used unethical means.

*

An encouraging event for Bhutto's supporters came with the release of his daughter Benazir from house arrest. She had been detained in Karachi for four months even before the death sentence was given in March, and her release was welcomed. Sind High Court ruled that the grounds for her detention were 'illegal' — an attitude which appeared contrary to that of the military régime. Benazir's release on 15 June was a boost to the morale of supporters and workers. As the only one of Bhutto's children in Pakistan at the time, with Begum Bhutto still under detention in Lahore, the 25-year-old Benazir alone bore the responsibility of keeping in touch with the people in the limited capacity which martial law permitted. Having been active in the election campaign before the elections were postponed the year before, she had established a rapport of her own with the people. A recent graduate from Oxford, having previously obtained a degree at Harvard, she had been thrust into politics after the July *coup* in 1977. Once she was free she attended the Supreme Court periodically. Her arrival created a stir and gave supporters a chance to meet with someone as close as they could get to Bhutto himself.

At first it appeared that the authorities would be glad to see Bhutto's fate settled quickly. But then a sudden adjournment in the middle of June at the time of Benazir's release, for the Chief Justice to attend an Asian Jurists Conference in Jakarta, Indonesia, made people start wondering. Many believed it was a delaying tactic and that therefore there must be some reason for it. Hurrying and delaying tactics were always carefully analysed, but really to no avail. It was impossible to see precisely what those in power had in mind.

Meanwhile, Bhutto from his cell was obliged to see the military régime and his opponents strengthen their position by pronouncements which put the prospect of free and fair elections even further away and definitely after his fate had been decided in the Supreme Court. He knew that all that was needed was to have fresh elections and there was a good chance that his party would be back in power: he would automatically be released and restored to exercise his position as Chairman of the People's Party. But General Zia had been negotiating with the other parties of the Pakistan National Alliance which had not seen the sight of power in Bhutto's time and hence were thirsty for it, to form a coalition government. It seemed that in so doing he wished to gain some degree of respectability by incorporating civilians into his set-up. However, this attempt failed because the parties could not agree. Therefore, on 25 June, in a speech to the nation, Zia announced that he himself would form a federal Cabinet of twenty-one 'men of talent' which would replace his present council of advisers. In practice it meant that most of the advisers remained, only they turned into 'ministers' overnight. Of the nine components of the PNA four rightist parties joined the Government — the Moslem League whose Chief was the Pir of Pagara, the Jamaat-i-Islami headed by Maudoodi, the Jamaat-i-Ulema-i-Islam under Mufti Mahmud and the Pakistan Democratic Party (PDP) headed by Nasrullah Khan. The last three joined in August.

Those who had refused to collaborate were Wali Khan's party — the National Democratic Party (NDP), under the leadership of Sherbaz Khan Mazari, with Wali Khan's wife as vice-president; the party of Asghar Khan — Tehrick-i-Istiqlal — which left the PNA in the autumn of 1977 and to which Kasuri had temporarily belonged during his estrangement with the PPP, and the Jamaatul-Ulema-e-Pakistan (JUP) headed by Maulana Shah Ahmed Noorani. They continued to grumble on the sidelines and at times to criticise the military régime.

Power was moving into the hands of some of those who had opposed the creation of Pakistan in the first place. As strict Moslems the League felt the creation of Pakistan would confine the strength of Islam to the top western and top eastern parts of the Asian sub-continent, whereas there would be a better chance for converts in an undivided India. Bhutto's supporters and he himself believed their tenure of power was indeed ironical. They called them 'mullahs', the Urdu for priests, indicating that as such they should not be meddling in politics. The Moslem League believed in following a strict code of ethics according to Islam. Their intention, therefore, was to introduce Islamic laws, and 'nizam-i-mustafa' (system of the Prophet) as it was called. Under these laws there were to be strict penalties for crimes such as rape, adultery, theft, as well as consumption of alcohol, according to what was prescribed in the Koran. Unlike other penal systems, where the penalty is theoretically meant to fit the crime, under Islam it was to be of sufficient severity to act as a deterrent. For a long time afterwards Zia and the members of PNA talked of the introduction of nizam-i-mustafa as their main goal ... along with elections.

The renewed promise of elections seemed less attractive since Zia made it clear that certain preparations were necessary: for instance, drawing up fresh electoral rolls which would separate Moslems and non-Moslems and, people believed, would create more division amongst Pakistanis. The Christians objected to being relegated to what they termed second-class citizens. The ban on political activities remained. The process of accountability, focused on Bhutto, had to be concluded. And along with this process, 'Other measures to ensure positive results of the elections were also being taken,' said Zia. The implication of such statements Bhutto felt was that Zia would merely preserve his own tenure of power. Free and fair elections would return Bhutto to power and Zia and his associates could not tolerate this. By saying that steps to ensure 'positive results' were being taken, Bhutto, not unnaturally, assumed that this was a direct attack against the People's Party. He believed that Zia himself was rigging the elections by manipulating the outcome of the poll, if and when it came. To Bhutto, Zia's sanctimonious talk about austerity, greed and lust, calling for the people to abstain from the two latter and practise the former, in the 25 June speech was nothing but a joke. But it was an important speech and heralded the approach of Zia's second year in power. Finally, in this speech Zia informed the people that a 'White Paper' in three volumes would appear shortly to tell the people about the misdeeds of the previous government. Volume I was on the conduct of the general elections in March 1977; Volume

II was on Bhutto's alleged misuse of the media. Volume I appeared on 25 July, a month after the speech. Volume II came on 28 August. The third volume, outdoing both the others in its vindictiveness, appeared much later.

The formation of his new Cabinet took place auspiciously on 5 July, the anniversary of the *coup d'état* when General Zia first assumed power as Chief Martial Law Administrator — the CMLA. Such had been the vacillations in his statements, he was by now nicknamed 'Cancel My Last Announcement'. Instead of remaining in power for 90 days, Zia had been there for 365. Bhutto's enemies were getting used to the taste of power. There was no one in a position to remove them.

*

When the court reassembled after the two-week adjournment — unwanted by Bhutto's supporters — matters were made worse when it was reported in an Indonesian newspaper that the Chief Justice, whilst abroad, had discussed the trial and, as Bhutto said, prejudged his case by saying that it had 'nothing to do with Pakistani politics'. Since one of the arguments of the defence was that the trial was politically motivated to eliminate the former Prime Minister, he was outraged. He said that Anwarul Haq was 'far too committed to and identified with' the martial law régime and its objectives to decide his appeal 'impartially and without bias'. This was one of Bhutto's barrages of attack against the Chief Justice which were to emerge from the death cell, Rawalpindi district jail, at intervals during the course of the appeal. But Anwarul Haq replied in dulcet tones in a court order to the effect that there was nothing prejudicial in his comments to the press — he was merely informing the journalists in Indonesia about the independent position of the judiciary in Pakistan — and that he had 'no personal bias whatsoever' against the appellant. He said it was his endeavour to ensure that the appeal was decided 'impartially and in accordance with law'. Bhutto remained unconvinced and felt that the Chief Justice was acting as the spokesman for the Chief Martial Law Administrator. To him it was just another indication that the course of the appeal was being subjected to a similar kind of partisanship to that of his trial. Anwarul Haq deemed himself competent to remain on the bench; there the matter ended.

D.M. Awan read the evidence of the confessing accused which was in Urdu — his Urdu being better than that of his colleagues. Finally it was time to read Bhutto's own in camera statement. Whereas Bhutto was generally sceptical about the impartiality of the bench, or more especially the Chief Justice, not all his supporters shared his opinions. When an indication came that the Supreme Court was not going to follow the same procedure as the trial court they fell upon it with alacrity as an indication that this bench was showing independence and integrity. Such an occasion came with the reading of Bhutto's own statement. At the outset there was speculation and panic that at this stage, since the statement had been recorded in camera, the appeal might be held in camera as well. The justices adjourned the court early to consider the matter.

When the following day they returned and the Chief Justice announced that there was 'no compelling reason' to adopt the same procedure as at Lahore and keep the contents of the statement secret, the departure from the Lahore trial was welcomed. In fact Bhutto's speech appeared as an anti-climax for those who believed that some state secrets had been disclosed, thus preventing its publication at the Lahore trial. Instead, what emerged was the statement of a man — and a former Prime Minister — who was refusing to defend himself in view of what he considered to be the bias and partiality of the court. This time his words, 'So you call this justice, so you call this a trial?' fell upon attentive ears, since the court was full of anxious listeners and journalists. Bakhtiar pointed to the prejudicial way in which the sixty-seven questions put to Bhutto were phrased, making them difficult to answer. 'There is bias oozing forth from every sentence, every question,' he said. The judges listened attentively to the statement; some appeared surprised that its contents might have constituted sufficient reason to conclude the trial in camera.

What went on behind the scenes was always a matter of speculation. What transpired to make Mian Abbas backtrack on his statement, no one knew. What made him do it again was also a mystery, although, of course, people had their suspicions. When Mian Abbas appeared in public at the hearing in

September 1977, looking broken, he openly stated that his confession as to his part in the murder had been extracted from him under duress, after one week in detention. Although the prosecution did not set out to establish a direct link with the Prime Minister and Mian Abbas, it was important for its case to establish Abbas's own role. The Lahore judgment had made nothing of his retracted confession, stating that anyway his earlier testimony alleging his guilt was corroborated by the direct testimony of other witnesses and circumstantial evidence. But even so, it helped their case when Mian Abbas's lawyer stood up in court, produced a piece of paper from his pocket and stated on behalf of his client that he would like to submit that his client maintained that the prosecution case was substantially correct. He then sat down.

The local press made capital out of his changed statement, announcing it in bold headlines in the newspaper and on radio and TV. The defence's only consolation was that a man who changed his statement three times, making 'so many somersaults', as Bakhtiar said, could hardly be a reliable person and that accordingly his statement should be discounted altogether. In private, Mian Abbas's lawyer made no secret of the fact that pressure had been exerted on his client from the 1st to the 9th July; the statement was read in court on the 10th. Also in it was a tell-tale line begging for mercy and that his life should be saved: many believed that if he had been guilty he should have been asking for mercy for the crime he had committed in the knowledge that it was punishable by death. But this did not help Bhutto, who felt that the authorities had put pressure on Mian Abbas to change his statement and were still meddling in his appeal and not allowing the course of justice to proceed unhampered.

There was another alarming aspect to be considered. This related to the bench itself. The retirement of one of the nine judges was considered by Bhutto and his supporters to be an outright manipulation of the bench. They believed it would alter the balance of the votes which would ultimately be cast. What was worse from their point of view, it appeared that if the right steps had been taken, Mr Justice Qaiser Khan would have been happy to be appointed on an *ad hoc* basis — a common enough practice and something which could have been accomplished by the stroke of a pen. Upon instructions from Bhutto, his lawyer complained to the Chief Justice about the retirement of Qaiser Khan. But he replied that since the defence had not made the request, he had not wanted to take it upon himself to appoint Mr Justice Qaiser Khan on an *ad hoc* basis as the appellant had already expressed dissatisfaction with the bench. The defence replied, somewhat curtly, that it was not with the bench that his client had shown his displeasure, but with the Chief Justice himself. Even though the voting balance could only be a matter of speculation, Qaiser Khan's retirement on 30 July left a four-four split, in which case pessimists said the Lahore verdict would stand.

Later many maintained that if only the appeal had been concluded before this retirement, the outcome would have been very different. Many said it was the lengthy appeal which would cost Bhutto his life.

Qaiser Khan's retirement caused anxiety not only on account of his own disappearance but also because it could set a precedent for the retirement of future judges when their time came. This added to the suspense over the timing of the appeal and its conclusion. Dr Naseem Hassan Shah, the judge with the squeaky voice, and Mr Justice Waheeduddin Ahmed, who constantly yawned, were both due to retire in November. But could the appeal go on much longer, people asked themselves? November was a long way from 30 July, the date Qaiser Khan retired. But even so, panic set in amongst Bhutto supporters and it was felt that the proceedings must not be delayed. Every visible procrastination was construed as an indication that the other judges would also be retired.

*

When it came to bias and malafides the defence's two other grounds of attack, the judges moved more uncomfortably in their high-backed chairs. Bhutto's in camera statement had already shown what he thought of the trial. The instances in the 18 December application were also cited. Some judges thought nothing of the behaviour of Maulvi Mushtaq; others appeared more concerned. But a slur on their brothers in the judiciary was not easy to bear and no judge seemed anxious to concede that the bench had been biased or that any irregular practice had taken place in the trial.

Bakhtiar launched forth in his dissertation against the present military administration, describing how Zia had said there would be no witch-hunts or arrests of political prisoners. But he met a chilly reception from the Chief Justice. The latter appeared to think there was nothing wrong with Zia's comments about Bhutto being a murderer, stating that Mr Bhutto, as Prime Minister, had also commented on the trial of one of his opponents while it was in progress. Nor did he agree that there were one-sided reports against Bhutto in the newspapers, as Bakhtiar submitted. All justices protested that anyway, whatever was said or whatever publicity was given against Bhutto in the local press, their minds would not be prejudiced or tainted by it. 'We have a lot of sympathy with what you are saying,' one judge said, 'but we will not be influenced by outside propaganda.' Bias and malafides were sore points; it seemed much more likely that if the verdict in Bhutto's trial were to be overturned, it would be on account of the many defects which had emerged from the testimony of the prosecution witnesses.

Bakhtiar presented additional arguments on conspiracy, submitting that there could be no conspiracy because there was no consensus of mind. It was an important point which the defence felt it necessary to highlight, at the expense of possibly labouring it. At one point Justice Safdar Shah stated, 'We are suffering from indigestion of facts now. We have digested them ten times over.' But Bakhtiar believed it was vital to convince the judges that there was no conspiracy and that Masood Mahmud was unreliable. In so doing the involvement of the Prime Minister could not be sustained.

Bhutto's senior defence counsel, weary after his prolonged reading, left the floor temporarily to Ghulam Ali Memon to argue on more points of law. Insofar as legal aspects were concerned a great weakness, the defence believed, in the prosecution's case was the fact that so much of the evidence rested on hearsay and circumstantial evidence.

The defence finished arguing on 20 August. At the end of Bakhtiar's submissions he made three applications. The first was for Welch to be re-examined to verify whether his testimony would change if he gave it as a Christian; the second was for Colonel Wazir Ahmed to be summoned to testify that the contents of the letter he had sent regarding the lot number of the ammunition used were true; finally came the most important request: for additional witnesses to be summoned. It was more and more apparent that since the judges maintained they would be considering only what was on record, it would be helpful to have the testimony of defence witnesses to balance that of the prosecution witnesses. The defence counsel had in mind to call Rao Rashid, General Tikka Khan (who also would be in a position to talk about the scruples of the military if pressed) and former Foreign Affairs Minister Mr Aziz Ahmed. All three had knowledge of Masood Mahmud's activities and would have been in a position to throw a different light on his testimony. More than ever before the defence now realised that by boycotting the trial Bhutto had forfeited the right to call defence witnesses, which would give a different picture from the one which emerged from the one-sided testimony of the prosecution witnesses. But it was up to the judges to permit the applications. Needless to say the prosecution vehemently opposed them.

The defence lawyers were relatively confident with the way the appeal had gone. Bakhtiar mumbled his thank-you to the justices for a 'very patient hearing' as he shuffled his papers, collecting them up. He was obviously tired and anxious to sit down. Lawyers, the public and the judges were all weary. With all that had been said the defence believed that if justice were done there was a strong case for acquittal.

It was clear that the court would have to break for part of the month of fasting of Ramzan, to be concluded by the feast of Eid. As it was, Bakhtiar had made his concluding arguments in August without his customary sip of water from a glass placed on a shelf in the podium. Under Islam nothing was meant to touch the lips after sunrise before sunset. No one was quite sure who observed the fast but in public most pretended that they did. The defence changed its venue for taking tea and coffee during the break to a private room to prevent photographers and newsmen from publicising to the opposition that they might be sitting drinking tea and eating sandwiches throughout. It was a small matter and inconsequential throughout the course of the appeal. But it made the break for Eid welcome.

Even so, Bhutto's supporters were still anxious about the retirement of the judges. They regretted bitterly the wasted two weeks when the Chief Justice was in Jakarta. The three-week break brought the appeal well into the autumn. People stopped talking about the appeal winding up in August. Early October was the given date.

6

THE REJOINDER

Bhutto was kept busy during the painful month of fasting in August. As promised by General Zia, a White Paper on the Conduct of the General Elections in March 1977 appeared on 25 July. There had been a certain amount of apprehension before the appearance of this first White Paper. People wondered what proof the military régime had unearthed regarding the alleged rigging of the elections. It was also feared amongst Bhutto's supporters that pressure would have been exerted on some of his former government officials to make incriminating and distorted statements. The statements of over 900 people were recorded: conspicuous by its absence was the statement of the man in charge of the conduct of the elections — the former Chief Election Commissioner himself. Everything he was alleged to have said was given in reported speech by the Secretary to the Election Commission, which it would appear inevitably detracted from its reliability.

In fact, when the document eventually appeared there was a certain amount of relief in Bhutto circles. It could almost have been a joke, they felt, but for the obvious implications of a document which was designed to discredit the former Prime Minister in the eyes of the people. It was a great volume which was so fat that an abridged version had to be supplied. This rather reduced the desire of some people to read the original volume since most would probably take a short cut to avoid over 1,000 pages of print. The text itself ran to just over 400 pages, the rest of the White Paper being taken up by 342 annexures which were copies of documents reproduced from Bhutto's government archives. The introduction to the White Paper commented sarcastically on 'the very full record' left by the Bhutto régime. 'In a strange way, Mr Bhutto seemed to believe in his own indispensability and success. He and his associates, therefore, were not afraid of reducing things to writing.' 'The documents speak for themselves,' ran the text, 'few comments are needed.'

But many believed that ultimately, few of those people who condemned Bhutto for rigging the elections would have fully perused this document. If they had done so, it was felt they would have reached very different conclusions. A shorter clipped version, a government précis, might give a different impression, but the long version, in the opinion of many, showed nothing more offensive than the preparation of an election campaign, which would be customary in any democratic country during and before election time. In places Bhutto had clearly vetoed any idea of foul play. For instance, in the National Assembly on 7 January 1977 when he announced that the election would be held in two months' time, Bhutto categorically stated:

'I know that politicians like to avoid elections as much as the generals like to avoid wars, but the point is that political battles have to be fought. I hope that the coming election will be a clean and a fair one.'

The White Paper quoted this in its entirety, but instead of giving Bhutto the benefit of the doubt and agreeing that he did want to hold fair elections, but that things might have got out of hand, it insinuated that this was merely Bhutto's publicity image, whereas behind the scenes he was busy planning to rig the elections. It made much of the fact that Bhutto had been preparing for the elections since 1974. Bhutto conceded after the elections on 28 March that although it was not his government's policy to have any manipulation or rigging in the election, 'there might have been irregularities at some places. It happened even in civilised countries like the U.S.A.,' he said. But even this did not sound convincing to the architects of the White Paper, who laid each and every misdemeanour at the feet of the Prime Minister.

The White Paper also reproduced instructions for fair play. Bhutto wrote to his Chief Minister of the Punjab in the following terms with regard to the appointment of returning officers and other election officials. He said they were to be of the 'right type' and 'dependable'. 'It has to be fully ensured,' he wrote, 'that persons of biased political leanings are not selected.'

Despite instructions in this vein the White Paper tried to portray Bhutto as the arch-rigger *par excellence*. In a chapter entitled 'The Image Makers', the White Paper outlined propaganda tactics, at all times trying to cast a bad light on any normal publicity move.

'With elections on his mind,' said the White Paper, 'Mr Bhutto took a relentless interest in the propaganda apparatus and drove the machinery with a hard hand to achieve the assigned goal. His political associates and a bevy of professionals in the media/departments obliged ungrudgingly.'

The White Paper tried to find fault with Bhutto's tours, the celebration of the 'week of x ... y ... z ... or 'such and such' new ventures, ballet performances for political projection and poster publicity. It saw Machiavellian design in the attempts to present to the public the efforts and achievements of the PPP on the one hand, and to expose the opposition and as Bhutto said 'make it look ridiculous'. Obvious election stunts were made out as the actions of an arch-autocrat. Little consideration was given to the obvious fact that if Bhutto had been the autocrat, as depicted by other military régime propaganda, he would have had no compunction in not holding elections at all, or at any rate in not leaving himself in a position to be overthrown by a military *coup* should anything go wrong. Insofar as the White Paper was concerned, all blame went to the top.

The White Paper described as 'thumping' the victory of the PPP at the 7 March polls when it won 136 seats in the National Assembly as well as 15 uncontested seats in Sind, and 4 in Baluchistan; whereas the PNA secured only 36. Somewhat gleefully, in this final chapter headed the 'Aftermath', the White Paper stated that this massive victory vitiated the credibility of the elections with the result that the opposition boycotted the provincial assembly elections which were due to be held on 10 March. Soon after, on 13 March, the White Paper described how Bhutto at a high-level conference held in the Prime Minister's house opened the discourse in distressed language:

'Why have you done this to me?' he began, meaning accord-

ing to the White Paper's analysis 'that the civil administration
had overplayed its hand'.

The White Paper itself never managed to give an explanation
for the cautionary remarks of Bhutto to his subordinates
whenever there was a mention of cutting corners. One such
remark occurred in the margin of a letter which talks about a
plan to help the government party in the election campaign.
Bhutto has written, 'I am not thinking of my elections, I am
thinking of the requirements of modern government.'

At times too, the text of the White Paper contradicted its own
documentary evidence. It stated categorically that no publicity
was permitted to the leaders of the PNA opposition, whereas
the PPP basked in it. However, it also reproduced a document
with various suggestions to the Prime Minister regarding the
elections. By the side of the point 'Opposition parties and
candidates will have to be given time on the Radio and TV'
Bhutto has commented, 'We will have to give the "leaders"
some time, some reasonable time.' Bhutto's supporters saw a
great deal of dishonesty in the White Paper, twisting and dis-
torting the real position and painting everyone else as snow
white, whereas Bhutto was intended to emerge black as pitch.
Another note contained a suggestion that 'irritants' could be
removed; whereas 'we cannot compromise on fundamental
issues like land reforms and income tax,' read the note, 'minor
issues like customs and excise departments and anti-smuggling
laws' could be revised. Bhutto had advised consultation with
the Finance Minister, 'but,' he had added, 'do not allow the
crooks to get away.'

Bhutto's own character emerges from some of his comments.
Many have criticised his magnanimity, stating that he forgave
corrupt people far too easily and allowed them back into the
fold — people who would ultimately turn on him. With little
relevance to the text the White Paper included a request from a
favour seeker — Pir Mohammed Ali Rashdi — for the
advancement of his son.

Bhutto stated, 'We are responsible for Rashdi and all his
sons, because he told Ayub Khan to get me shot. That is life.
What more can we do for this loyal band of faithfuls?' Himself
astute and a politician, he was well aware that he moved on
shifting sands.

In its Epilogue the White Paper gave sarcastic comments at the expense of the fallen leader with visible delight.

'Throughout his tenure in office,' it claimed, 'Mr Bhutto seemed to have been deeply conscious of his sense of history. He claimed not only to be a student of history but also a maker of history. In a sense he was right.'

It described Bhutto's reluctance to call fresh elections because, he said, it would amount to conceding 'their false charges that I am a manipulator and rigger of elections'. And he did not want to go down in history with that appellation. Again the White Paper could not avoid the temptation to give a further dig at Bhutto. It defined 'history' in two ways: firstly, the conventional dictionary definition; secondly, that used by Napoleon — 'What is history but a fable agreed upon?' For those who were not aware of Bhutto's admiration for Napoleon, they were now reminded of it; need the White Paper say more? Indications such as these made the average reader aware that the White Paper not only set out the documents which 'spoke for themselves' to prove Bhutto's rigging, but in its commentary added little touches to malign him.

In Bhutto's opinion the intention of the White Paper was to destroy his reputation politically at a time when he was already condemned to die for his alleged part in the murder, and he believed that the White Paper had been released in order for the sympathies of the people to be adversely affected. He still maintained that as Chief Justice of the Lahore High Court, Maulvi Mushtaq Hussain had no business being Chief Election Commissioner as well. To him the whole document was just part of the character assassination campaign which had been going on ever since the *coup* and the contested election result. When the White Paper was released it received enormous publicity in the local press and appeared on sale in the bookshops and bazaars.

But it was obvious to most observers both before and after the appearance of the White Paper that its consideration of rigging had not been accompanied by an awareness that the democratic process is a very sophisticated mechanism which cannot easily be grafted onto any society, especially one which has not yet fully emerged from the bonds of feudalism. Bhutto knew this as well as anyone, and that complete fair play would have been a great deal to expect of people with comparatively little political experience. 'My promise alone is not enough,' he said. The White Paper, quoting a report after the 1951 elections which complains of rigging and stuffed ballots, stated dismally, 'Time does not seem to move in these parts, perhaps it travelled backwards in the "new Pakistan" ' — as if it were the easiest thing in the world to get the adults of a developing country of so many millions of people to go docilely to the polling booths. Bhutto, as a shrewd politician, clearly wanted to win the elections, as would any leader, and accordingly made an all-out effort. But a great number of people believed that the hue and cry about the allegation of rigging was out of all proportion in a society where the parliamentary system had hardly had time to take root.

Despite the documents it produced, the White Paper did not establish that Bhutto stage-managed an enormous rigging operation to secure his tenure of power; yet the dubious actions of subordinates, a certain amount of over-confidence and possibly high-handed use of state machinery combined to make Bhutto's enemies portray him as the manipulator of all times, at a time when they too could be called to account for their own actions.

*

In his cell, Zulfikar Ali Bhutto read the White Paper very speedily. Even before its publication he was conscious that he would have to write a reply or a 'rejoinder', as he called it. In Bhutto's opinion there were many false accusations contained in the White Paper, which the military régime was circulating at home and abroad in four languages, including Arabic. What was its relevance to the Arab states? he asked. They did not have a system of parliamentary elections based on adult franchise and probably could not care less whether or not the elections were rigged. 'If I were an Arab Monarch or an Arab Sheikh I would say, so what?' he wrote.

But more important still was Bhutto's belief that the White Paper was pertinent to the hearing of the appeal in the Supreme Court. He believed that these 'white lies', as he called them, had been released at a particular time to poison the minds of the public and possibly the judges against him. When he was being tried for conspiracy to murder it seemed to be hitting below the belt to condemn him for rigging the elections, especially when the charge relating to rigging filed against him was pending in another court. Yet Zia was grinding through his process of accountability and this was just another aspect of it. In this respect, the Pakistan People's Party felt particularly aggrieved to be the sole object of the White Paper since its own plentiful allegations of rigging by the Pakistan National Alliance were not included. A newspaper writer in the government-controlled press side-stepped people's complaints by saying that the White Paper only concerned the conduct of the elections and the PNA did not conduct the elections. Bhutto in the Rejoinder was quick to point that that neither did the PPP but the Election Commission, which was why he believed it was so vital to have the statement of the Chief Election Commissioner which was lacking. Clearly, he believed, if one party's alleged misdeeds were being exposed, so should those of the other. Bhutto thought that it was not entirely coincidental that of all the manifold alleged cases of rigging in the constituencies, the only one to receive an entire chapter of forty pages devoted to it was the charge against none other than Bhutto's defence counsel, Yahya Bakhtiar. He scorned the singling out of Bakhtiar, believing that this was yet another indication that the authorities were not oblivious of the effect this White Paper might have in the minds and sympathies of the people, while his appeal was being heard. Bhutto believed that it was quite possible that Bakhtiar had received this special attention because of his own bad relations with Maulvi Mushtaq.

Furthermore, the White Paper was more closely related to the appeal itself than at first appeared. With the prosecution stating that Bhutto committed the murder through the agency of the FSF it was therefore in its interest to paint as unsavoury a picture of the FSF as possible. And the White Paper took it upon itself to do this. Whilst discussing the conduct of the FSF during the elections it stated that Mian Mohammed Abbas, as a sub-inspector of the force, was responsible for setting up a squad which was designed to disrupt and break up meetings of the opposition political parties. It also stated that Intelligence Bureau Chief Rao Rashid, together with other officers of the FSF, had responsibility for setting up squads of 'bomb blasters, sharp-shooters, and knife-runners'.

This, Bhutto believed, corresponded exactly with the sort of activity alleged to be carried out by the FSF in the murder trial, not surprisingly bearing in mind that the authorities appeared to have already given credence to Bhutto's guilt. Everyone knew that Mian Abbas was a co-accused and a co-appellant and the role and activities of the FSF were the subject matter of the appeal. Bhutto therefore stated that his case had been prejudiced by portraying the FSF in such a manner, when the defence case was that it was not used for criminal activities. He also believed that involving Rao Rashid in the activities would detract from the bona fide reliability of his affidavit filed in Bhutto's favour in the Supreme Court. Throughout the White Paper he was depicted as Bhutto's right-hand man, which would accordingly diminish his impartiality.

Bhutto therefore saw fit to write his Rejoinder as a court document 'to keep the record straight and for such action as this Hon'ble Court deems fit in the interest of justice'. It went without saying that if it had not been submitted as a court document it would have been illegal as Bhutto had no right to write anything other than court material. As it was, the writing of the Rejoinder was not publicised, lest its completion be thwarted by a sudden sweep on Flashmans, where it was typed.

Many people write their memoirs in jail, where they have solitude and time; solitude Bhutto may have had, but he did not have much time and was anxious to get his Rejoinder out as soon as possible after the White Paper. He would have liked it to be out in a month, but in fact it took two. Nor were the conditions in which he worked conducive to writing a document of this nature; in normal circumstances to refute allegations of rigging it would be necessary to consult documents and files, to have time and space. Yet this document was written without proper light, by hand, 'with the paper resting upon my knee', with no books other than the newspapers, the White Paper itself and his memory for consultation. It was extremely hot in August and Bhutto himself was observing his fast. In solitary confinement for almost a year by this time, his memory and attention to detail were remarkable. Inevitably, people found faults with it. They said it was rambling, that Bhutto appeared paranoid; but people criticise only too easily when they are not in similar circumstances and the comments do not detract from the feat of producing a document such as this in like conditions. In it the genius of Bhutto is apparent even to his enemies. It is witty, informative and poetic. Those who tossed it off lightly, as though it were produced in a light and airy office with a team of secretaries typing away, have completely the wrong picture of the sort of aid and assistance upon which Bhutto was able to rely. Even the lawyers were almost too busy to give it much attention.

Bhutto noted down points with which he had to deal, scratching them out on the front page of the White Paper when he had finished. He put a line through pages of the White Paper which he believed were irrelevant or which contained aspects he had already covered. He did not go consistently through the White Paper page by page but rather took themes and developed them as his fancy took him. At times Bhutto scribbled his own comments on the commentary of the White Paper, scorning and deriding it.

Bhutto's Rejoinder — over three hundred typed foolscap pages — contained about 80,000 words. Each day he wrote between five and six foolscap pages (on both sides of the paper in small, crabbed handwriting) on the large, coarse paper pads brought to him by his lawyers; sometimes, writing late into the night, he wrote more. He also corrected what he had written the previous day, often making considerable alterations to the typed version which was brought to him by the lawyers on their daily visit. The lawyers maintained that the document was court material and therefore believed it was well within their brief to act as the go-betweens. When later it was stated that the document was 'smuggled' out, Bhutto and his lawyers took great exception to this insinuation, with its inference of illegality. Bhutto said that he had sat writing it in his cell for all his guards to see.

Obviously a great deal of the Rejoinder deals with the allegations in the White Paper. Since Bhutto had no other documents to rely upon it was fortunate that he found it beneficial to use the White Paper itself to refute the accusations of rigging. In a defiant manner he defended even those who might have let him down – a surprising revelation to those who believed that Bhutto was nothing but selfish and arrogant, caring little for those around him. In fact, many believed that he defended his colleagues too staunchly. However, he did make it clear that 'another dishonest and misleading device followed [by the White Paper] is to put down all and sundry views emanating from all quarters in such a way as to make the reader believe that the views and opinions are mine'. 'Fortunately,' he added, 'sufficient contradictions have surfaced in this unethical methodology to dispel the impression.' He also said that 'documents telling the truth have been suppressed or destroyed', leaving those which have been 'specially selected and doctored' to implicate him. To those who believe Bhutto should not have taken up the defence of his subordinates along with his own, the question of accountability arises.

The White Paper admitted and Bhutto quoted it as saying that he had made it clear that he did not want anything done on polling day which he would regret for the next five years. But was he to be blamed if his subordinates did not obey his instructions? 'I am not responsible for each and every thought and idea born in the minds of officials or non-officials of our fertile Indus Valley,' he said. Or were his instructions merely cosmetic ones, which is how the White Paper tried to portray them, mindful that he had got his 'do or die' plan up his sleeve? Clearly the present military régime thought uncharitably that he was entirely to blame. Yet even so, Bhutto pulled out all the quotations in the White Paper which vindicated both himself and his Government, moving away from the false idealism of the White Paper that free and fair elections are easy to achieve. These arguments throw an entirely different light on the picture.

However, the most interesting parts of the Rejoinder are the digressions. To the casual reader, discussions about delimitation of constituencies, the Larkana 'plan' — the model plan for winning an election which Bhutto allegedly authorised for his own constituency when in fact he says it was drawn up by a friend and admirer and related to a neighbouring one — as well as matters of party funds which, though vital for his defence, hold less attraction than his political discussions. Naturally Bhutto took full advantage of his opportunity to 'speak' to the outside world for the first time in a long time. Once released, it would be a way of keeping touch with the people and making them aware of his views.

He justified his broad analyses on the following grounds:

'Without the total sweep, this paper would have lacked political perception and been unworthy of its author ... Beyond the imperatives of being duty bound to present a picture in balance it would have been a disservice to the reader to circumscribe the repast,' he wrote, as though he were anxious to offer the reader as large a feast of his writings as possible.

The Rejoinder was interspersed with anecdotes and recollections from the past. Bhutto related how one of Ayub Khan's favourite topics of conversation with the Germans used to be the comparison of Prussia with Pakistan — the point in common, it appeared, being the large standing army and the three wars which, however, Prussia had won and Pakistan had lost. Clearly there the similarity ended but apparently it amused Ayub Khan to mention it. Bhutto discussed at length the relationship between the civil and military authorities. This stemmed from a discussion of the role of the military in Baluchistan. This was also of particular interest to Bhutto since he found himself the target of criticism from the military régime for having kept Baluchistan under the army for too long. He refuted this and said that it was the military which insisted on staying. Undoubtedly he felt pangs of anger at being criticised by the Army for measures which the Army itself insisted upon; the more so, since the man latterly in charge was one and the same — General Zia ul Haq. Bhutto also appeared to feel that it was about time the Hamood ur Rehman report was published. This document, drawn up after an enquiry into the 1971 war, again mentioned in the White Paper, revealed, Bhutto said, the story of rape, plunder and loot which was carried out by the Army against the Bengalis. Its publication had not taken place since it was considered by Bhutto and the Army that it would do irreparable damage to the already tarnished reputation of the Army. To have lost the war was one thing, to have plundered its way through was another. Bhutto was not feeling so magnanimous towards the Army at this stage and felt tempted to speak up in more detail; yet he refrained, ever mindful of the sensitivity of the issue.

In satirical fashion he ridiculed the present régime, referring to it as the Junta — the coterie or Tommy-gun Dictatorship. At no time did he call it a government. Sometimes his comments were almost too subtle for the reader. He referred to martial law as 'being heavily made up with cosmetics' and so the people could not clearly see the face. Yet now, he said, 'the wig and false teeth' of the present martial law had been removed. His reference to the wig is, of course, the judiciary, and the false teeth are the prominent teeth in the flashy smile of Zia ul Haq. Once given the bait, he travelled far in his discussions. He talked about *coups d'état*, military dictatorships and the inherent dangers thereof. He called Pakistan coup-istan and invented a new word 'coup-gemony' — which he believed was as obnoxious as hegemony.

He exposed the double standards of the régime and the farce of accountability, which was applicable to one side only. 'Double standards have been applied by this régime in double dosage,' he wrote. The White Paper 'is so one-sided as to close even the other eye of Lord Nelson'. He believed that all criticism was directed at his tenure of office, but that the military régime was oblivious of its own failings. 'Our sins are no longer on the agenda. The diary of the Junta is being written from the moment of that midsummer's night,' he wrote, referring of course to 5 July 1977.

He reviewed the political situation, the abeyance of the Constitution and the lack of elections. Here again the discriminatory nature of the régime could not pass without comment:

'Every illegal stratagem has been employed for the past fourteen months to eliminate the Pakistan People's Party in order to pave the road for positive results,' he wrote, deriding Zia's promise to hold elections.

Bhutto did not want to let his own achievements go unrecorded. He emerged as a man who was indeed conscious of the role he played in shaping the destiny of his country.

'My government made the Nation walk out of the jaws of death. We faced and overcame gargantuan problems in the power of the people. We brought confidence in the place of chaos, and stability from the shambles of dismemberment.' Bhutto's own part cannot be overlooked. 'My services to the cause of our people are a mirror in front of them. My name is synonymous with the return of Prisoners of War, with Kashmir, with the Islamic summit, with the Security Council and

Zulfikar Ali Bhutto in 1977 during the People's Party election

General Zia ul Haq, Chief Martial Law Administrator

Zulfikar Ali Bhutto, former Prime Minister of Pakistan

Benazir Bhutto, Mr Bhutto's
daughter

Begum Nusrat Bhutto the day before the
appeal judgment was announced

In the bar room during the tea interval in the Supreme Court of Pakistan
Left to right: the late Ghulam Ali Memon, Rao Rashid Khan, D. M. Awan

Left to right: D. M. Awan, Aziz Ahmed, former Foreign Minister, and
Yahya Bakhtiar, Bhutto's senior defence counsel

Above: Benazir Bhutto campaigning for her father's life, September 1978

Opposite: Mr Bhutto with the Iranian Prime Minister, Amir Abbas Hoveyda, in Teheran in 1977. They were executed within days of one another in April 1979

Below: Shahnawaz and Mir Murtaza Bhutto, the former Prime Minister's sons, at a press conference in London, February 1979

The grave of Zulfikar Ali Bhutto at Garhi Khuda Bux near Larkana, now a place of pilgrimage for his supporters

with the proletarian causes.'

These statements, termed arrogant by his opponents, were Bhutto's method, from a death cell, of illustrating that whatever the humiliation to which he might be subjected, he was confident of his place in history. 'My name and my reputation are safe in the custody of the people and in the heart of history,' he wrote in his conclusion to one chapter.

Bhutto's consideration of governments — military and civilian — brought him to a cherished topic: that of foreign affairs and the national interest. He turns to discuss the most pressing problems facing his country: the Pakistan-Afghanistan relationship; the Nuclear Re-processing Plant; the Non-aligned Conference and relations with India. These were all issues which were explosive or current during the month of August at the time of the writing of the Rejoinder. They therefore came within the sphere of the national interest. Bhutto was eager to put forward his own views. It is evident how dearly he would like to have been dealing with the issues themselves instead of analysing them from his death cell — but then he also believed that but for the military *coup d'état* Pakistan would not be in the mess he considered her to be in at present.

Nearest to his heart was the Nuclear Re-processing Plant Agreement. His discussion followed in the wake of the visit of David Newsom, the United States' Political Secretary, and Monsieur Jacomet, the French special envoy of Giscard d'Estaing. It was clear by this time that modifications were about to be made in the agreement which Bhutto had himself negotiated with the French Government in 1976. By means of this agreement, which had had the approval of the U.S.A. when it was reviewed by the International Atomic Energy Authority at Vienna, Pakistan was to be supplied with a nuclear re-processing plant which would, of course, give her the capability of making a bomb, although ostensibly the agreement was to be used for peaceful purposes. His frustration at seeing his policies handled by the military régime can only have been slightly alleviated by the chance encounter on an aeroplane of his daughter Benazir with the special envoy, Monsieur Jacomet, himself on his way back to Paris via Karachi. Even if Bhutto could not give his views on the subject and the military had isolated the Bhutto family from political contact, this was an unforeseen meeting which probably would have annoyed the authorities had they known about it. Bhutto made no secret of his cherished aim to get nuclear capability for his people, especially in view of the threat and preponderance of India. 'What difference does my life make,' he wrote, 'when I can imagine eighty million of my countrymen standing under the nuclear shadow of a defenceless sky?' The fact that the military clung to the bid to gain nuclear technology indicates its acceptance of the value of the policy initiated by Bhutto.

Bhutto was also concerned with the relations between Pakistan and Afghanistan. Zia's unconditional release of Bhutto's old foe Wali Khan, whom he had jailed for high treason because of his secessionist activities, was seen as showing little foresight. What Bhutto objected to was that he had been freed without the recognition of the Durrand Line as the official border between the two countries. This meant that Pakistan had lost the quid pro quo. Bhutto had himself been negotiating an agreement along these lines with the former government in Afghanistan before the *coup* in April 1978 and this had already been confirmed by a Joint Communiqué. Moreover, Pakistan had lost the initiative with an Afghanistan as yet untested with its new Russian-backed people's government. Bhutto therefore saw the prospect of the border dispute being reopened.

The former Prime Minister was also concerned by the Non-aligned Conference which met in Belgrade in mid-August. When invited to the previous meeting held in Sri Lanka in 1976 Bhutto refused the invitation. He now felt that it was a gross indignity for Pakistan to attend the conference as an observer. He himself had consistently pursued a policy of non-alignment, trying to break away from the 'most allied ally' relationship with the U.S.A. which Pakistan was obliged to adopt in its early existence. But attending the conference as an observer meant, in Bhutto's opinion, that Pakistan was going in through the back door. Either she should go in through the front door or not at all, he believed. He fully advocated in the Rejoinder that Pakistan should forthwith leave CENTO, a line later adopted by the military régime. Then and only then would she be able to attend a conference such as that of non-alignment in her full right as a non-aligned power and not as a mere observer.

In addition, Pakistan's attendance in the capacity of an observer set a dangerous precedent, he believed, for India to attend the Islamic Summit conference in the same manner. Although a Hindu nation, she had more Moslems within her borders than were living in Pakistan and this might furnish a pretext for getting her foot into Moslem affairs at the Islamic summit conference. Ever since its inception Pakistan had been searching for an identity separate and apart from that of India. At last she was beginning to find it by strongly identifying herself with Islam and the Arabs. India's intrusion in this regard would inevitably restore some of the old inferiority complex, by being observed by her neighbour in a conference which Pakistan believed was its sole Islamic preserve. On no account did Bhutto wish to see this happen. As Chairman of the Second Islamic Summit Conference when the Moslem and Arab countries were hosted by Pakistan in 1974, Bhutto found this issue particularly sensitive.

Both as Foreign Minister and Prime Minister, Bhutto had always adopted an anti-India stand. It had been a way for him to rally his people. Twice in the Rejoinder he proudly stated how he brought back 90,000 prisoners of war from India with honour and regained 5,000 square miles of land. He believed that India was a threat because of its preponderance and the unsettled dispute over Kashmir. Therefore, he grasped upon any slight accommodation which Zia might have made with India and used it to show his people the danger that Zia might ultimately give way to India and compromise Pakistan's vital interests. He refuted the *canard* that he himself had made a secret clause in the agreement signed in Simla in 1972 with Indira Gandhi over Kashmir. He objected to the terminology of India as a 'dear and great neighbour' used recently by Zia. He liked no mention of partnership between the two countries. The problems between India and Pakistan, he wrote, 'will not be dissolved by a dance.'

At the time he wrote about these aspects of foreign policy, since they were themselves in the news, he kept adapting what he wanted to say in order to keep up to date with the latest events. It was no mean task, but he wanted his document to be of the highest standard to surpass what he called 'the tissue of lies' contained in the White Paper.

Bhutto's own knowledge of world affairs and the library of his mind are evident. It was almost as though he had used his own vast and magnificent library at Karachi from which to draw his inspiration. In keeping with his own sense of destiny, he concluded the Rejoinder with a recollection of two gifts which he received on his twenty-first birthday — one was the biography of Napoleon — the other Karl Marx's communist manifesto — both men who had made history in their time, and subsequently. Ironically too, they indicated the combination and to a certain extent conflict in Bhutto's own life — the man of aristocratic background fused with his belief in socialism for the masses and all power to the people. His last words, however, relate to the fight for liberty and are taken from Ostrovsky's *How the Steel Was Tempered*, with which Nehru concluded the book he himself wrote in jail before he took power in independent India, *The Discovery of India*:

'Man's dearest possession is his life, and since it is given to him to live but once, he must so live as not to be seared with the shame of a cowardly and trivial past, so live as not to be tortured for years without purpose, that dying he can say, "all my life and my strength were given to the first cause in the world — the liberation of mankind".'

Clearly Bhutto felt this was apt in his present situaton. In a previous chapter he recalls a meeting with Lord Brabourne — the Governor of Bombay in undivided India when he was a child, when the Governor called him a 'poet and a revolutionary' — 'and that is how I shall remain,' he wrote, 'until the last breath has gone from my body.'

Bhutto wrote the Rejoinder in a remarkably short time. But the adjournment of the Supreme Court after Bakhtiar had finished his arguments on 20 August, before the typing of the document had been completed, meant that its submission to the Supreme Court had to be postponed until the court reassembled in September. By the time this happened, two more events made alterations to the Rejoinder essential: the next White Paper on the alleged misuse of the media under Bhutto has been issued on 28 August. Bhutto, therefore, wrote a Postscript. He believed that the timing of the release of this White Paper had been utterly stage-managed. Sitting in his cell he saw that the date of the release was given in the Urdu version on a small piece of white paper stuck on the cover and front page. Peeling it off, he found that the date of August concealed the date of April. This White Paper had been ready since then, but he believed the military régime had chosen to issue it at what it believed was an auspicious moment. This fact was duly mentioned in his Postscript.

Then, barely two days before the event, Zia announced that he would assume the Presidency of Pakistan on 16 September, the day the court was due to reassemble, so Bhutto felt compelled to write an Addendum, again castigating Zia and his military régime, describing Pakistan as an 'Animal Farm'.

Just before the Rejoinder was ready to be submitted in court, the lawyers, earlier pressed for time, took a look at the legal aspects, in particular Bhutto's scathing comments about Maulvi Mushtaq, who had a chapter devoted to him in his role as Chief Election Commissioner. Despite the invective Bhutto felt justified in using, Maulvi Mushtaq was also a Chief Justice, and in the close-knit fraternity of the judiciary it was feared that the remarks about a brother justice might offend the Justices of the Supreme Court at the crucial stage in the appeal. Bhutto concurred in the advice offered to him and made the necessary alterations, reluctant, however, to delete remarks which he believed were warranted.

As the Rejoinder was about to be submitted, a lawyer stood up in court and protested about prior publication of matters relating to the appeal in the newspapers — more especially in the pro-Bhutto newspaper *Musawaat*. The complaint seemed merely a pretext for firm action to be taken against the Rejoinder, because at the same time 1,000 copies were seized whilst under print in Lahore, before the document had in fact been submitted to the Supreme Court. Later the number was reported to be 900, no doubt to account for the ones that were secretly sold on the literary black market to Bhutto supporters. A small news item in an anti-Bhutto newspaper announcing the seizure appeared on the same day as the lawyer's complaint that any prior publication of court material constituted contempt of court. Anxious that the Rejoinder should receive as much publicity as possible and be widely circulated, people supporting Bhutto had seen to it that it was printed in anticipation of its acceptance by the Supreme Court. However, when it was submitted to the Supreme Court, the Chief Justice took exception to the prior publication and whilst accepting it on the court record, forbade publication of the document. Any publicity given to the Rejoinder whatsoever amounted to contempt of court, punishable by six months' imprisonment according to Pakistani law, stated the Chief Justice. Bakhtiar was severely censored for 'smuggling' the document out and allowing its publication before its submission to the Supreme Court. He argued that it was not being publicised but merely printed.

The ban, however, did not prevent the Rejoinder reaching many people, particularly foreigners. It went to Delhi, Hong Kong, New York. In London it was on sale locally as a giant pamphlet. Ultimately, an enterprising Indian printed it as a book and it came back into the news several months later, as Bhutto's book written whilst he was in jail, called *If I Am Assassinated* — a fitting title taken from the text of the Rejoinder when Bhutto in poetic style contemplates the future, ever mindful that as a condemned prisoner his death might not be far off.*

* Later it was printed by the Bhutto Memorial Trust as 'My Testament'

7
POLITICAL ACTIVITY

'My sons will not be my sons [Bhutto wrote] if they do not drink the blood of those who dare to shed my blood ... Who are my sons? My sons are the masses.'

An outstanding characteristic of Zulfikar Ali Bhutto was that he had been able to inspire love in the people and he was a popular leader in the true sense. However, it was all very well for him to have the support of his people even in his hour of need, but it had somehow to be shown in real terms how substantial that support was. It had to be marshalled into some form of expression to let the military authorities know that its own hold was only skin deep, inspired by fear. It was also necessary for supporters to be encouraged and kept informed about the Chairman, his state of health and general condition. With the ban on political activities this was not easy, and ultimately most of the people, suppressed, frightened and, not knowing in which direction to act, resigned themselves to letting the judicial process take its course. As soon as gallant supporters emerged they were swept into prison and lashed.

Informal meetings of the political parties were permitted but these did not really reach the people. Nor did they amount to much more than a general discussion of policy without of course being able to put into effect the policies put forward. The Central Executive Committee of the People's Party met every three weeks or so and constantly demanded the immediate release of its Chairman and Acting Chairman, Bhutto's wife, Begum Nusrat Bhutto, as well as free and fair elections. When Benazir was free she was able to manage the organisation of the party informally; if and when her mother were to be 'disqualified' from taking part in political activities it was said that Benazir would be the next Acting Chairman. Having not held political office herself she could not be disqualified. Many looked to her as the future head of the PPP, if, 'God forbid', as the people used to say, the Chairman was not there to run the party himself.

'Disqualification' tribunals were a feature of Zia's régime which appeared to detract from his promise of 'free and fair' elections. These *ad hoc* tribunals had been set up in order to examine the conduct of past office-holders and, if they were found to have acted in an untoward manner, they were disqualified from taking part in any political activities for the next seven years. Often the alleged crime committed bore no relation to the period of time when the office was held. Those brought before the disqualification tribunals had no right to legal defence counsel. The tribunal itself consisted of a brigadier and a magistrate. It was also stipulated that even those who had been brought before such tribunals and found 'not guilty' could be called again. Once summoned, even before the case was heard, the person in question had to refrain henceforward from the limited political activity which was allowed. Bhutto's supporters believed that Zia was out to 'disqualify' most of the PPP before elections were (if ever) held. It was either disqualification for former office-bearers, or straightforward arrest for many party workers. The members of the PPP complained bitterly about the double standards used by the military régime, since only the People's Party was the object of scrutiny and, they believed, vendetta.

However, once disqualification or arrest took place, 'acting members' of the central and provincial committees were immediately appointed. There was little difficulty in finding people who would swell the ranks of the PPP. They stated jokingly that if a PPP ticket were placed on a lamp-post and an election were held, the lamp-post would be elected. Or, they said, if all the Bhutto family were arrested, put forward Bhutto's servant and he would be elected. Despite the fact that the leader was in jail condemned to death, the PPP still retained considerable support — an unusual phenomenon in the fickle political climate of the Asian sub-continent. Only Indira

Gandhi amongst Asian leaders managed to retain a similar love amongst her people, once fallen from power. The other political parties who were 'out in the cold' because they had not collaborated with the martial law authorities in the formation of the government — in particular the National Democratic Party led by Sherbaz Khan Mazari and the Tehrick-i-Istiqlal headed by Asghar Khan, began to murmur about the need for elections. In general the political parties were in disarray, and still the PPP was considered to be the premier party if allowed to campaign freely. It also suffered a splinter group breaking away under Bhutto's former Minister for Religious Affairs — Maulana Kausar Niazi. From then on the PPP consistently maintained that it would not permit those who had left the fold to return. It virtually implied that those who were not sincere in their support of the Chairman, the party were well rid of. Some also said that without the Bhutto family the PPP would amount to nothing of its former strength.

Almost as if to test his might, on 28 August 1978 Zia partially lifted the ban on political activities. Meetings were allowed to be held 'within four walls'. This was an open invitation for the PPP to show its strength and was an opportunity to come into contact with the people which could not be lost. As Benazir was the only politically active member of the family at liberty in Pakistan, it fell upon her to be the spokesman of the party on behalf of her father. Just prior to her tour she spent the festival of Eid at Larkana, meeting the people as was the custom, and as her father had done each year and on the very day of his arrest on the conspiracy to murder charge the previous year. She visited the graveyard of her ancestors and said prayers at the marble tombstones. On 10 September she set out to tour Frontier Province — the last time she had visited this Province was in the company of her mother, when she merely acted as companion. This time she was making the speeches. The PPP had large support among the people in Sind and Punjab but Frontier Province, carved out of the mountains bordering on Afghanistan, had been under the sway of Wali Khan, who looked towards the tribes in Afghanistan for their allegiance. However, even his strongholds, such as the towns of Mardan and Sherpao, came out in large numbers to welcome Benazir, or 'one without an equal'. Crowds shouted enthusiastically 'daughter of Pakistan' as she appeared. The kind of reception which she received was an indication of the reserve of support which the People's Party still enjoyed. Thousands welcomed her at towns like Abbottabad, Peshawar, Swat, Mansehra, Kohat, as well as Mardan and Sherpao. The response was spontaneous, enthusiastic and heart-warming. As a token of friendship, at each town she visited she was given a piece of cloth and garlands mounted up around her. Often the address of welcome was already framed as a picture and was presented to her after its delivery. Slogans in favour of the former Prime Minister were raised; Benazir wore a cap resembling that worn by her father and her speeches were applauded with hope and enthusiasm by spectators packed tight in the boiling sun. There was a sense of excitement about being able once more to prepare the large, coloured marquees — 'shamianas' — with the red, black and green PPP flags. The symbol of the People's Party was a sword and many felt 'Zulfikar Ali', meaning the Sword of Ali, would once more fight the way to the victory of the people.

Although meetings within four walls only were allowed, the large courtyards of the houses in Frontier Province, looking like mini-forts, meant that thousands were able to cram in to glimpse Benazir even if they could not hear her. Some came out of curiosity; most out of support for their Chairman. For Benazir it was an exhausting and exhilarating experience, similar to that she had undertaken during the election campaign the previous year before Zia put a halt to elections altogether. Then she was campaigning for the political future of her father; now she was campaigning for his life.

But arrests by the Government followed in Benazir's wake. Ten or fifteen lashes and one year's rigorous imprisonment was the usual punishment for holding a demonstration, which often happened after a meeting, or for having delivered fiery and militant speeches. The former Governor of the Province, a retired Major-General, who had fought in two wars against India, and had been highly decorated for his services, accompanied Benazir on the tour. He too made fiery speeches, saying that the waters of the Punjab flow down from the Attock river and so too must revolution (the Attock river forming the border between Frontier Province and the Punjab and which is joined at Attock by the Indus). Thereupon he found himself in jail in the Province's capital of Peshawar. Too old to be lashed, he was sentenced to one year's rigorous imprisonment. In disgust he returned his medals to the military authorities.

In view of the upsurge of enthusiasm and open support shown for the PPP it was not altogether unexpected when the ban was reimposed and meetings were restricted to committee members. Arrests took place against those who shouted 'Jeeay Bhutto' — 'Long live Bhutto' — the general complaint by the military authorities being that this caused 'a law and order' situation. Other parties held meetings but there was not the same mass support. Often their meetings were confined to hotel rooms. Nor did they pose the same threat to the military régime.

These meetings were heart-warming to Bhutto: he was only too aware that generally a fallen leader rapidly loses support. In spite of disorganisation caused mainly by massive arrests which inevitably had a disruptive effect on the party, Bhutto actually increased his popularity. People forgot about the complaints and grievances which they might have harboured against him whilst he was in power. His opponents scorned this show of support for him and even suggested that people were paid in advance to attend the meetings. But sympathy flowed in to Bhutto in adverse circumstances. It is unlikely that the poorest people understood exactly what ill their leader was undergoing, but they knew that a great wrong had been done to him and that it must be righted. The Appeal in the Supreme Court when it recommenced on 16 September, the day after Benazir had finished her tour, was comparatively remote. However, as long as power was in the hands of the military, the success of the Appeal would be the only avenue of escape for Bhutto and at this stage people were still hoping for a favourable outcome. The people could show their support for him, but they could not free him.

And so, as the prosecution began its submissions in the Supreme Court, Benazir began to tour again. After Frontier, she went to Rawalpindi, Lahore and Sargodha in the Punjab, where she received enormous and enthusiastic receptions, despite the reimposed ban.

Finally the authorities had had enough. Before being allowed to address a meeting of workers in Multan, some 500 kilometres from Islamabad, she was arrested at the airport on 4 October as she arrived from Karachi, where she had taken a few days' rest. She was issued with the detention order on the plane itself and taken at once to Islamabad in a small twin-engined Cessna plane. On account of her refusal to go unaccompanied on the plane — her companion was Yasmin Niazi, the daughter of Bhutto's dentist — she was forcibly dragged across the tarmac of the airport, clothes torn and feet cut in front of horrified onlookers, to be dumped in the Punjab. Her detention order stated that she had caused a 'law and order situation' in Rawalpindi, Lahore and Sargodha. The authorities had given her three days' respite in Karachi before arresting her; clearly since the alleged crime was committed in the Punjab it was there that she had to be confined. It was also significant that arson and pillage broke out in Multan when she was not allowed to speak, whereas she maintained that there was no law and order situation in the other places she had visited. She seemed anxious about being taken to the Punjab to the court of Maulvi Mushtaq Hussain after the sentence passed by the Punjab judiciary on her father. Ironically, one of the judges who presided over her court case when it came before the Lahore court in December was one of the five who had condemned her father to death in March that year.

Even more arrests followed this tour. The fear of the lash was ever present, men believing it made them impotent. However, at this time the people appeared to stop caring. A new dimension in protest developed. There was a certain solidarity in suffering. In early October four people burned themselves, soaked in kerosene. The sight of a charred body appeared on the front page of an Urdu newspaper. The only way anti-Bhutto elements could rationalise these self-immolations was by saying that the people were paid by the PPP to do so on the assurance that they would be saved. They could not account for the four deaths. The question came — would anyone subject himself to such a painful and humiliating death if he were promised all the money in the world? The Government found it hard to believe that people would go to such extremes for Bhutto and were sceptical of their actions. Bhutto, from his cell, was aware that the people still cared. The self-immolations at the time were seen as a clear sympton of Pakistan's desperation. However, they did not recur and people resorted to more conventional forms of protest in favour of their Chairman, such as slogans and processions.

Benazir Bhutto therefore began another bout of house arrest. Begum Bhutto had requested at the end of July that she be moved from Lahore to a house in Islamabad so that she need not take the airplane each week from Lahore to Rawalpindi to visit her husband. She suffered from low blood pressure and often fainted in the plane. It also meant that since Benazir spent most of her time in Karachi or Islamabad she was able to see her mother more often than when she was in Lahore. As both she and her mother now came under the jurisdiction of the Punjab they were detained in the house together in Islamabad, which had already been declared a sub-jail. Armed police paced up and down. The road was cordoned off at each end with stones and there were sentry-boxes for the policemen. No one except servants was allowed to pass, and occasionally they were searched. Family visitors from Karachi had to obtain special permission to visit. Like Bhutto they were in camera, incommunicado. Benazir read books voraciously. Her mother, in detention for so many months, spent much of the day preparing food for Bhutto, to whom they would sometimes refer as 'Chairman' in conversation. Whereas Begum Bhutto was more or less conditioned to her confinement Benazir, after her months of freedom since June, was frustrated at once more being detained, this time in a house which was not their own and which afforded little of their home comforts. Occasionally they emerged onto a balcony to wave at friends and supporters, to the annoyance and frustration of the police. Yet they were always aware that undue annoyance caused to the police would mean certain facilities might be denied. They knew as well as anyone that the first privilege to go could be the precious meeting once a week with Bhutto.

Just after Benazir's re-arrest the whole family was issued with letters from the Federal Land Commission making enquiries into the declarations they had made with regard to the amount of land each member owned. Descending as they did from one of the largest land-owning families in Pakistan, the Bhutto family used to own virtually the whole province of Sind. In the process of time this had diminished but Bhutto still owned vast lands centred on the village of Larkana in the heart of Sind, about 350 miles from Karachi. Their feudal origins were apparent. Larkana was near the ruins of Moenjodaro, meaning 'Mound of the Dead' (which showed the presence of an Indus valley civilisation dating back more than 2,000 years B.C.). The Bhutto family often referred to Moenjodaro to show that if there was one thing they were not, that was newcomers and upstarts. With perhaps a degree of arrogance, they considered themselves to be one of the old-established families of Pakistan. In this area they ruled as it were by right. And it was not unnatural — the transformation from a feudal pyramid society to a modern egalitarian one overnight has never been easy. Bhutto was as much aware of this as any of his colleagues or his critics.

At the cost of surrendering part of his lands, he had put forward land reforms in 1972 and 1977. This formed part of his programme of nationalisation and socialism in order to move in the direction of a more equal society, away from feudalism. The process was painful for those who felt they lost out; moreover, many argued that the reforms were in fact nominal for the most wealthy. But Bhutto believed the process had to be accomplished and it was, therefore, the grossest insult to him and his family to be accused of fraud and cheating with regard to his own lands. He maintained that he had acted in accordance with the law and had requested officials to make sure that his lands were scrutinised like any others. Benazir was told that she had declared 519 acres instead of 506. The family were all threatened with *ex parte* decisions if they or a representative did not appear. As they were not in a position to brief a representative, nor was a lawyer who came specially for the purpose allowed to see them and they were not free to attend themselves, they believed that these actions were unfair and humiliating. A later White Paper revealed how the Bhutto family 'flagrantly violated' the land reforms, describing how Bhutto 'got away' with 389.24 acres of land, as though if he had wanted more land for himself he could not have made the reforms less stringent.

As it was, Bhutto said his family relinquished 45,000 acres in 1972 alone, 6,000 or 7,000 belonging to Bhutto himself. The court case was kept in the background as just one more thing on their minds, at the time the prosecution was quoting extensively from law books and taking its time in the Supreme Court.

Whether it was sensational news like the immolations, or factual information about Bhutto's lands, or just general reporting about the Appeal and Pakistan's political situation, it received fairly wide coverage in the foreign press. To many in foreign countries, Pakistan was remote and there seemed little reason to become unduly perturbed by the vagaries of its political ruling élite. But such had been the allegations of unfairness about the trial of the former Prime Minister that the attention of foreigners had been drawn to observe in particular how the Appeal was conducted.

If people in Pakistan found their lips sealed for one reason or another and felt they could not speak out in favour of the deposed leader, the same was not true for foreigners. They did not have the same limitations. Foreign journalists could be outspoken, more so than the diplomats although they had to be careful not to appear biased. The Government appeared to bear a particular grievance against the BBC, which it considered was totally biased in favour of Bhutto, and sometimes the Pakistani press said as much in its editorials. Nonetheless, just as the military authorities could not prevent the arrival of appeals for clemency when the death sentence was announced, so they could not prevent observers from arriving to attend the hearing of the Appeal and see for themselves how things were going. The military régime was obliged, by the norms of international courtesy, to give them a cordial welcome. Moreover, since it continually stated that the judiciary was independent and that the trial had been conducted according to the prescribed rules of justice, it could hardly appear anxious to thwart foreign scrutiny of the Appeal, and indeed never did.

Bhutto had many friends amongst the foreign diplomats and was well respected. He also had friends dating from the time when he studied abroad, such as Professor (later Lord) Trevor-Roper at Oxford, who were prepared to speak out in favour of him. However, the Pakistani authorities seemed to attach so much importance to what the foreigners had to say that invariably their views were refuted in the Pakistani press. This happened with Hugh Trevor-Roper's article when it appeared in the *New York Times*. Trevor-Roper, having been asked by the Bhutto family to secure the advice of one of the best and most respected English criminal lawyers, had been instrumental in John Mathews' attendance at the trial in November the previous year.

At the beginning of the Appeal, a French lawyer, Monsieur Etienne Jaudel, belonging to the International Federation of Human Rights, came for a few days. Later he wrote a lengthy report in which he said, 'There appear to me to be in the decision of the first judges, very serious anomalies with regard to the general principles of human rights which authorise to every accused the right to a fair trial ...' He went on to say that it appeared from the interviews he had had with foreign correspondents that the debates were held in an atmosphere of hostility both towards Bhutto and his lawyers — 'a fact which appears contrary to the concern for objective and impartial justice'. 'History will judge the judges,' said another French lawyer, Monsieur Robert Badinter, who came for a few days in August. Although they were in attendance for only a short while, the presence of foreign lawyers reminded the judiciary and the authorities that the rest of the world was keeping an eye on the proceedings.

Ramsey Clark, former Attorney-General of the U.S.A. under President Johnson, came while Mr Bakhtiar was still on his feet. He was one of the few Americans who actually admitted that the CIA could well have been involved in destabilising the Bhutto régime. On his return to the U.S.A. he put the question to some students at Stanford University, California: 'As Americans,' he said, 'we must ask ourselves this: Is it possible that a rational military leader, under the circumstances in Pakistan, could have overthrown a constitutional government without at least the tacit approval of the United States?' He attended the Appeal for a few days and on his return wrote a sympathetic and favourable article in a journal, *The Nation*, stating: 'The evidence presented against Bhutto, even if believed, would not support a verdict of guilt.' Certain aspects of the article were however refuted in the Pakistani press.

As most of the foreign observers belonged to human rights

groups they were anxious to meet Mr Bhutto and see what his state was and examine his conditions of confinement. Amnesty International also showed concern. Clark put forward a strong case, saying that he had been allowed to visit condemned prisoners in Chile and other Latin-American countries. But 'no' came the answer from the General himself, with whom he had been granted an interview. According to Clark, Zia said that allowing him to visit the former Prime Minister would make the trial into a political issue, and it was merely a criminal one. It was in fact fairly obvious that no foreigner was going to be allowed to see the former Prime Minister, come what may. The authorities did not seem to realise that they were creating an image and an aura of mystique around him. Denying impartial observers only made the people more anxious to see him and more suspicious of the conditions of his detention.

Another well-wisher who had appeared on the scene was the son of a former Prime Minister, who had been rudely sent into exile on a plane by the instigator of Pakistan's first military *coup d'état*. Although a capitalist and well established as such in the U.S.A., the visitor claimed that he had been a friend of Bhutto's even though he abhorred Bhutto's socialist policies. However, now he was concerned only that Bhutto's life should be saved. He had come to Pakistan in the hope that Zia would grant him an interview with Bhutto and that he would be able to persuade Bhutto to renounce politics in return for his assurance that his life would be saved. Had this sort of encounter ever got as far as Bhutto he undoubtedly would have rejected it out of hand: his honour was worth more than his life, which he was not prepared to bargain for. But no such interview took place. The well-wisher returned to the U.S.A.

The attention of Britain in particular was drawn towards Pakistan, partly because of the large number of Pakistani immigrants living in Britain, but also because of the presence of Bhutto's elder son — Mir Murtaza — who was now twenty-four and had left Pakistan soon after the *coup*. He and the other two children were temporarily 'exiled' in London. The younger two, Shahnawaz and Sunham, were not initially involved in politics and concentrated on finishing their studies abroad. Murtaza, who had a degree from Harvard, had interrupted his course at Oxford, and was active in the campaign to 'free

Bhutto' run from London, and was later aided by Shahnawaz. They also visited various countries to enlist support, particularly among the Arabs. They tried to make people aware of the facts of the trial and the possibility that their father might not get justice and that, regardless of appearances, the military régime might still be intent on hanging him. They encouraged well-wishers to make clemency appeals when the time came and kept them in touch with the situation, from which even they were remote. Both the sons were in a much freer position to distribute literature which would give people the other side of the picture to that portrayed by the Pakistani Embassy in London and elsewhere.

The Rejoinder was the most important document to disseminate to journalists and diplomats. It was reproduced in the form of a large pamphlet and circulated on sale for fifty pence, until finally the book was launched. Murtaza was also connected with the production of the London edition of *Musawaat* — the pro-Bhutto newspaper which, in Pakistan, underwent considerable censorship. In London it could afford to be far more outspoken. There was also of course, an opposition newspaper — the London *Jang* — again the British counterpart to that produced in Pakistan. Murtaza was anxious for as much literature as possible to be distributed to keep the people in touch with the plight of their Chairman, his father. He, too, could be more defiant in his pronouncements and when, for instance, an article derogatory to his father appeared, as one did in the *Far Eastern Economic Review* in an interview with Wali Khan, Murtaza was in a position to reply to it.

Occasionally items appeared in the Pakistani press alleging that Murtaza was living lavishly abroad and criticising his statements. The charge brought by the British Government against Shahnawaz for a hoax call that there was a bomb in 10 Downing Street was given wide coverage in Pakistan. The Bhutto family maintained Shahnawaz's innocence and believed it was another manoeuvre on the part of the military régime to embarrass them. Often they felt Murtaza's statements to the press were misquoted in Pakistan to make it appear as though his opinions differed from those of the rest of the family. As it was, communication was difficult between England and Pakistan, especially when mother and sister were confined as well.

Ultimately there was little the governments of foreign countries could do apart from appealing for mercy when judgment was given. Constrained by diplomatic protocol, they were obliged to concede grudgingly that the trial was Pakistan's internal affair. Whereas people in Pakistan might have no other preoccupations than Bhutto, clearly foreigners had problems of their own to deal with. A brief interview with a head of state was a bonus. It could hardly be expected that they would take as much notice of the plight of Bhutto as his supporters thought the case merited. The judicial process prevented direct comment and criticism, which would constitute contempt of court. Although they had more freedom of action it was almost more frustrating than being on the spot in Pakistan. (Ironically, just at the time of the execution the two brothers organised a legal conference in London when most of the lawyers who attended the appeal and other prominent legal experts from different countries reviewed Bhutto's Appeal and trial. Their findings did not correspond at all with those of the Pakistani judiciary.) Murtaza had been advised by his father not to return to Pakistan because he would undoubtedly find himself in jail and anyway he could be of more use outside the country championing the cause, arranging rallies amongst the many Pakistanis abroad.

As a bid to keep Murtaza in touch with his feelings Bhutto once wrote him a long letter: at times it was as though Bhutto were talking to a historian, ever mindful of his place in history.

'My biggest achievement was to awaken the down-trodden people of the country,' he wrote, 'and to give them a vote in the affairs of the State. I took them out of the shame of 1971 and restored their honour.'

At others, he wrote just as any father would write to a son.

'I hope that you are looking after yourself and making good friends. Tomorrow your mother and sister are coming to see me ... in this crisis, and it has been the worst seen by us, your mother and your sister have been shining pillars of strength.'

Yet ultimately, regardless of the support of his family and the people, Bhutto had to face his tribulations alone.

'We all know that I am innocent. We all know that I am the victim of a deep, sordid conspiracy. Yet the humiliation and the insult cannot be ignored,' he wrote. 'The important thing is

that time will pass, the most important thing is that I must pass
through it with honour. Whatever the end, it must be faced
bravely.'

8

THE CASE FOR
THE PROSECUTION

The way in which the prosecution presented its case was closely scrutinised in Bhutto circles. If it presented its case badly, then the defence believed it might be an indication that the judges would acquit. However, if the prosecution attacked their arguments strongly then the prospect of an upheld verdict would have to be faced. Bhutto's supporters were still convinced that there were more than judicial fingers in the pie of the prosecution's case. The defence hoped it had sufficiently destroyed the prosecution's case, thereby making the death sentence impossible.

The learned Special Prosecutor — Ejaz Hussain Batalvi, slightly balding and with a parrot-like nose, began his submissions with panache. Ironically, he commenced on the day General Zia ul Haq assumed the Presidency of the country — 16 September. In the morning the Chief Justice listened to Batalvi's submissions. In the afternoon he saw to it that Zia ul Haq was sworn in as President. Zia's assumption of the Presidency was ominous. It would mean that in the event of an upheld sentence, as the chief executive he would be the only one with power to commute. Strangely, no one talked of the significance of replacing a President who had been appointed in Bhutto's time with one who had appointed himself and whose hostility to Bhutto was by now apparent to all. With the wisdom of hindsight, along with Qaiser Khan's retirement, some of Bhutto's supporters believed that it was one more reason why the appeal should have to be presented swiftly, instead of letting the military régime entrench itself still further. Yet, still retaining a false sense of confidence in the legal process, the defence remained optimistic throughout the prosecution's submissions.

Batalvi was meant to take two weeks to present his case. However, it soon became clear that he was going to take considerably longer. Ultimately he took two months, prolonging the appeal still further.

In his opening statement he started off, hard and strong, against the defence, who in turn murmured that his 'speech' had been prepared for him. Batalvi took exception to any such insinuation. Even so, as a more articulate orator than Bakhtiar he made his submissions with aplomb. It was clear that the prosecution had been busy during the three-week break.

Nonetheless, spectators thinned out. People generally were not nearly so interested in what he had to say. Plain-clothes policemen sat on the prosecution side. Batalvi reiterated the prosecution's case as presented in the Lahore Court. He pointed to clear motive by Bhutto on the grounds that Kasuri 'positively insisted' that Bhutto's name should be taken down in the First Intelligence Report. The speeches which Kasuri had made in the National Assembly criticising Bhutto were resurrected as constituting motive for Bhutto to want to do away with a man whom the prosecution termed his 'political opponent'. Kasuri's lavish praise, his changing colours, were all accepted as being part of the plan to avenge himself on the former Prime Minister for the death of his father.

'The case is,' Batalvi said, 'that Kasuri became a permanent thorn in the reputation of the Prime Minister; a perpetual thorn,' he added, 'which was damaging the democratic reputation of the Prime Minister as a socialist.' Such bitter criticism to the effect that 'you destroyed Pakistan' and comparisons with Hitler were unpalatable and unbearable for the appellant, Batalvi argued.

'But politicians are used to criticism,' Dorab Patel observed dryly.

Batalvi countered this remark with the assertion that it was very difficult for judges to place themselves in the position of the appellant, which to some looked like a statement that they were not competent to pass judgment on the actions of another. Upon the question by another judge: 'What was the point of getting Kasuri silenced?' Batalvi replied that it was twofold: firstly his tongue would be silenced, secondly it would deter others. But the judges did not think this was a substantial enough reason. Safdar Shah remarked, 'How would people be aware that he had been murdered for this reason?' to which Batalvi hazarded a guess: 'They have a sixth sense.' But even the Chief Justice appeared a little sceptical. 'If the case rested merely on motive,' he observed, 'then you have no case.' But, said the learned Public Prosecutor, in cases of conspiracy, motive had to be taken into consideration. Batalvi persisted, 'The appellant was very sensitive about his personal image'; he recalled how since 1971 Bhutto had been trying to change his image from the time when he served under Ayub Khan in an élitist set-up. Yet still this was not an impressive argument. Safdar Shah gave his opinion to the court that there was nothing unnatural about caring for one's image. Batalvi also stated that Kasuri had been pressurised into rejoining the PPP, maintaining that the 'dirty dog' document showing Bhutto's contempt of Kasuri was a forgery. Kasuri's surveillance was again considered to be something out of the ordinary — points, the defence believed, it had sufficiently refuted.

Insofar as conspiracy was concerned, Batalvi pointed to the 3 June incident as being the 'last straw'. He did not reconcile the inconsistency that on the one hand Bhutto was charged with hatching the conspiracy around mid-June with Masood Mahmud, and on the other, according to Masood Mahmud's own testimony, Bhutto had already hatched the conspiracy with his predecessor. Batalvi tried to create suspicion around the 'long interview' which preceded Mahmud's appointment as Director-General of the FSF, as though a long interview before such an appointment were out of the ordinary.

With regard to the actual definition of conspiracy, Batalvi wished to move away from Bakhtiar's contention that there could be no conspiracy because all the participants in the murder had themselves stated that they acted under duress from their superior officers. He asserted that as opposed to a 'contract', a conspiracy could still be in existence regardless of duress because of the presence of a guilty mind, *'mens rea'*, he said. It was not important for the prosecution's case that the approver had scant knowledge of the plans, nor that he had been unaware of the Islamabad incident. The learned Special Public Prosecutor stuck to the Lahore judgment's argument that the agreement did not have to be reached at one time alone or even that an express agreement had to be proved. It could merely be implied by subsequent conduct, acts or 'by anything said and/or by writing by any one of such persons'. The whole definition was so vague as to make the conspiracy once alleged by one person difficult to disprove, according to the prosecution.

Batalvi violently disagreed with the defence's demand for a 'double test' with regard to an approver's evidence. All he believed was necessary was for the evidence of the approver to be corroborated; it was unrealistic, he said, to try and ascertain that the approver was reliable since the very fact that he had deposed to save his skin meant that he was indeed a man of 'depraved character'.

'Worse witnesses than him have been believed,' stated Batalvi in answer to Mr Justice Waheeduddin's query as to whether or not such a witness could be believed. However, Safdar Shah interpreted this unfortunate comment as meaning that Batalvi was submitting that the judges did not know their job if they swallowed all manner of lies wholesale. Batalvi, hardly anxious to provoke the judges, said that this was not quite the point he was trying to make. And the Chief Justice concurred that a witness's unreliability was made up for by his evidence's corroboration by another witness, as was Masood Mahmud's by Welch and Saeed Ahmed Khan.

Whereas the defence had stated that Saeed Ahmed Khan's own confessed alleged involvement in channelling the investigation made him an accomplice, the prosecution believed that he was an 'innocent' agent. The fact that in so doing he was shielding assassins, since the matter under investigation was a murder case, did not, the prosecution believed, make him in any way an accomplice. He was one such independent witness according to the prosecution who therefore could corroborate the testimony of Masood Mahmud.

The prosecution still maintained that since Saeed Ahmed Khan was in a position of such close contact as Bhutto's Chief Security Officer, all his actions and initiatives inevitably came from the Prime Minister. 'The appellant,' he said, 'was the mastermind from the beginning.' In his initial synopsis Batalvi put forward a series of hypotheses: firstly, could the three confessing accused have hatched the conspiracy without Mr Bhutto? Answering his own question: 'No,' he replied, 'because they had no motive or grudge to kill Kasuri.' He then put another question: Could, after the occurrence, the other accused — the three confessing accused and the two approvers — control the investigation in the manner in which it was controlled by Saeed Ahmed Khan? Again 'No' came the answer, 'because Saeed Ahmed Khan was on the personal staff of the Prime Minister; Mahmud's allegiance furthermore was to the Prime Minister and not to the other accused.' Lastly, 'Why' he asked, 'did Saeed Ahmed Khan control the investigation?' Clearly, Batalvi submitted, he did not do it for the other accused because he had no allegiance to them; therefore, he concluded, it must have been for someone else, i.e. the Prime Minister. Batalvi pointed to the 'extraordinary interest' taken by Bhutto in the investigation of the murder case, through the intermediary of Saeed Ahmed Khan. 'There are two interpretations,' Batalvi announced: (a) is that of the defence that Saeed Ahmed Khan was doing it all on his own and that he was a busybody; (b) is that everything he did was on the instructions and in the knowledge of the Prime Minister.

'Now' said Batalvi, giving no further thought to (a), 'assuming (b) is correct, there are two further interpretations; one that with the name of Mr Bhutto mentioned he was keen to clear his name; two that No, it was not that innocent but motivated by a desire to suppress the evidence and the investigation. One could say,' submitted Batalvi magnanimously, 'that all these efforts were being made to clear Bhutto's name, which from his point of view would support the contention that Saeed Ahmed Khan was acting as an innocent agent. But,' he added, 'if it were all an innocent effort, then why was there an effort to create security around the FSF for the investigators?' Here Batalvi assumed as proven that there was an effort to steer the investigation of the murder away from the FSF. It was on record that 7.62 mm calibre ammunition was the calibre of the spent cartridges; and it was also on record that the FSF used this ammunition ...'

Still in the midst of his synopsis, at the mention of this technicality he was warned by Safdar Shah not to deal with peripheries and to keep to the substance of the case. 'You are dealing with irrelevancies,' he cautioned, 'and are falling into the same trap which you have criticised.' At which the Chief Justice proffered the advice, 'Yes, don't get derailed at this stage.' Batalvi, ever on the defensive in the face of criticism, protested that he was only clarifying a point raised as a question by a learned judge. He was going to experience the same sort of comments to which Bakhtiar had been subjected throughout his submissions. Bhutto's supporters kept a close watch on the comments and remarks of the judges, eager to detect signs of incredulity as Batalvi proceeded along the well-worn road of the prosecution's case.

Batalvi was anxious to point to the Prime Minister's involvement. He maintained that there was no connection between the FSF and the Chief Security Officer *vis à vis* their relationships with the Prime Minister. If Saeed Ahmed Khan was trying to protect the FSF was he doing it for the FSF or for someone else? he asked. The only link, he said, between the FSF and the Chief Security Officer came in the person of the Prime Minister. But the more he relied on Saeed Ahmed Khan's channelling of the investigation away from the FSF, the further he moved from being able to say that he was an 'innocent' agent. Ultimately he had to rely on the assumption that Saeed Ahmed Khan was directing the investigation merely to clear the Prime Minister's name in order to make him into an 'innocent' agent. This interpretation, equally applicable to the 'extraordinary interest' Batalvi claimed that the Prime Minister took in the case, was not however, granted to Bhutto. Saeed Ahmed Khan's trips to Lahore, during which he was seeing the officers concerned in the investigation, as well as the correspondence with the Army seeking information as to which units had the same calibre of ammunition, were all shrouded in suspicion, Batalvi maintained, and were not capable of an innocent interpretation from Bhutto's point of view, although from Saeed Ahmed Khan's they were.

The prosecution case that the murder was not properly investigated was one of its most important grievances. Batalvi pointed to the manner in which the investigation was conducted before the tribunal according to the testimony of the policemen; how in the Shafi ur Rehman tribunal only favourable material was produced and only publicity was given to this material, adding, of course, the role of Saeed Ahmed Khan. Nonetheless, Batalvi was forced to concede that in spite of all the alleged interference the findings of the tribunal were significant, thus pointing to the fact that its conduct, controlled or otherwise, did not prevent 'significant' findings from being made. It established that the spent cartridges were 7.62 mm calibre according to the ballistics expert's report. Producing the Shafi ur Rehman report as Supreme Court Exhibit 1, Batalvi outlined its findings:

> firstly, that the attack was directed at the life of Kasuri and incidentally, his father was injured and died;
>
> secondly, that in view of the identity and type of weapon used it appeared that the occurrence which took place three months before in Islamabad had common inspiration, motive, even if the perpetrators were not the same;
>
> thirdly, that the motive behind this occurrence was political;
>
> fourthly, the perpetrators of the crime were well organised, well equipped and resourceful, going persistently after the life of Kasuri.

But nothing was done with the report, Batalvi complained. Its non-publication was deemed by the prosecution to be an indication that the Prime Minister had something to hide; although its findings did not incriminate him and even included the controversial paragraph 15 in which Kasuri had named four groups of people who might have had a motive to kill him. Batalvi pointed to the hierarchy of control over the investigation which was inefficient and not properly conducted. He again laid emphasis on the non-investigation of the FSF. He believed this could have been investigated on the grounds that it was known that the ammunition was of 7.62 calibre although the defence had continually maintained that since it was known that this type was in use by other units as well, there was no reason for them to go directly to the FSF.

One of the biggest problems for the prosecution to solve was why the spent cartridges recovered did not correspond with the guns allegedly used. Batalvi felt himself on difficult ground when the time came to reconcile the fact that the cartridges did not tally. He tried to make up for this by saying that when the spent cartridges were recovered they were not sealed (in a packet) and therefore no reliance could be placed on their genuineness. Once time passed between recovery and sealing, he said, it threw into doubt their genuine nature. Therefore, he concluded that they had been substituted:

'I am not in a position to say positively,' he stated, 'that there is positive evidence of substitution, but there is a mass of evidence to suggest substitution.'

He was unable to substantiate the evidence any further. Nonetheless, by maintaining that the bullets were the same used for both Islamabad and Lahore attacks without there being any mention of substitution at Islamabad, the prosecution case contained a vital contradiction which some of the judges were to accept and which the defence would later use as one of the most glaring errors on the face of the record.

'There is a high probability that the empties have been changed,' he went on to say. 'There is a case for strong inference.'

In many instances the arguments of the case became a series of claims and counter-claims; the defence had claimed that Ghulam Hussain's TA Bill was not forged and pointed to the fact that Ghulam Hussain had only mentioned it when the defence had asked for it to be brought on record; the prosecution maintained that it was forged. To counter the charts produced by Bakhtiar indicating that Ghulam Hussain's testimony was not reliable, the prosecution produced its own charts. The defence had stated that the logbook showed the jeep in question was being used by another member of the FSF at the time of the attack; the prosecution claimed that the entries in the log book had not been admitted by the person who had made them, nor by any other person who could verify the handwriting and that, therefore, they were not admissible as evidence.

According to the prosecution, the testimony of all the other witnesses stood the test. The fact that many witnesses could not remember certain details or got dates wrong was inconsequential. Nor was the idea of torture or inducement entertained. With regard to Masood Mahmud, the prosecution dismissed lightly the defence's objection that he had been retained in government service on the same high grade as his post in the FSF, as well as being in detention throughout the trial, which could be considered a form of inducement to depose against the Prime Minister. Batalvi made nothing of this, stating that it was enough incentive to have the prospect of a pardon before him: obviously the greatest inducement any man could have in order to concoct all manner of lies, the defence believed.

In his remarks about bias, and the allegations against the Chief Justice of Lahore and his court, Batalvi submitted that it was based on 'venom' and was unfounded. He appeared outraged. It was, he said, nothing more than 'slanderous and scurrilous abuse'. Batalvi pointed to what he termed 'prejudicial advice' given even before the proceedings had commenced by Bhutto's defence counsel. Therefore, who was biased? he asked, the judge, the accused or the senior defence? Batalvi submitted that the accused's mind had been poisoned against the Chief Justice and accordingly a paranoia set in. It must have been poisoned to an extent where the ordinary and day-to-day observations of the bench must have been misconstrued and misinterpreted.

At this point there was an interruption from the bench. 'Certainly some of the observations were quite obnoxious.'

Batalvi proceeded to deal with the issue of supersession, a cause the defence argued for Maulvi Mushtaq's hostility to Bhutto. But strangely he began on an adverse tack. He stated that there was no legal or constitutional law for following appointments in strict order and any judge would know this. He wanted to submit that Maulvi Mushtaq was not expecting to be appointed and therefore could not have been disappointed, or for that matter, hostile to Bhutto for not having been appointed. But his submission did not sound favourable to the learned justices.

'It is a bad practice to supersede a senior man,' Waheeduddin remarked ponderously.

Continuing his submissions Batalvi was once more interrupted, this time by the Chief Justice. 'In common parlance the non-appointment of a senior man would be supersession.' Still Batalvi maintained that it was a non-issue. Yet the Chief Justice was anxious to point out that a lot of bitterness and discontent had been created by supersession and that it was considered as destroying the institution of the judiciary. 'Therefore,' he said testily, 'don't go on harping about this,' somewhat angry that Batalvi should persist in this line of argument. Giving his own remarks on the subject the Chief Justice concluded that the best safeguard against expectation of promotion was to ensure that it comes in due course. In order to make up for his colleague's apparent insensitivity to this issue which came close to the hearts of the justices, Rehman piped up just in time, 'Yes, otherwise it is an open invitation to adventurers.' There the discussion ended and it was clear that the judges did not want to hear more of Batalvi's arguments regarding supersession. He turned to other incidents of bias, none of which he believed vitiated the trial, as the defence claimed.

One he chose to discuss was the press conference when Mushtaq had declared that the trial was being held in the full light of day. Yet the justices clearly wanted to hear about the more unpleasant incidents and Dorab Patel called upon Batalvi to refer to them.

None of the issues Batalvi tried to submit were a manifestation of bias against the accused. Regarding Bhutto's dissatisfaction with the bench, Batalvi pointed to the safeguard afforded to him by letting him be tried by five justices. 'Nowhere in the world has a person been given the right to select his own tribunal,' he declared, as if Bhutto had asked to choose the judges, as opposed to requesting that the trial be transferred to another bench. Batalvi maintained that the points raised in the 18 December Application by Bhutto were taken care of in the court. The dock, he said, was justified because of Bhutto's remarks with foreign correspondents.

The Chief Justice found the allegation that the record had been manipulated a very serious one. 'Who has been manipulating it?' he queried.

But Batalvi maintained that this was all part of the accused's attempt to malign the judiciary. It was the accused's word against five judges, he submitted, all of whom were under a constitutional oath. But he did not answer the accusation. Instead, Batalvi asked more questions.

'Where would we be if we accept that the judiciary is suspect?' he demanded. 'Do we accept the word of the accused against those five judges? We must protect the judicial institutions,' he asserted. 'If we permit allegations like these, then the jungle prevails.'

Batalvi, an exuberant speaker, became quite excited at the thought of this. Yet most were aware that five judges could not be held to be above such an allegation, regardless of the outcome if, as Bhutto believed, there was good reason for the accusation in the first place. He merely submitted that it was Bhutto's inherent distrust and dislike of the judiciary, shown by the amendments put forward in his tenure of power limiting the terms of office of the Chief Justices which caused Bhutto to malign the judiciary so that he could say, 'Look, didn't I tell you in advance that I wasn't going to get justice?' ...

The allegations against the administration, Batalvi believed, were groundless. Whether or not Zia had stated that Bhutto was a murderer would not prejudice his trial. The judges all maintained that anyway they would not be prejudiced by material not on the record.

Throughout the weeks of his submissions Batalvi pursued his aim: to prove that all the appellants were rightly accused and that their appeals should be dismissed. He took his time reading from law books and citing many cases of Indian and Pakistani law.

For the first time during the course of the appeal the intended murder victim appeared in court. Ahmed Raza Kasuri made brief and infrequent appearances. His non-attendance during Bakhtiar's submissions was not entirely coincidental since he had been in the U.S.A. and Britain for the best part of three months with, as he said, the aim of publicising the Lahore judgment and explaining that the trial had been conducted fairly and that Bhutto was the murderer of his father. Although a lawyer, he said he was acting in his private capacity and that his tour of the U.S.A. did not amount to contempt of court. In a press conference given soon after his arrival back in Islamabad, he said that he was championing the cause of his father's murder, not so much because it was his father, but because the case was representative of all the murders Bhutto had committed. His hatred of Bhutto was evident; so too was his belief in his own political talents, and he said that the former Prime Minister had surrounded himself by pygmies.

Bhutto supporters scorned Kasuri and said that the whole of

his tour of the U.S.A. had been paid for by the Government. Kasuri said that he had gone as the guest of the Pakistani communities in the United States. Bhutto's supporters believed that it was quite contrary to justice to have the son of the murder victim publicising the case abroad while the appeal was being heard in the Supreme Court of Pakistan. Kasuri sat in court nervously, fidgeting with his hands, which were clasped in his lap; occasionally he looked round, casting disapproving glances at the defence. Once he even ventured into the bar room where the defence lawyers took their tea, and sat uncomfortably at the end of the table with a friend or associate. However, he appeared little interested in the proceedings and rarely stayed more than an hour. Sometimes he came at ten to one just as the hearing was about to adjourn. He wore gaudy checked suits which his opponents said he had bought in the U.S.A.

Batalvi had virtually repeated the prosecution case verbatim on facts and merits. However, he had to fight to make his points. One justice in particular, Mr Justice Safdar Shah, looked alternately surprised and incredulous at some of his submissions. Others too, showed open signs of disbelief. The learned Public Prosecutor concluded his remarks by saying that the judgment given was the only one which could possibly be used. 'All are equal before the law,' he said and he submitted that since the sentences were in accordance with law, the appeals should be dismissed.

Batalvi finished arguing before the next break for Eid in mid-November. The defence, believing that he had not proved the prosecution's case, felt relatively confident. They considered that he had made no substantial improvement in the case, which they believed they had shown to be wholly untenable. So much was hearsay and uncorroborated evidence: viewed objectively, they maintained that the evidence did not prove the former Prime Minister guilty beyond reasonable doubt. Any explanation of the inconsistencies was based on conjecture. Very few believed, in view of the doubts thrown on the whole story, that it would be possible to sentence the former Prime Minister to death again.

However, the time taken by Batalvi alarmed the defence. Bhutto's supporters again began to worry about the retirement of the two judges whose terms expired in November, as clearly the appeal would not now be over by then. Mr Justice Naseem Hassan Shah was due to retire on 19 November and Mr Justice Waheeduddin Ahmed a few days later on the 22nd. In order to forestall what had happened with Mr Justice Qaiser Khan, whereby the Chief Justice had implied that because the defence did not ask for the renewal of Qaiser Khan's term of office he did not want to take it upon himself to retain him, the defence made it quite clear that it would like both judges kept on the bench. Dr Naseem Hassan Shah's leanings were uncertain, but Mr Justice Waheeduddin had shown himself in favour of the defence's submissions. Clearly they could not keep one without the other.

Bhutto made an application to his senior defence counsel. This was transmitted to the Chief Justice with a request that these two judges be retained on an *ad hoc* basis. However, the Chief Justice kept everyone in suspense until just before the break for the next festival of Eid. Before the court rose Mr Bakhtiar asked what had happened to his application. Thereupon the Chief Justice replied that the defence and public would read about it in the press the next day. This seemed a little curt and a few minutes later the Chief Justice relented his abruptness and replied that the application had been granted and both the judges would remain on the bench. The relief felt in Bhutto circles did not compensate for the fact that Qaiser Khan had not received the same treatment. In addition, if anyone could have foreseen what was going to happen to Waheeduddin Ahmed, they would willingly have seen both judges go gracefully into retirement.

The break for Eid was supplemented by a further break because Mr Chief Justice Anwarul Haq had once more been 'called upon' to assume the acting Presidency in the absence of the President abroad. Bhutto made a further complaint about this since he still maintained that in doing so the executive and the judiciary were fused in the person of one man. With not a little venom he concluded his letter to the Chief Justice by wishing an unelected President a happy Eid from a former elected President. This was characteristic of Bhutto. He knew what his rights were and he intended to assert them even from a death cell. Anwarul Haq assumed the Presidency this time not because the President had gone to Austria for medical treatment, as had happened before, but because the President — in the person of Zia ul Haq — had gone to Mecca to perform Haj — the pilgrimage necessary for devout followers of Islam. Rumours circulated that because Zia commandeered a plane for his trip 400 worthy pilgrims were deprived of their right to go. Zia's performance of Haj was widely televised. He also made a trip to Saudi Arabia. It was said that one reason for his visit was to discuss what the Saudis' position was on the fate of Mr Bhutto.

However, it appeared likely that the appeal would be over by Christmas. It remained for the defence to make its right of reply and the judges would then retire to write their judgment. Rumours circulated that they would make a rapid decision in order to announce the judgment at Christmas when the western world was making merry and would not be in a position to expend its energy on finding out what was going on in Pakistan. But most informed people realised that by this stage it was futile to make prognostications: anything could happen.

9
THE DEFENCE'S RIGHT OF REPLY

The defence counsel began to exercise its right of reply after the break for Eid and the time when Anwarul Haq was acting President during Zia's three-day visit abroad. The return of Mr Bakhtiar to the podium in front of the eight judges was welcomed by Bhutto's supporters, who were weary of the loud voice of Ejaz Hussain Batalvi and his obviously unpleasant submissions. A welcome spectator also arrived. This was Begum Nusrat Bhutto herself, following her release by the Lahore High Court from house arrest after nearly eleven months' detention. As with Benazir's first release, the court ruled that the grounds of her detention were illegal. The people were delighted; so too were the photographers, who had a chance to amass a new collection of portraits of her. All the newspapers were heartily sick of having to reproduce the same out-of-date photographs whenever mention was made of her in the local press. She quickly made an appearance in the Supreme Court to unruffle the feathers of the prosecution and the judges who, since Benazir's arrest, had not had the proceedings observed by any member of the Bhutto family. Her dignity, grace and charm were magnetic. Once again, as when Benazir was free, the bar room became an attraction for PPP workers, who came more to see the Begum than to hear the appeal.

But events took an unexpected turn. Mr Yahya Bakhtiar was only able to argue for three days before Mr Justice Waheeduddin fell ill with a haemorrhage near his eye. Initially the court was adjourned for a few days, then for a week. No one was particularly worried. During this time the defence busied itself preparing abridged notes in order to finish the appeal quickly upon the return of the judge, lest he should have a relapse. At sixty-nine he was already well past retirement age and was only remaining on the bench to finish hearing the appeal of Mr Bhutto. But this illness heralded a crucial state in the appeal when the mood of the defence went from optimism to pessimism and back again.

In the meantime Bhutto himself was not well. His teeth and gums had been giving him great trouble. In his letter of 15 October to the jail superintendent he had written: 'It is imperative that I be shifted to a hospital for proper medical treatment, as recommended by the doctors' — on 4 August — the last time he had been examined. But it took him several more weeks to have the kind of dental treatment he wanted and in which he had faith. This was made possible by the sudden and surprising release of Dr Niazi once more on bail.

Niazi's own court case had shown sufficiently that there was no substance in the charges against him and he had been released on bail on 10 November. It seemed that the Government had little to gain by keeping Niazi in jail; at any rate the judiciary did not think so and although the charges against him were not dropped, he was allowed to resume his practice. In the months which followed, like those which preceded his arrest, Niazi was kept under strict 24-hour-a-day surveillance by the intelligence authorities to remind him that the arm of martial law was long. As Niazi was released at a time when Bhutto's teeth were particularly bad, Bhutto immediately requested permission to be treated by his own dentist. Niazi had the mobile equipment to which Bhutto was accustomed. Because he had persistent gum problems Niazi used to follow Bhutto about the country when he was Prime Minister, to be ready when the next bout of treatment was due.

However, even this simple exercise took time to accomplish. Permission was granted for Dr Niazi to see Bhutto, cancelled the next day and then granted again. When the permission was cancelled Bhutto declared that henceforward he could not eat, such was the pain he was in. What he needed was regular treatment and this was never forthcoming. Because the authorities believed Niazi was 'involved in politics' another dentist appointed by the Government had to be present also. Professional disagreement between the two caused the government dentist to submit a report stating that Niazi's diagnosis was greatly exaggerated, which Niazi believed was tantamount to accusing him of professional dishonesty. However, he was able to give periodic relief to Bhutto and also pressed for Bhutto to be given the medical tests he required because he believed that Bhutto's general state of health had been severely affected by the prolonged infection of the gums. Niazi for one believed that sufficient attention was not given to the most important aspect of the former Prime Minister's life, his health. This new drama over Bhutto's health occupied people's minds during the adjournment of the Supreme Court.

But Bhutto himself, despite his discomfort, was more concerned with what was going on in the Supreme Court. The illness of Mr Justice Waheeduddin Ahmed was more critical than had at first appeared. The burst blood vessel near his eye severely damaged his vision and balance. He was examined by a board of doctors from Karachi, Lahore and Rawalpindi. On the strength of their report the brother justices concurred unanimously that it was imperative for him to take the prescribed amount of rest, which was tentatively four to six weeks. It could be longer but it was unlikely to be less. The justices also made it clear that they would not be in a position to wait for his recovery to resume hearing the appeal — one of the reasons being that the appeal had already been so long-drawn-out that a further delay might cause them to forget parts of the arguments already presented. Mr Justice Waheeduddin from his sick bed wrote a letter indicating that he would like to resume hearing the appeal on his recovery, but if the court felt that it could not wait that long, then the bench should be reconstituted without him. Bhutto's supporters interpreted this as meaning that he washed his hands of the whole case if they were not prepared to wait for him, but his brother judges said that, realising he was not well and that the case must be concluded, he had given a clear indication for them to proceed without him.

The announcement by the Chief Justice that Mr Justice Waheeduddin would no longer sit on the bench was violently opposed by Bhutto's defence. Mr Bakhtiar said that this was tantamount to removing the learned judge when he had expressed his desire to finish hearing the appeal. His appointment on an *ad hoc* basis had been specifically for him to finish the case in question. The Chief Justice, supported by the other justices, said that it would not be practical to wait that long, nor would it be fair on their brother Waheeduddin, who might suffer a relapse on account of the strain. The altercations in court were angry and hostile. Bakhtiar virtually pleaded to wait for the judge in view of the fact that the court would probably take a recess for Christmas. He even suggested he would submit written arguments which could be read to the ailing judge. But the Bench was unmoved: the appeal was to continue without Waheeduddin. Both sides were obviously aware that Waheeduddin's departure would alter the voting strength, reducing the bench yet again from eight to seven. From having believed at the outset that they were in the majority with a 5-4 vote in their favour, Bhutto's supporters now believed that they were in the minority with a 3-4 vote against them. At present, this was all speculation, but it was a powerful demoraliser. People began to wish the appeal had been concluded long ago, even before Mr Justice Qaiser Khan was retired. Both defence and prosecution had taken their time, but it would be the defence's case which would lose out.

Bhutto felt so strongly about the removal of Waheeduddin that he decided to play his last trump card — he requested that he should be allowed to speak in his defence; if such permission were not granted, he intimated in a letter to the Chief Justice that he would be obliged to withdraw the power of attorney given to his advocates to act on his behalf and would accordingly finish the right of reply himself. The letter to the Chief Justice also once more enumerated the causes for his dissatisfaction with the Chief Justice's own conduct — chiefly his assumption of the acting Presidency on two occasions and the press statements made whilst the Chief Justice was in Jakarta. The Chief Justice, although admitting that Mr Bhutto once more directed the full force of his invective against him in person, only read out, however, that part of the letter in court which dealt with his request to speak. Somehow, the immediate impact of Bhutto's gesture was detracted from by the Chief Justice's calm protestation that he and his brother judges had no reason for not wanting Mr Bhutto to speak at the appointed time, but that meanwhile it would be best if Mr Bakhtiar himself concluded the legal arguments.

Bhutto's defence team had at this point undergone serious pressure and strain. They had been obliged to argue points in law regarding the removal of Justice Waheeduddin with only half a day's notice, although this itself was an improvement on what the Chief Justice at first prescribed, which was half an hour for the tea break. It appeared a disaster to have gained a judge from the arms of retirement, only to lose him in the clutches of illness. The mood of confidence was gone. They felt they had lost the case.

A last-ditch effort by Begum Bhutto to secure a review of Waheeduddin's departure as well as pressing for medical facilities to be granted to Bhutto to facilitate the writing of his own speech, foundered in a near misunderstanding between client and lawyer. Bakhtiar believed the applications, drafted by another lawyer in Lahore, were not tenable in law and would damage their case. The matter was resolved by an impromptu meeting in the jail with Bhutto, Begum Bhutto and the defence counsel. Mystery surrounded the whole matter because no one in the court was told what was in the applications nor how the apparent rift was healed so easily. Perhaps it had something to do with the warning given by the Chief Justice that if the defence team did not return from their impromptu meeting with Mr Bhutto before 11.30 the court would deem the defence had concluded its arguments and would retire to write the judgment. It seemed futile to waste time on what could only be termed a difference of opinion at this critical stage in the appeal.

The attention of Bhutto's supporters was distracted from the disappointment they felt over Waheeduddin's retirement by the assurance that Bhutto would be allowed to speak. He would be removed from his 'in camera' position for the first time since the trial at Lahore was made secret on 25 January. It remained to be seen when and in what manner he would appear.

Bakhtiar was jostled through his remaining arguments. But with Waheeduddin gone away the defence were not anxious to conclude in a hurry since time, with a possible change in the political situation, could only be on their side. It was an idle hope, as it was clear that the military régime was establishing itself even more securely in the seat of power.

The justices were getting weary and each day Mr Bakhtiar was asked how much longer he would take. Although continually protesting that he would need 'a couple more days' the lawyers behind the scenes were busy searching up new points to make in order to prolong the proceedings and make as thorough a defence as possible.

To a certain extent they also galloped through the concluding arguments due to their own diligence. Instead of reverting to reading laboriously from law books, the defence team had extracted the relevant cases and typed out notes of the submissions Bakhtiar would make. Photocopies were made for the judges to peruse as Bakhtiar read, which made the going much easier and quicker since they had the material in front of their eyes. Done in anticipation of the return of Justice Waheeduddin in the realisation that he might once again fall ill, it seemed pointless not to use the carefully prepared notes. In his submissions, Bakhtiar made loud protestations of the unproven guilt of his client and the unsustainable submissions of the prosecution.

Meanwhile Bhutto in his cell was preparing to make his comeback into the public eye. So long had he been absent from it that people were apprehensive about the way he would act and what he would say. Some said that he would appear contrite, others still that he would not be capable of arguing for a morning, such was the state of his health. He had been supplied with various documents and was busying himself with pad and paper to make his submissions.

Bakhtiar gave what he called his summation speech on Sunday, 17 December. He had been told positively to conclude then and his client would appear on the 18th. Although Bakhtiar had not finished all the legal arguments the Chief Justice, expecting to call Mr Bhutto on Sunday, was prepared to put this off only for one more day. Mr Anwarul Haq appeared heartily sick of the whole proceedings and yet managed to maintain the dignity and decorum expected of a man holding such a high office in the Supreme Court. He seemed to take the appearance of the former Prime Minister in court in his stride although he himself had been subjected to harsh and cutting criticism by Bhutto. His indifference was almost uncanny.

On 16 December, as people in the western world looked forward to Christmas and its festivities, it was announced in Pakistan's Supreme Court that the former Prime Minister would address the court on Monday, 18 December, after the tea break at 11.30 a.m. People could hardly believe the moment would come, finding it difficult to conjure up the appearance of their former leader. Bhutto himself, when the time came for this long-awaited appearance, was a bit surprised at the short notice he was given, but there was nothing to be done. If he wanted to appear, appear he must on the date given by the Chief Justice of the Supreme Court. It was just another small but painful reminder that he was no longer in control of his actions.

Bakhtiar concluded his submissions, reiterating his statements at the outset of the appeal. His words echoed those on the first day.

'It is a false and fabricated case,' he urged, 'which intended to eliminate the most popular national leader,' the reason being, he went on to say, that the 'vested and chauvinist' elements knew that he could not be eliminated politically or through the democratic process of elections.

With all the effort at his command, he continued:

'The prosecution has miserably failed, and,' he added, 'its diabolical conspiracy to eliminate Mr Bhutto has been fully exposed to the whole world.'

Bakhtiar outlined and pinpointed the submissions he had made during the course of the appeal on motive and conspiracy. He talked about Kasuri and described the lack of motive for Bhutto to want to kill this political 'nonentity'. Nor was there any proof that there was a conspiracy in which the former Prime Minister was involved. The only man to allege a direct connection with the Prime Minister was wholly unreliable, as was Kasuri himself. Masood Mahmud had been arrested on the day of the *coup* and remained — uncharged — in detention and in government employment. He pointed to the falsehood of the other witnesses and once more highlighted contradictions in the prosecution story: in particular the two gunmen, bullets in four places, two batches falling both sides of the hedge and the other two nearly 190 feet apart.

At this time the prosecution organised a demonstration to show that by holding the gun in a certain position it was possible for cartridges to be flung over the hedge. However, they were unable to account for the finding of the bullets nearly 190 feet apart on the other side of the roundabout. Bakhtiar reminded the court that the shell cases did not come from the guns allegedly used. He did not think much of the prosecution's suggestion that these had been substituted, asking the court to accept this thesis on the basis of high probabilities. The other main points were brought out — the log book, the jeep, the by-lane (whether Ghulam Hussain was there or at the scene of the attack), the TA bill and most of the other important points mentioned during the appeal were briefly summarised. They were well rehearsed arguments and Bakhtiar felt reasonably confident as he concluded:

'This is a most important decision your lordships are going to make.'

Almost before he had time to sit down, the response of one judge was heard. 'In our lives probably ...'

Foreign correspondents busily taking notes during the proceedings and eagerly procuring copies of his final speech sent this news back to the rest of the world, a world which by now had its attention focused fully on the Bhutto trial in Pakistan in anticipation of the appearance of the man himself.

10

BHUTTO'S APPEARANCE

The appearance of the former Prime Minister on 18 December in the Supreme Court created a sensation. As he emerged, accompanied by his defence counsel, into the packed and buzzing court room, there was silence. Loyal supporters rose to their feet as a mark of respect to their leader. People had been waiting to enter the court room since 7 a.m. Mr Bakhtiar still had some concluding remarks to make which he did in the first two hours of the morning session. Never before had he addressed such a crowded court. People unable to get seats were squashed into the aisles, sitting on radiators and on volumes of law books in the pit of the court in front of the podium. Many were dismayed to find on entering, in spite of their long wait, that some of the seats had already been taken by Intelligence Officers. At strategic intervals, particularly on the aisles, were large, surly, plain-clothes policemen so placed that they could prevent any contact with the former Prime Minister as he passed. Relations of the justices had also been allowed prior entry, which annoyed Bhutto supporters, who mumbled in audible tones about the inequality of equality.

During the break for tea between 11 and 11.30 few dared to leave their places for fear of not being able to squeeze in again. The court authorities were officious about people who left and then wanted to return. Even journalists were given a rough time although they could not really be refused entry. With a seating capacity of about 100, between 300 and 400 new passes had been issued. Many anxious spectators had to be turned away at the door but there did not appear to be any discretionary behaviour. Bhutto's servants from Karachi and Larkana managed to get in to see their master. If people wanted to see Mr Bhutto they just had to arrive early and sit squashed together throughout the proceedings. Mostly European foreign correspondents came, as well as numerous journalists from local Urdu papers. There was a handful of diplomats who had applied through their embassies for seats to be reserved for them.

Emerging from his death cell to see the world for the first time in nine months Mr Bhutto was still a commanding figure. Renowned for his taste in clothes, he appeared beautifully dressed in a well-cut, expensive suit. Only on one day did he wear the 'national' dress of Pakistan — the shalwar kameez. However, his clothes hanging loosely were ample proof that he had lost a great deal of weight while in jail. Although his gums had improved and were less swollen, his teeth were discoloured.

As the justices came in and everyone rose, the Chief Justice, curious to see Mr Bhutto after such a long time, gave him a long, hard look. Without further delay he called on him to address the court. Mr Bhutto looked pale and trembled slightly as he came to the podium. When he began to speak it was as though it was after a very long time.

For a man reputed to be arrogant Zulfikar Ali Bhutto appeared almost humble. In his opening sentences Bhutto showed immediately that he was not going to start on a great invective either against the court or the military authorities. He appeared intensely sincere, a man who had come earnestly to put forward his point of view. He thanked the court for this right which he felt had been denied him for so long.

'Not only my life but according to my objective appreciation, far more is at stake.' he said.

'My reputation, my political career, the honour and future of my family and above all the future of Pakistan itself are involved. This is my view. It might be a mistaken view but it is an honest and sincere view and I am not trying to dramatise or exaggerate it.'

He assured the court that he would not go over ground which had already been covered by his defence, but he did want to deal with issues which he believed only he could answer. He apologised in advance if he did stray from the point or went over old ground by mistake. He hoped the court would appreciate that for such a long time he had been kept in a 7 ft by 10 ft cell 'and in this court room I feel a little dizzy,' he said. 'I can't adjust myself to the momentum and the people.' Looking round the court room he exclaimed, 'Yes, it's nice to see people.'

There were rumours that Bhutto would attempt to scandalise the Government, particularly Zia ul Haq, but in his opening remarks he made it quite clear that this was not to be the basis of his submissions. He gave assurances that he would scandalise neither the institutions of the country nor any individual.

'Why should I scandalise the institutions?' he asked. 'In the first place, precious few institutions are left to scandalise and I have been deeply connected and associated with the institutions of this country, trying to build them up.'

He appeared tempted to talk about the 1973 Constitution and its suspension. He said that the judgment given by the Supreme Court in Begum Nusrat Bhutto's petition challenging the validity of martial law was a 'positive' judgment. This was Bhutto's way of giving a limited degree of approval to a judgment which obviously did not go in his favour. However, he thought that the judgment would have been better if a time limit for elections had been fixed and provision had been made so that the Constitution could not be amended arbitrarily. The judges moved uncomfortably in their chairs, hoping that Bhutto would not stray into irrelevancy. But having touched upon this and his fears for regionalism, proliferation of parties and the break-up of the country, Bhutto returned to his main theme.

He was getting used to talking again, talking in public, in front of people who were listening. However, one spectator was agitated. Not far away, sandwiched in between the members of the prosecution, sat Ahmed Raza Kasuri. He winced and grimaced as Bhutto spoke. At the time when Bhutto was talking about the Constitution he turned to one of the prosecution and in a loud whisper said something to the effect that surely Bhutto could not be allowed to go on much longer. The young lawyer assured him confidently that the Chief Justice would let him speak for a while and then would shut him up. But the Chief Justice did not shut Mr Bhutto up. Instead he showed surprising patience with Mr Bhutto's at times lengthy discourse. On the first day, speaking for just over one hour, Bhutto outlined what he intended to deal with in his defence. At times he elaborated on certain points since he was not sure how much time would eventually be granted to him to speak.

He wished to refute certain aspects of the Lahore judgment, particularly the paragraphs which condemned him as a Moslem in name only; arising from this was the question of his temperament and character. He talked about the nature of insults and how they were a matter of interpretation. He described how when at Christ Church, Oxford, his tutor advised him to take three years as opposed to two over his proposed course of studies in jurisprudence since 'even an English boy' would require that amount of time, Bhutto felt insulted by this slight on his potential as an Asian. He therefore said that he would take two years, and subsequently passed his examinations with high honours. 'I have not been brought up to insult people,' he said, 'nor do I expect to be insulted.' He took great exception to his description as a compulsive liar since he considered there were no grounds for this title.

Since Bhutto believed that the case against him had grave political overtones, he was anxious to touch upon what he termed the 'social conditions' prevailing at present and those in his régime. He pointed to the use of the telephone as evidence against him.

'The telephone has become the greatest persecutor against me,' he said. It was either that, or the fact that 'these people were terrorised by Mr Bhutto' which was used against him to incriminate him. But he believed far worse was going on under the rule of martial law.

'In my time there was a parliament in existence,' he said. He went on to say that there was democracy and critical speeches could be and were made in Parliament. He said that the prosecution stated that the subordinate police were reluctant to proceed with the FIR since the Prime Minister's name had been mentioned. But, Bhutto said, supposing the Chief Martial Law Administrator's name was mentioned today in a FIR in connection with a murder case, would not a subordinate policeman say, 'Take it easy, maybe you are wrong?' It was not a small matter to include the name of the chief executive in connection with a murder charge. Moreover, Bhutto pointed out, the FIR did not indict him. It was merely said in the FIR that it might be remembered that Mr Bhutto had made a speech against Kasuri in the Assembly. This was not an indictment. It could, at best, be reason for motive but was not a motive in itself.

'However difficult the conditions are under civilian rule,' he said, 'they can never be compared to conditions under martial law.'

Obviously aware that he would not be permitted to stray too far in the political sphere of discussion, he cleverly inserted sentences and phrases which would fall on attentive ears. Much like the Rejoinder, he was aware that this was a God-given opportunity to speak and he must say as much as possible while time permitted.

Bhutto's main task was to defend himself on the conspiracy to murder charge, and he wanted to deal extensively with motive and conspiracy to show that he had no motive and there was no conspiracy. He also wanted to make known to the people just how the Lahore trial was conducted, especially with regard to the in camera proceedings when few people knew what happened. He pointed to the prosecution's reliance on high probability to incriminate him. He wished to show that there were inherent contradictions in the judgment against him. The fact that whether the criticisms which had been levelled against Bhutto were true or false, it was alleged that they still constituted grounds for Bhutto's desire to eliminate Kasuri. This was one such instance of a contradiction.

He touched briefly on his achievements and pointed out that he was not new to politics and was used to being criticised.

He described how he had been in the National Assembly in Pakistan for over twenty-two years. 'So,' he said, 'it cannot be said that I was thin skinned in politics.' Later he pointed to far more virulent critics than Kasuri, including Wali Khan and Asghar Khan.

At times while he was speaking, Bhutto appeared tired and wearied by the ordeal. Sweat began pouring down his face. When he came to the question of what he termed his maltreatment since his arrest over fifteen months ago, some people believed that he wept.

'I don't like to talk about it,' he began. 'I am embarrassed. My people will be embarrassed. There will be a sense of trauma.'

At this he hung his head and shook with emotion. His jaw

trembled and tears welled to his eyes, but none rolled down his cheeks. Undoubtedly he was overwhelmed and he thumped the podium with his fist, calling upon God in his mother tongue of Sindi to keep him from losing his confidence.

'Believe me,' he said, 'I have been very shabbily treated.'

He regained his confidence and lifted his head proudly to proclaim:

'I am not a rootless phenomenon. I have done no harm to this country. I am treated like a criminal when I am not a criminal. I am treated worse than the other co-accused. For ninety days I have not seen sunshine or light. I was put into the death cell on fifteenth October and kept there for ten days because two prisoners had run away. What connection had this with me? I am not going to run away from my country. I am not leaving my roots.'

He described how his former Chief Minister and ex-Governor of the Punjab, Ghulam Mustafa Khar, had warned that they were after his blood and advised him to go. But he had refused, saying, 'You go, if you want, but I am not going.'

The Chief Justice seemed anxious to make a connection between Khar's own departure to London and Bhutto's statement, but Bhutto assured him that he had nothing to do with Khar's actual disappearance. He referred also to the incident when on 13 September, just after he was released on bail before his arrest by the military, a foreign journalist, as an admirer, had advised him to leave. But Bhutto said it was not life as a life. There had been many attacks on his life and he was not afraid of losing his life.

'Everyone who is made of flesh has to leave this world one day. I do not want life as life, but I want justice.' He had not come to speak for pity, nor for mercy but for justice, indivisible justice, he said. 'The question is not that I have to establish my innocence; the question is that the prosecution has to prove its case beyond reasonable doubt. I want my innocence to be established not for the person of Zulfikar Ali Bhutto. I want it established for the higher consideration that this has been a grotesque injustice. It puts into the shade Dreyfus and everything else.'

Bhutto believed that the treatment which he had undergone formed part of the malafides. 'Only a sick and depraved régime could have treated me like this,' he said. 'They keep on saying I want to be treated like a Prime Minister, that I still think I am the President. My Lord, I am a humble man. It is not a question of my wanting to be treated as President or Prime Minister. I want to forget that I was Prime Minister because that is the consideration, the obsession, which lies at the basis of this case.'

He went on to talk about the criticism of his conduct in court. 'I have been called a compulsive liar, where are the lies? It has been said that I am a Moslem only in name, where is the evidence?' Later in his submissions on the final day he returned to this slightly tongue-in-cheek, and said that now he must be a stateless person because the Constitution provides only for Moslems and minority non-Moslems. There is no provision for someone who is a Moslem only in name and, he added, there must be many Pakistanis in that predicament.

He referred briefly to the trial at Lahore itself — the dock constructed to seclude him, his illness during the trial, the fact that he believed what he said was not brought on record; the observations by the Chief Justice in the secret proceedings at Lahore, which Bhutto believed showed regional bias and if disclosed would have a disastrous effect on the sentiments of the people. 'These observations,' Bhutto pointed out, 'were denied in the Supreme Court by the prosecution.' (When, in Lahore, Bhutto had referred to A.K. Brohi — at present Minister for Law and Parliamentary Affairs — as the 'friend' of the Chief Justice, the latter, according to Bhutto, had replied, 'How can he be my friend, he's from your province [i.e. Sind] not my province [i.e. Punjab]?') Mindful that provincial sentiment was strong in Pakistan, Bhutto believed these remarks brought out one of the worst forms of bias. He intended to return to all these points in detail on the days following — time permitting.

The Chief Justice, Mr Anwarul Haq, surprised all those who had murmured 'bias' throughout the appeal. He conducted the proceedings in a fair and reasoned manner, occasionally joining in the repartee with Mr Bhutto. Bhutto himself continually showed profound gratitude at having been given the right to address the court and declared that he had confidence in the Supreme Court. He accepted what was his right as though it were a gift. 'I am in your hands,' he said. He seemed hardly able to believe it when the Chief Justice said he could have as much

time as he needed to present his defence as long as his statements were relevant. Relevancy was the point at issue and the
Chief Justice was not going to let Mr Bhutto have quite everything he wanted.

Bhutto said that he would like to talk a little about the future
of Pakistan because 'Pakistan today is in a very precarious and
critical condition. You may say "This is a very vain man, a
boastful man." But don't you see the void in the country? It is a
barren void. There is no direction. The balance of power has
shifted so much and is shifting so fast that the sub-continent is
in a new political crisis of great magnitude.'

This seemed a little too close to sensitive political issues and
away from the case and the Chief Justice interrupted. He said
that it would be very useful for them as citizens of Pakistan,
especially with Mr Bhutto's knowledge of foreign affairs, but it
was hardly within the scope of the case. Mr Bhutto accepted
this observation. But it merely revealed that here was not just an
alleged 'murderer' but indeed a man of brilliance and expertise.
It was almost as though the Chief Justice was saying — well,
whether or not we uphold your death sentence, it would be nice
to benefit from your knowledge of foreign affairs, but actually it
cannot be squeezed into the relevancy of the case.

It was much the same as when Bhutto said just before his
arrest in September General Zia came to him and asked for his
advice on the future framing of the Constitution, surely knowing full well that soon he was to be charged with conspiracy to
murder.

Bhutto, a man renowned for his oratory, put all his energy
into making his defence, despite the fact that he was obviously
unwell. He said that it was only his spirit and determination
which had kept him going because he was a leader — an
ordinary man would have disintegrated long ago. But he was
obviously overcome by the occasion, as were members of the
audience, who wept at seeing their former Prime Minister in
such circumstances. At times he had difficulty in putting his
thoughts together.

He pointed to his own haggard appearance and concluded his
first day's submissions by saying that he was not permitted to
sleep. He recalled how for three months in Kot Lakhpat in

Lahore there were lunatics next door who shrieked and made maddening noises all night.

'When I first came to the prison here they were throwing pebbles onto the roof. Every fifteen minutes I could hear the noise on the tin roof. They used to collect the pebbles in the morning and throw them at night. There is a parapet next to my cell with a military guard on it and a tin roof. They jumped on it with their boots and that keeps happening because there is not one guard but a number of guards. I thought at least last night they would spare me, but they did not. They turned off my water for twenty-five days, only yesterday did they restore it.'

The first appearance of Mr Bhutto was undoubtedly the most moving. It had broken the spell. He had come out of the death cell to see the people again. And the people had seen him.

*

Bhutto went from strength to strength each day. On the second day he looked far more relaxed and composed. Whereas he only spoke for just over an hour on the first day and stopped, sweating and pale, about fifteen minutes before the court was due to adjourn, on the subsequent days he showed that he was getting used to talking; he had regained his equilibrium. Even when his defence whispered to him to stop he replied — 'I *am* tired, but I must go on.' His honour was worth more than his life.

Apart from Bhutto's actual appearance, what he had to say was important. He began his submissions on the second day at 9 a.m. rather than 11.30. The first point he wished to reject was the description of himself as a Moslem only in name which appeared in the Lahore judgment. While he was about it, he also pointed out objectionable parts of the judgment which he clearly knew by heart. When his defence counsel were anxious to prompt paragraph numbers he replied impatiently, 'I know all these paragraphs.' At other times he appeared grateful for factual correction and assistance from his counsel. He began by a dissertation on the history of religion through the ages as part of his rebuttal. However, the Chief Justice interrupted him.

'This is all very interesting, but would you like to come to the point?'

Bhutto then said he felt strongly about the criticism of his faith which was a matter between the individual and God. It was an embarrassing and painful matter and he felt showed bias by innuendo.

'In Islam an elected leader of the people alone can be a repository of the trust of the Government.'

He was elected as the leader of the Moslems of Pakistan in 1970 and the Lahore Court had exceeded its limits when it observed that he was unfit to have been elected the leader of the Moslems. This was 'a clear manifestation of bias,' he said, and 'vitiated the whole finding of the court'.

Bhutto also disposed of the title of 'principal accused' when dissecting the Lahore judgment and its offensive aspects. He could never be the 'principal accused' since this title was reserved for those actually involved in the shooting. The judges seemed readily to concede this point. Moreover, the terminology of 'arch culprit' showed the biased mind of the court, Bhutto believed. The judges intimated that if they found these remarks were not necessary for giving the judgment they would be expunged. One justice remarked:

'Prima facie we give you our tentative view that these paragraphs in the judgment of the Lahore High Court were not relevant, nor were they factually correct.' Bhutto felt so strongly about the slight on his religion that he said he would have preferred to go to the gallows rather than be insulted in this manner. 'My Lord,' he said to the Chief Justice, 'you are not in my shoes. You do not know how much these remarks hurt me.' What with the trial and the judgment of Lahore High Court, Bhutto later said: 'I would have preferred death as the result of revolutionary justice. I wish they had done it, because it would have been better than facing this trial.'

The former Prime Minister outlined what he as a good Moslem had done for his people. He had solved the 90-year-old Ahmedi problem.*

He described how the 1973 Constitution had provisions

---

* This sect had never had its status determined as to whether or not its followers were Moslems since they did not adhere to all the principles of Islam. The ruling pronounced in the National Assembly in 1974 that they were not Moslems put an end to the controversy

according to Islamic ideology. Furthermore, for the first time the annual pilgrimage of Moslems to Mecca was made free for everyone. He reminded the court how he had made Friday the day of rest and changed the Red Cross into the Red Crescent. Prohibition had also been enforced which, Bhutto said, again smiling, might be reconsidered in view of all the rupees spent on illicit whisky from India.* The Chief Justice picked up this point. 'You mean you are having second thoughts?' he enquired. Bhutto said that he most certainly was having second thoughts about it and it would be well worth reconsidering. The European onlookers thought that perhaps Bhutto — ever human — had other benefits in mind as well. When prohibition was introduced at the National Assembly, it was reported that Bhutto displayed his sense of humour.

'So you want no more gambling, then all the game houses will be closed; so you want no more dancing — then all the night clubs will be shut; so you want prohibition — then I introduce prohibition ... but [taking a large cigar out of his pocket]— you will not prevent me from smoking a good cigar from time to time'...

Most important of his achievements was that he had been invited by the late King Faisal of Saudi Arabia to become Chairman of the second Islamic Conference. 'And I am still Chairman,' he declared defiantly. If there were to be another Islamic Conference he made it clear that he would have to attend as the chosen Chairman until the election of a new one. It would be up to the jail authorities how this was arranged, but he would have to go, he said, again laughing at the predicament in which this would put the authorities.

The judgment had stated that Islam did not believe in the creation of privileged classes. Bhutto wanted to make it clear that he was well aware of this fact and had been fighting against them and the vested interests. It was because he had opposed them that he was in his present predicament.

He said that the FSF was not used for a personal vendetta. It was a Federal Police Force created by the National Assembly to maintain law and order. Even in advanced countries crimes

* The black market price ranged from 500 to 600 rupees per one litre bottle — about £20 to £30 sterling

took place, but this did not mean that each and every offence could be laid at the door of the Chief Executive. 'If this case is filed as untraced,' he said, 'I should not get it in the neck.' Merely because cases were untraced it did not mean that the Government was responsible for the crime, as was assumed in this murder charge. Bhutto said that even if he had wanted to plan such a murder he would have got loyal people from his own village and not called on members of the FSF who, according to their testimony, were reluctant and only committed the crime under pressure. But, he said, he was a modern man and would not dream of doing such an abhorrent thing. Later, he pointed to other murder cases which had been filed untraced, notably the assassination of the first Prime Minister of Pakistan, Liquat Ali Khan. Also, he felt tempted to talk about the murder of the son of the Sardar of Mengal, a powerful Baluchi leader, which had also been filed untraced. But he refrained, saying that one of the generals knew all about it, implying that the Army was itself involved. He said that a number of political murders had taken place under martial law but if they remained untraced it did not mean that the Government would be held responsible. According to the judgment the whole matter of motive provided a very thin link, Bhutto believed. Whereas many other witnesses were interrogated, Bhutto never was. He was merely arrested. Surely the 'principal accused' should have been interrogated first? he asked. If he were the principal accused people should have come straight to him after the *coup*. All persons concerned were taken into custody and there was preponderant evidence that pressure was exerted on the witnesses. He enumerated paragraphs which the judges had to find quickly in their copies of the judgment as he moved swiftly from one to the next. He was anxious to remind the judges that in the report submitted before Mr Justice Shafi ur Rehman, when the investigation into the murder took place after the incident, Kasuri had suggested four groups of people who might have had a motive to kill him. The point had already been made by the defence but Bhutto saw fit to reiterate it. The witnesses introduced by the prosecution, he said, were tainted witnesses with dirty hands. They were not independent.

He also pointed to the Lahore Court's ready acceptance of the evidence of the man on Moslem oath whose names were Melvin

Rupert Welch. 'Melvin Rupert Welch,' he cried, looking round the court room. The audience appreciated the irony in his own condemnation as a Moslem only in name and the knowledge that this witness had been found to be, not unexpectedly with such names, a practising Christian, which thus made his testimony questionable.

From discussing how Saeed Ahmed Khan and Bajwa were the ones interceding on behalf of Kasuri to get him back into the Prime Minister's favour he passed to the 'dirty dog' document. Bhutto ridiculed the idea that he would have had time to think of forging these uncomplimentary remarks on the night of the *coup* to establish some sort of alibi for himself. He was reminded of the admission in the White Paper on the conduct of the elections in March 1977 'that he left a very full record of all his papers behind'. This made him think of his own Rejoinder and he requested the Chief Justice to permit the document to be released to the public. He objected to the fact that it had been termed 'a smuggled document', and pointed to its relevancy to his appeal. The Chief Justice, however, still seemed displeased that the Rejoinder was 'under print' before it was submitted to the court. Bhutto, in an engaging manner, asked if when the Chief Justice was in a 'better mood' he might reconsider his decision. There was almost an atmosphere of familiarity between Bhutto and the bench, each known to the other for a very long time. He returned to the discussion of his case. He submitted that he had been given the opportunity to address the court in the interest of justice since justice was higher than the record, he said. He believed that the record of the Lahore Court was 'defective, tampered, tailored', more especially as he later said his own testimony had not been correctly recorded. He once again stated that he had come for equity and justice.

Bhutto believed it was important for him to show that he had no motive to kill Ahmed Raza Kasuri since, with motive gone, the basis of the alleged conspiracy would fall. And there was no motive, he said. Kasuri was a nobody. He was a sycophant. Rather than accept Kasuri's statement that Bhutto became hungry for power after the 1971 war with Bangladesh, Bhutto showed how Kasuri could be seen to have been hungry for power. He changed parties three times in a career spanning ten years. As well as having in the past been thrown out of other organisations he was asked to leave the People's Party because he was becoming unbearably difficult. He had made a concerted effort to return to the party by praising the Prime Minister to the skies. But he never constituted a threat to Bhutto. Bhutto recalled the damaging statement of General Zia, made in September 1977 to a foreign newspaper, the *Kahyan International*, when he said that he could understand the reason for killing someone like Mr Bhutto. If Kasuri had been like Mr Bhutto, then killing him would have been understandable. Bhutto read out the exact quotation given in a press cutting. 'What is repulsive,' Zia had said, 'is that Mr Bhutto stooped so low as to arrange the murder of a nobody, a certain Kasuri.'

It was towards the end of the morning on the second day. 'I cannot continue, I am very tired now,' Bhutto murmured to his defence. He rounded off the morning's submissions with a poignant defence of his innocence with regard to motive and Kasuri.

'I have no motive, no reason whatsoever to do away with this man. The question is this, why should I want to kill him? My level of political antagonists is much higher. I have not picked small quarrels, small fights ... I tried to be good to this boy. I tried to train him like I tried to train so many others ... I have no motive. Not a scintilla of evidence can show that I have any motive to kill this boy. I wish him well even now.'

Bhutto went on to say that the framers of the murder had gone too far and 'really I am grateful'. A perfect case could have been constructed if three or four very brilliant people had got together in a room to frame a case.

'But they came [the present régime] in their hurry, in their venom against Bhutto ... in their excitement, their inexperience, to get me — and I am glad because it has been an overkill. God has saved me. He came to my rescue,' he said, 'because of all these anomalies in the case. It is bazaar gossip.'

Again he expressed gratitude for his hearing.

'I can't judge what is in your minds, but yesterday in half an hour or an hour I saw objectively that you were giving me a patient hearing. I said "Thank God, at last after one year I have been allowed to say something." Now you have done me this favour and you have given this right to me. You can even hang me now.'

Again he made a last statement on motive.

'I have no motive, my fight is with big people on big issues.' He seemed exhausted. The court was stunned at listening to the defence of a man who had been their Prime Minister and now had been convicted as a 'murderer'. As he sat down and the court rose, people rushed to greet him or shake hands before the net of police closed in and he was removed from their sight once more.

*

Mr Bhutto began his third day of submissions with an apology. He had arrived late. Whereas on the two previous days he was directed into a closed-in van with a chair for him to sit on, this day he was motioned towards a police van already crammed with police like a 'tin of sardines', he said. He asked why he should not be allowed to use the vehicle in which he had come on the two previous days, which was standing vacant, apparently waiting for him. No reason was given. Bhutto refused to enter the crammed van.

'My honour is worth more than my life and unless you give me a valid reason for changing the procedure I will go back to my death cell,' he said. There was an altercation between the police. Finally he was allowed to travel in the van. It was all unnecessary harassment and provocation and the Chief Justice expressed his dissatisfaction both with the fact that the proceedings had been delayed and that Mr Bhutto had been inconvenienced.

Bhutto added to what his lawyers had said on the man who turned State's evidence in order to save his own life — Masood Mahmud — currently languishing in the civil and military hospital with no apparent illness. It was vital to Bhutto's case to discredit the statements of Masood Mahmud, his being the word which linked the Prime Minister with the crime and involved the Federal Security Force in the murder. He pointed out that Mahmud was not one of his appointees and having a record of good service there was no reason for him not to have been promoted as Director-General of the Federal Security Force. He explained how he used to delegate authority. 'Trust begets trust,' he said, and he continued to do so until the person proved untrustworthy. Insofar as concerned Masood Mahmud there appeared no reason for him not to have been given such an appointment. The question was decided on merit and the Foreign Minister at the time, Mr Aziz Ahmed, had confirmed that Masood Mahmud was a good officer and had served with him. Bhutto denied the statement by Mahmud that he had put pressure on the Director-General to take the post. Nor would Bhutto have exerted pressure on him, as Mahmud alleged, to perform the murder, threatening that his wife and children would be in jeopardy, especially as, according to his testimony, Mahmud had been reluctant to take the job in the first place. Bhutto later said that during the PNA agitation he had entrusted the security of his own children to Masood Mahmud. He would hardly have done so if he, as alleged, had himself threatened the man's wife and children in the past. Bhutto attacked Masood Mahmud's claim that he used to meet the Prime Minister frequently. If that were the case it would hardly have been necessary for Bhutto to send a message about the task to be undertaken through Saeed Ahmed Khan, the Chief Security Officer, as the prosecution case alleged.

Following in the footsteps of his defence counsel Bhutto wanted to show that Mahmud had made a large number of improvements on the statements made by him to the magistrate compared with what he said in court. The most obvious incident was at Multan when the Prime Minister denied having seen Mahmud on the morning of 11 November, as had Mahmud's driver, who denied having taken Mahmud to the house where Bhutto was staying. This account did not appear in Mahmud's previous statement. Nor would he, Bhutto said, ever have called anyone 'at six-thirty in the morning', as Mahmud alleged, since it was a highly uncivilised hour.

Bhutto said that Mahmud was supposed to be a conspirator with him and yet according to his statements he did not know any of the plans. He did not know Ghulam Hussain, who was to execute the plan. He was supposed to have reminded Mian Abbas about the task but he did not know what the plans were nor how they were to be put into operation. Bhutto said that Mahmud's evidence was not viable, valid or plausible. He said that the evidence fell to the ground because it was 'a tissue of lies' — a 'concocted story' — 'a bad novel'. After his arrest on

5 July 1977 Mahmud had been questioned for forty days until he decided to make his 'clean breast' of the supposed misdeeds of the FSF and submitted a 100-page statement to the Chief Martial Law Administrator. This itself was odd, Bhutto felt, since this declaration could easily have gone to a lower authority. Furthermore, despite the facilities available to Masood Mahmud, which included the use of a stenographer, important details were omitted from his statement. On his own showing he had not disclosed all the facts when he was granted a pardon and, Bhutto said, was accordingly disqualified from being an approver.

'There was no agreement,' he said. 'It is all a fantasy to involve me. There was no motive, no conspiracy — it was all the figment of a malicious imagination and of a sick mind. Masood Mahmud stood condemned by his own statements, as was Saeed Ahmed Khan.'

According to the prosecution case Saeed Ahmed Khan's actions made him guilty and innocent at the same time. As Bhutto's Chief Security Officer he had interceded on behalf of Kasuri to get him back into favour with Bhutto. But Bhutto made nothing of this, saying that many people requested an audience with him — Kasuri was not unique, nor were Saeed Ahmed Khan's intercessions on his behalf the only ones to be made. The prosecution had made much of the personal file kept on Kasuri but in fact, Bhutto reminded the court, these files were automatically opened on political personalities and there was nothing unusual about it. He said that with regard to the ammunition allegedly used by the accused it was not possible for the prosecution to rely on 'high probabilities' to say that the spent cartridges were in all probability substituted. This, he believed, was not sufficient proof. Bhutto spoke at some length, pulling apart the evidence of the witnesses and pointing out inconsistencies, most of which had already been mentioned by his defence counsel. However, he added his own touch and appreciation of the situation.

In the midst of adversity Bhutto still managed to retain his sense of humour and injected jokes into his delivery. He recalled that when General Zia ul Haq seized power in the *coup* of July the previous year it was the first time civil servants were taken into custody. 'Perhaps next time judges will be taken also,' he said, smiling at the bench. The spectators were amused; the judges were not.

Clearly Bhutto believed that the reason so many witnesses had spoken up against him was because they were in the hands of the Government. 'It all depended who had the power,' he said. He illustrated this point with a story about a rich man in Talpur who was visited by a poor man anxious to have alms. The rich man said that he would give as many gold pieces to the poor man as hairs came out of his beard when he himself pulled it. At this point in the narration, making expansive gestures with his arms, Bhutto characterised the actions of the rich man pulling his own beard. 'I am sorry, you are unlucky,' the rich man replied, as no hairs came out in his hand. 'Wait a minute,' cried the poor man, 'let me try with my hand.' The audience laughed, appreciating full well that the poor man would have seen to it that a whole handful of hairs would be pulled out. 'So you see,' declared Bhutto, 'it all depends which hand, which beard', and thus who is in control of the situation.

Throughout his submissions Bhutto could not seem to get over the fact that he was being allowed to speak in public. To have an open trial, he said, was not merely a matter of publicity. People had always fought to have a public trial so that, as he had said in the Lahore trial, justice was not only done but could be seen to be done. He concluded his remarks on this day with another expression of gratitude to the judges for having allowed him to speak.

'When talking about taking the life of an innocent man,' he said, 'at least hear him.'

*

The fourth and final day of Bhutto's appearance in the Supreme Court saw the return of Ahmed Raza Kasuri, the intended victim of the murder. Once again he sat with the prosecution, this time in the second row. Before the proceedings people were already aware that he was as hostile to Mr Bhutto as ever. There was a letter in the morning's newspaper to the Chief Justice from Kasuri's mother, asking permission for her son to speak in the Supreme Court to clear the 'wild lies' made by the main appellant in the murder case. In loud tones Kasuri expressed his desire and, as he believed, right to address the court. However, when the matter was taken up by the Chief Justice, Kasuri was reprimanded before the court. The Chief Justice pointed out that as a witness Kasuri had been given every opportunity to speak at the trial and that he, as an advocate, should be aware of that. There was no question of a witness being allowed to speak at this stage in the appeal. 'You ought to know better,' he stated. He further said that Kasuri should have advised his mother not to make the request. Kasuri seemed disgruntled with this rebuff and later on caused a disturbance in the court by trying to speak to the prosecution. A police officer prevented him, which Kasuri found objectionable. 'I am trying to speak to my lawyer,' he said. But Mr Rehman was forced to make it clear that he could not receive instructions from Kasuri since he represented the State, not Kasuri. The Chief Justice said that he sympathised with the sensitive feelings of Kasuri over the case since it involved the death of his father, and suggested that if Kasuri would like to leave the court the plain-clothes policeman at his elbow would be glad to assist him. Kasuri remained silent for the rest of the proceedings, only occasionally muttering under his breath.

Most of the audience were aware that this was the last day on which they would be able to catch a glimpse of Bhutto. The carnival atmosphere which pervaded the earlier days was replaced by one of urgency at seeing as much of the former leader as possible. The court was even more packed than on previous days; latecomers had no chance to enter the court room.

Bhutto seemed in even better form than on the previous days. As usual he appeared immaculately dressed, with his silk shirt and silk handkerchief setting off a well tailored suit. This time he had a pink rosebud in his buttonhole and carried a second one which he gave to his wife. The Begum had sat through all the proceedings and looked radiant as she watched her husband speak.

Having dealt with conspiracy and murder, Bhutto now addressed himself to the more personal aspects of his arrest — what he termed maltreatment and the bias of the Lahore court which tried him. He took particular exception to the dock to which he was confined in the Lahore court — he had referred to this on the first day, comparing it with the trials at Nuremberg. He believed that the German generals were treated with greater dignity and respect than had been meted out to him at the trial. He described how the dock to which he was confined in the court was not only a humiliation but a physical impediment between him and his lawyers.

'On my left was a superintendent of police and on my right was an Intelligence Officer and they were all ears. If I was going to say "good morning" to my lawyers they leaned forward to listen. They watched everything I wrote. They were like vultures. Never before had a dock been constructed in the Lahore court,' Bhutto said.

He pointed out that the situation whereby he had sworn at his counsel, Mr. D.M. Awan, would never have arisen if he had been in a position to talk freely with his lawyers. Bhutto summarily dismissed the prosecution's statement that the reason for the construction of the dock was to prevent him from giving a press conference. 'I have been harpooned into a false case,' he expostulated. 'I gave no press conference.' He excused his words with the press by saying that it was merely an informal chat, not a formal press statement.

Of course the main proponent of bias in Bhutto's opinion was the Chief Justice himself. Bhutto referred to the antipathy between the two of them, dating from 1963. It was no coincidence, he believed, that Mushtaq was the same man who tried him in the Lahore camp jail in 1968.

Bhutto referred to Mushtaq's remark to foreign correspondents at his press conference on 2 November 1977 when he said that the trial would be conducted in the 'full light of day'. He compared this with the situation when the time came for him to make his defence. At that time he wished in particular to talk about two subjects, why the case had been brought against him and the bias of the court — but then the court proceedings were summarily held in camera. Bhutto took exception to the remarks of one of the judges to the effect that 'you are being tried by us, not by the public' when Bhutto showed his dissatisfaction that the trial was to be concluded in camera. He pointed out once more that a public trial is the right of every accused and this was one of the reasons why he was so grateful to be given the chance to speak in the Supreme Court. Bhutto reminded the court that there was no reason to hold the trial in camera. It did not relate to children or incest, which legally constituted good grounds for having a secret trial. When at Lahore he had mentioned in court that possibly Lord Halsbury, in his voluminous legal commentary, referred to the fear of public disturbances as a reason for a secret trial, he was aghast to see that this reason was inserted in the order supplied to him, as it were upon his own suggestion and as an afterthought by the court. There was no law and order situation, he said, since the court was like a fort, swarming with Intelligence officers. 'Justice is not a cloistered virtue,' he announced.

Bhutto also referred to the lack of attention given to his application of 18 December outlining bias and requesting the transfer of his trial to another bench. He objected especially to being told initially to argue this application without legal counsel in chambers at the start of the trial after the Christmas break on 9 January. Bhutto believed that he had had no alternative but to boycott the remainder of the trial. He was by then convinced he was not getting a fair trial and on the basis of the bias, he believed that anyway the trial had become null and void. He maintained, as he had stated before, that the record of what he said in court was not a faithful transcript of what he actually said. It was for this allegation that he had been called a compulsive liar in the Lahore judgment, although he claimed that the stenographer made it clear to him that he was not taking down all he said.

On the subject of his illness, Bhutto again complained bitterly that he had not been given proper treatment whilst in Kot Lakhpat in Lahore, nor in Rawalpindi. He gave a chronology of his illnesses which caused him to be absent while fifteen prosecution witnesses were examined. On account of the combined attack of malaria, influenza and colonic trouble with a temperature of 102°, Bhutto was very ill and the court was compelled to adjourn for a few days. The court's effort to conduct the proceedings from 8 to 4 as opposed to normal court hours from 8.30 to 1, in order to make up for time missed, was uncalled for. He pointed out that it took one hour to come to court from Kot Lakhpat and if the order had been put into practice it would have meant an exhausting day for client and counsel. All this was a culmination of insults. Once again Bhutto cried, 'I am not a rootless phenomenon', and drew attention to the trauma and agony in Pakistan.

He also said that there was no reason for him to be taken to a death cell. This was an extension of bias against him since others who had been convicted were allowed to remain in their cells. He enumerated the preparations for his hanging which were undertaken at Kot Lakhpat. There was extraordinary activity. Sirens blared; the gallows were oiled. Again Bhutto managed to inject humour into even the most gruesome eventualities. Eager to trap the commanding officer into an admission that the jail was swarming with commandos, he said that he knew they were there because he had heard their boots. 'But,' came the reply, 'they had taken off their boots.'!

Bhutto reiterated that he did not want special treatment.

'I want to be under the law, but not underground the law.'

Because Bhutto believed that the case was now 'smashed to smithereens' he did not feel it was essential to discuss the social realities and double standards in detail. He did not enter into describing the malafides of the administration although he wanted to produce newspaper statements to show that the *coup* was a 'manifestation of bias' against him. The Chief Justice, however, made his usual plea that no notice would be taken of information not on the record. Bhutto's last word on the case was that it stood on no legs, not even on hollow or clay legs.

Although the Chief Justice had made it clear that a discussion on the future of Pakistan and the political situation was not relevant to the case, Bhutto tried to touch upon a few issues. 'The nation is in a delicate and very precarious position,' he stated once more, echoing sentiments expressed on the first day and criticising the martial law régime and especially its arbitrary amendment of the Constitution and the disqualification tribunals. He said that solutions which were valid in a certain time span became irrelevant after that time span had elapsed.

'Martial law demartialises the nation,' he cried. 'It is a breach, not a bridge.'

The Chief Justice did not let him speak long on this topic. 'Unfortunately we cannot give this advice to anyone,' he remarked stiffly. Bhutto took the point and returned to conclude his case.

'Justice is indivisible,' he said. 'It is absolute ... It cannot be bargained for. Either a person is innocent, or he is not. There is no via media ... no compromise ... The prosecution has failed to prove its case.'

He concluded by asking the court to uphold the majesty of law, not the matron of martial law. He ended by reciting the poet Ghalib and a verse in dialect, sitting down weary after his four-day performance.

His appearance had been electric, sensational. It seemed that he had played his last trump card and won. But legal technicalities had to be tied up: judgment had yet to come; only then would the value of Bhutto's appearance in court be known.*

*

Even on this final day, events were put back into perspective by the statements of the four confessing co-accused who had sat silently through Bhutto's submissions. On the third day their lawyers had requested permission for them, as accused, to speak. This was granted to them on the understanding that they would take five to ten minutes each. Each had prepared his statement. The first to speak was Mian Mohammed Abbas, the man who had changed his confession three times. A big man, he looked unhappy with his lot as he spoke slowly in measured tones in English. He reiterated the statement he had made on 10 July from jail, which had been read out by his lawyer in the Supreme Court, to the effect that he had been part of the conspiracy. He apologised to the family of the deceased, looking round to where Raza Kasuri sat. However, there was no indication in his statement that his orders came from the Prime Minister. What was clear was that Masood Mahmud was the 'hard task-master' and a 'bully', and the person who had forced him to commit the crime.

The next three spoke in Urdu — Inspector Ghulam Mustafa, Arshad Iqbal and Rana Iftikar Ahmed. They all said that they had taken part in the crime. Arshad Iqbal said that if any member of the FSF refused to obey orders he was given hell. Rana Iftikar said that those who wore the belt, i.e. the police,

* Bhutto's four-day appearance was later printed as a book entitled *My Execution*.

were supposed to be the weapons of oppression. Little did the people know that these people had no choice of their own. The junior officials were helpless, he said, and they could not afford to disobey orders. All stated that they had obeyed the orders of higher authorities. As well as incriminating the Prime Minister, they said that Masood Mahmud was to blame. But a rumour circulated in a local newspaper that on one of the days, one of the accused said to a guard when he was requesting to be given permission to go to the bathroom, 'If you maltreat me, I shall speak out with the truth.'

Whereas the four confessing co-accused all asked for mercy, Bhutto refused to do so. This was the last word any of them could have in their defence — they knew only too well that it would now be up to the judges to decide who was telling the truth and whose statements should stand.

Domestic matters were discussed in the last few minutes remaining of the morning session. Mr Bhutto was given permission to be examined by a doctor in whom he had faith, as well as the dentist of his choice, Dr Zafar Niazi. Niazi, who was present in court, came under attack by the prosecution because of his alleged involvement in politics; it was therefore considered advisable that another dentist should at least be present while Niazi was treating Bhutto.

Bhutto made his exit from the court quietly. He had gone almost before people realised. After the usual coffee session with his wife and lawyers he was delivered back to jail. During the break for tea and after the proceedings each day, he was allowed to spend ten to fifteen minutes with his lawyers. He would ask them how the morning's proceedings had gone, whether his arguments had been well presented and so forth. At one time, he said despairingly, 'And we built this country into a respectable nation!' Bhutto was still convinced that he, as leader of the people, was the man to shape their destiny.

For once during the course of the appeal, arguments were presented in the afternoon regarding the recalling of witnesses. The appeal was over on 23 December. No witnesses were to be recalled and there was to be no additional evidence. The appeal which had begun on 20 May was concluded. 'All's well that ends well,' said one judge, as he rose to leave the court room, giving a last long look at the defence. There was a slight smile on his face. The judges retired for a few days' rest and to write their judgment. The Chief Justice said that it had been a difficult case and the court now needed time to formulate its verdict. People felt relieved. The tension was over. The prosecution was still sure that it had made convincing arguments. The defence for the first time in a while felt optimistic. There was talk of acquittal or re-trial. The supporters of Bhutto could not believe that in view of all the loopholes and inconsistencies which both the defence and Bhutto had exposed, there could be any question of upholding the death sentence. Bhutto should be considered innocent until proved guilty according to common law, not the reverse, which seemed to have been the case in Lahore.

The lawyers returned to their homes. Flashmans Hotel was vacated. Bhutto remained in Rawalpindi district jail. There were fears that he would be transferred out of easy reach of his family but upon a request by the defence that he would not be moved, the court gave an assurance that he would remain in Rawalpindi. Yet signs again came from the Chief Justice that he was making statements about the trial — these appeared in the newspaper just after Christmas. Begum Bhutto wrote a letter objecting; the Chief Justice, for all his politeness, appeared unconvinced by Bhutto's submissions.

Bhutto spent Christmas Day — the birthday of Mohammed Ali Jinnah — alone. He was not permitted to spend New Year's Day with his wife and daughter. Soon after, on 5 January 1979, he celebrated his fifty-first birthday, again alone.

11

WAITING FOR
JUDGMENT

During the weeks that passed before judgment was given in
Zulfikar Ali Bhutto's appeal there was a hiatus in the Bhutto
legal camp. There was nothing much they could do but wait.
Many anticipated a change in the verdict; others feared the
worst.

In the sphere of politics there was movement. People
appeared to be straining under the political ban and were
anxious to manoeuvre themselves into the best position, ready
for the elections promised in 1979. Many were still sceptical and
believed that the promise of elections was just another aspect of
Zia's dilatory tactics to keep his own Government afloat. However, such was the general cry from all parties for elections that
it seemed it would be very difficult for Zia not to hold them,
although he still made it clear that there was no real point in
having elections until what he termed 'positive results' could be
achieved.

Furthermore, for so long — ever since elections were postponed in October 1977 and Bhutto was put on trial for conspiracy to murder — people were aware that whatever the
President said about elections there would be little chance of
their being held until Bhutto's fate was decided. Now for the
first time since the trial began, people could see that this was
soon going to be resolved, one way or the other. Once a final
decision had been reached there would undoubtedly be a massive scramble for people to redefine their positions and realign
themselves on the political spectrum. Before the judgment was
given, they still wondered whether or not Bhutto was indeed
'finished' politically, providing of course he was allowed to live.

As an indication of their optimism, PPP supporters still talked of the return of their Chairman to power.

As Bhutto himself had predicted, there had been a proliferation of splinter political parties. Although earlier in the year there had been a split in his own party when Maulana Kausar Niazi broke away to form his own group, Niazi now proclaimed, without the consent of the PPP, that he would once more join the Bhutto PPP to form a 'grand party'. The PPP continued to hold its Central Executive Committee meeting at regular intervals and generally castigated the Government for its ineffectiveness in domestic and foreign affairs. It held a special session on 5 January, and once more proudly stated its motto — 'Islam is our religion, democracy is our policy, socialism is our economy and all power to the people.' Special meetings were also held in various districts and prayers were offered for the release and long life of the Chairman. This was not just a matter of procedure — people really and truly did believe that somehow the gates of Rawalpindi district jail would open and that the Chairman would be free. Resolutions were passed demanding an early general election and the transfer of power to the people. The PPP was also convinced that if and when elections were held they would win; so too were many of their opponents. The disorganised PPP was still stronger than any other party, even in spite of the people who had been 'disqualified' from taking part in political activity.

The most obvious person for the authorities to catch in the disqualification net was Begum Bhutto, who was Acting Chairman of the People's Party whilst Bhutto — the Chairman for life — was in jail. In this capacity she had presided over one meeting of the Central Executive Committee of the PPP soon after her release. But as expected, two days later she was issued with a disqualification notice, the mere issuance of which prohibited her from further political activity. She was summoned to appear before the tribunal in Karachi in December but the proceedings dragged on well into the New Year. The charge related to the period 21 March to 5 July 1977 when Begum Bhutto was a member of the National Assembly, but the alleged offences were committed in 1976 and had nothing to do with her activities as a member of the National Assembly. It was generally assumed that she would eventually be disqualified.

After her release the Government filed an appeal in the Supreme Court against the decision of the High Court to release Begum Bhutto, which came to nothing. As it was, she was once more arrested on the eve of the verdict.

Obviously not anxious to lose her liberty, Begum Bhutto moved around Pakistan cautiously meeting workers. She made an exhausting trip to Quetta in Baluchistan, the only province Benazir had not visited when free. Benazir herself was kept under house arrest in Islamabad. Her detention order, due to expire on 3 January, was extended for a further three months. The court case to secure her release was argued tediously in the High Court in Lahore. Surprisingly, in mid-January the Sind High Court released Abdul Hafeez Pirzada, who had been in detention since the July takeover in 1977. The words of the order which released him were revealing:

It is clear that the detaining authority had not applied its own exclusive mind, but rather acted on the orders or advice of the high authorities and moreover, the consideration which was kept in mind was the *present political situation*, rather than the legal considerations that are to be borne in mind in the making of an order of detention under the law.

On this account, the court declared, the detention order was invalid and ought to be quashed. As with Begum Bhutto's release, the Government also filed a petition requesting that he be re-arrested on account of the prevailing situation but this was rejected.

Again the release was astonishing, firstly because it had set free a senior member of the PPP and a former minister; secondly, because as with the release of Benazir in June 1978, and of Begum Bhutto in November, it admitted that the military authorities had detained them illegally.

The same decision was also made in respect of Bhutto's cousin, Mumtaz Ali Bhutto, although he was detained on another charge. Subsequently he too was freed and the charge was dropped. Of the trio who had been together on the night of the *coup*, only Bhutto remained in prison. Mumtaz Ali Bhutto soon gained permission to visit his cousin. Pirzada also met his former Prime Minister as his legal counsel for various petitions and then subsequently as a member of the team of lawyers defending Bhutto against the conspiracy to murder charge.

Pirzada was kept under 24-hour surveillance after his release, followed at all times by the Intelligence authorities in conspicuous yellow jeeps, as were Begum Bhutto and Benazir when they were free, and a few other personalities regarded as suspect by the military authorities, such as Dr Niazi. The surveillance, apart from the harassing aspect of being observed continually, was ludicrous. Those under such close obvious scrutiny would be unlikely to do anything illegal and could easily escape the followers by driving fast if they really wanted to do so. For those who did the shadowing it was an unpleasant job since they had to sleep in the cars at night — at times during the winter — and in the early hours of the morning when it was very cold they could be seen pacing the streets to keep warm. On occasions, foreign journalists were followed for a day or two to check up on their activities, especially if they looked as if they were too closely involved with Bhutto's side. At times too, Mr Bhutto's lawyers received the same sort of treatment. Many regarded it as a futile exercise and a colossal waste of government petrol and manpower.

Rumours were rampant during this period. No one quite knew what was happening and so fantastic ideas were put forward: that Bhutto had made, was making or would make a deal with Zia; that the only reason for Begum Bhutto's release was for her to reach agreement with Zia; that Zia had visited Bhutto in jail; that Bhutto had appealed to President Carter to save his life. This last rumour was immediately refuted by Begum Bhutto before Bhutto's opponents had time to savour the delight of thinking that the former Prime Minister of Pakistan, who had criticised the U.S.A. for its possible involvement in the *coup*, was now grovelling at its feet. Zia ul Haq had his own share of rumours levelled at him. It was said that one of his sons had taken a job with the Bank of America in the U.S.A. for the exorbitant salary of 50,000 rupees (circa £2,500) a month and that lavish sums had been spent on a wedding party, when he was advocating austerity and moderation. It was also speculated that Zia would become a Field Marshal like Ayub Khan and would introduce his own system of government after forming his own political party. Rumours on both sides were hotly denied. But those papers which discredited the military leader had to atone for it by further censorship of their pages.

Within the Government itself there was much immobility and people considered the prospects of the Pakistan National Alliance. Many believed that all the PNA ministers were about to quit the Government because of their ineffectiveness. The PNA was reminded by the local press that it had kept none of the promises it had made on obtaining power: it had not remained united; prices had not been brought down to the 1970 level; and Islamic laws had not been implemented within seven days. The régime was continually maintaining that it was doing all it could to introduce the Islamic system. What this would amount to in real terms no one was quite sure, apart of course from the Islamic punishment of flogging, which was already being practised. 'We have plunged deep into the ocean for a pearl,' said PNA leader Mufti Mahmud. 'Either we will be successful or we will be doomed.' He also said that he would not mind if the Islamic system were to be established by an unelected Government, which clearly it would be.

Those who had broken away from the nine-party alliance, particularly the Tehrick-i-Istiqlal and the National Democratic Party, remained on the sidelines and called for elections. Whether they would be prepared to see the PPP back in power was a different matter — probably they envisaged that its support would have waned appreciably, and hoped that they would attract some of its votes by the fact that they had not collaborated with the military régime and were taking up a democratic stance by calling for a return to civilian rule.

After his release by the military régime, Wali Khan remained as an ordinary member of the NDP. However his wife, Begum Nasim Wali Khan, was influential as vice-president of the party. She herself had been subjected to a certain amount of embarrassment, having been charged with stealing underwear from Marks & Spencer in London in the summer of 1978. She had brazened out the charge and maintained her innocence, but the episode kept opponents amused for some time. Ultimately the NDP split, ostensibly because of collaboration of one faction with the military régime.

The JUP — Jamaatul-Ulema-i-Pakistan, headed by Maulana Shah Ahmed Noorani, said that the party left the alliance because of the 'undemocratic nature' of the Government.

Clearly, people were becoming weary of military rule with civilian collaborators and were anxious to have elected representatives. Others whose members were in the Government — the Pakistan Democratic Party and the Jamaat-i-Ulema-i-Islam — stated that their parties should come out of the Government. The remaining stalwarts in the Government were still the Jamaat-i-Islami and the Moslem League.

The Moslem League was itself in disarray. It had been the first to join the Army in the Government of Pakistan and had more or less forced the rest of the PNA to come in after it. But reportedly because of personal vanities it had splintered into four factions. Its former chief, the Pir of Pagara, left the Government towards the end of 1978, and formed his own Pagara group, which said it was quite happy to wait for elections until 1981. It was continually stated that an effort was being made to reunite the party, but without visible success.

With this apparent instability in the Government it was obviously in Zia's interest to get on with the business of handing power over to elected representatives. A few opponents of the Government optimistically pointed to the danger of a constitutional crisis and hoped that Begum Nusrat Bhutto's challenge to his assumption of the presidency filed in the Sind High Court would at least create an embarrassment for him. But like so many other petitions which were to be filed, it came to nothing. In mid-January, Zia talked of elections in an interview with a London journalist. His remarks were directed at the former Prime Minister.

'If people elect thieves, well, how can I stop that?' he asked. But in view of the general clamour he said he was not prepared to retain power for as long as it might take for a more 'vibrant' and 'patriotic' leadership to emerge.

The implication was that whoever was elected it would not be Mr Bhutto.

'Take Mr Bhutto,' he said, 'he had been elected the majority leader in West Pakistan. Just because Pakistan was split in two he claimed he was the leader and we put him on the chair. So if we elected him on the slogan of bread, clothing and housing and allowed him to ruin this country for seven years [in fact Bhutto was in power for five and a half years] who can we blame? Nobody but ourselves.'

Most people realistically faced the probability that this sounded the death-knell for Bhutto in an attempt to destroy 'Bhuttoism', since it was fairly clear that even if Bhutto were alive in jail his party would sweep the polls and release him. Only on the basis of the assumption that the death penalty would be upheld by the Supreme Court could Zia make the glib pronouncement:

'If death is upheld, I shall send him to the gallows. And if a release is ordered I will release Bhutto.'

The optimistic hoped in this instance that he would not prove true to his word ... or that better still the Supreme Court would release Bhutto, contrary to the wishes of the military régime.

It was obvious that Zia would have to consider carefully whether he could afford the instability which an execution might cause, as compared with the threat to his own leadership with Bhutto alive and at large in the hearts of the people, whether it be in prison, in exile or under house arrest. Although legally re-trial was a possibility, it would merely prolong the uncertainty and instability and did not appear feasible. Most thought Bhutto's fate would be decided one way or the other.

People also contemplated what would suit the justices: re-trial would save them from having to pass judgment, although any change in the verdict would cast aspersions on the Lahore Court's judgment. However, along with the judges' obvious desire not to impugn the integrity of the fraternity of the judiciary was the awareness that their judgment would be read and scrutinised throughout the world. Most assumed that they would not be able to afford a faulty judgment in an appeal of this nature when so much criticism had been levelled at the Lahore Court. The fact that other charges were pending against Bhutto was regarded as another way of containing him if the death penalty were not to be upheld — as another safety net for the régime to keep Bhutto in jail. Most of these were fairly insig-nificant — for corruption and rigging — but there was also a charge of high treason for the break-up of Pakistan, which was, however, withdrawn before judgment in the murder case was given. Yet was it withdrawn because the death penalty was going to be used anyway for the murder charge? supporters asked. There was no end to the deliberations Bhutto's suppor-ters made, trying to analyse the future course of events. Most hoped that if the authorities wanted to keep their leader out of the way, they would do so by the lesser charges. But it was far too optimistic an expectation.

At this time, in order to damage Bhutto's reputation further, there was also extraordinary activity on the part of the news media. Again this was capable of two interpretations — either it was because the death sentence was not going to be upheld and so the public had to be made aware of his alleged misdeeds, lest their euphoria at having him acquitted or even merely jailed might sweep him back into power when the promised elections finally came; or, as realists believed, this renewed attempt at character assassination of the former Prime Minister was another indication that the public was being prepared for the death sentence and a final effort was being made to discredit Bhutto in the eyes of the people, especially after his outstanding performance in the Supreme Court before Christmas.

Part of the propaganda was conducted on television. Early in the New Year a television programme was run called 'Story of Atrocities', which gave vignettes of the alleged tyranny of the Bhutto régime. Various people appeared on TV to impart their 'tales of woe'. It was an unprecedented opportunity for those who felt they had grievances against Bhutto whilst he was in power to speak up in front of TV watchers and radio listeners all over Pakistan. Although broadcast in Urdu the contents of the programme were given wide and prominent coverage in the English daily newspapers. Headlines such as 'Bhutto was afraid of being exposed' (for his part in the 1971 tragedy when East Pakistan seceded), said a veteran Moslem League leader, were the newspaper's method of giving a value judgment to the people. Since Bhutto was the principal target of this attack he was also held responsible for alleged murders in the PPP régime. Bhutto was called the worst type of 'jagirdar' — land-owner — and accused of not having the interest of Sindhis at heart. A retired major-general alleged that Bhutto believed he was synonymous with Pakistan and that anyone who opposed him politically was considered a traitor.

A journalist talked of his 'extremely cruel treatment in jail' because he presented the 'true self' of Bhutto in editorials, news and articles. Each day a new story appeared. Most prominent among those who spoke out against Bhutto was J.A. Rahim, the first Secretary-General of the People's Party when it was founded in 1967. Rahim had indeed been one of the founder members and had been active in the drafting of the election manifesto of the PPP. He was cultured and well read and reached a high position in the Bhutto Government, holding a senior post as Minister of Production. But Bhutto found it necessary to throw him out of the party, partly because, as he said, he was unpopular with the conservative generals, who called him a 'bloody commie' because of his left-wing leanings. Right or wrong, Rahim had no compunction in speaking out against Bhutto — a man to whom he had been devoted — at a time when he was in a death cell. Notably, the people who spoke out against Bhutto were his enemies and had an interest in so doing. But most believed that it was a vindictive act against a man who was perilously close to the gallows.

The most unsavoury aspect of the whole publicity campaign was that it came precisely at the time the verdict was expected. Very few condoned the TV series. A local newspaper spoke out and said that 'condemning a bad tradition can be helpful only if one is sure that no such incidents have been happening today and shall not happen in the future'. Bhutto's supporters echoed these sentiments. The newspaper also demanded that the 'progressive political elements' who were in jail should be brought onto the screen to tell the people what hardships they had been facing under the military régime.

Few doubted that the military régime had an ulterior motive in permitting this TV series to be shown when so much censorship took place in the pro-Bhutto newspapers. Censorship had been maintained in the Punjab on pro-PPP papers since October and the immolations. This was now extended to those in Sind where newspapers frequently appeared with some columns blotted out.

It was not long before a pro-Bhutto lawyer filed a contempt petition in court, alleging that whilst the verdict was unannounced, this TV series should not be publicised and thus poison the atmosphere against Bhutto. The people felt that whether or not he was to be destroyed physically, this was a last-ditch effort to destroy him politically.

When the contempt petition was admitted in the Supreme Court the justices, still engaged in writing the judgment, were grumpy, like moles that had been prematurely forced out of their burrows. They swiftly adjourned the hearing of the contempt case until after the verdict, because of the 'voluminous record of the hearing'. The TV programme was due to run for three months and the producers maintained that there was no information which had not already been publicised. In which case, said Bhutto's supporters, why publicise it at this particular moment? But the producers did undertake not to resume the programmes until after the announcement of the judgment.

At about the same time it was announced that some statements made by the former Prime Minister and engraved on a monument after the Lahore summit conference in 1974 had been 'accidentally' rubbed off during a cleaning operation.

Not content with the TV programmes, in mid-January another White Paper in a new series, promised as long ago as last July, finally appeared. As usual this was given full publicity, with headlines reading 'Bhutto undermined all institutions — sustained moves for authoritarian state; flattery for superiors', on the front page. The whole of the newspaper that day was taken up with highlighting the contents of the White Paper. As with the previous White Papers, newspaper coverage conveyed the gist to those who were neither willing nor able to obtain the White Paper itself. The exercise was repeated a week later when the next in the series appeared and again when the other two were issued at short intervals. The contents were even serialised.

Like the TV series, people believed that these White Papers were scandalous, appearing at the precise moment when they did. Each volume — less fat than the first mammoth White Paper on rigging — was accompanied by documents drawn from Bhutto's files. The first White Paper in this series dealing with the performance of the Bhutto régime concerned Bhutto, his family and associates, and dealt mainly with his alleged misuse of public funds. Begum Bhutto said that the contents were a 'pack of lies'. Most of the charges had been made already immediately after the *coup* in July 1977 and Bhutto had replied to them in detail in the small rejoinder which preceded the main Rejoinder countering the charges of rigging. Other charges, for instance, relating to the question of his Indian citizenship, had been thrashed out legally in courts long ago. People seemed to forget that until 1947 they were all Indian citizens and that Bhutto had been one of the first to apply for a Pakistani passport. Issues were merely raked up in a further attempt at smearing Bhutto's reputation in the eyes of those who were not familiar with the whole story. Bhutto was also criticised for having turned on Ayub Khan, his 'former boss, benefactor and hero', and notably for not having attended his funeral. Bhutto had offered condolences and probably wondered whether Zia would be present when his 'former boss, benefactor and hero' mounted the gallows. Clearly what Bhutto needed was the opportunity and facilities to reply to all the allegations.

The second White Paper, coming a week later, dealt with the way in which Bhutto allegedly harmed the basic institutions. 'Legislature and judiciary crippled', 'Executive debased' were the headlines of the newspaper the day after its appearance. Bhutto, however, believed that the present régime's own actions with regard to the basic institutions were 'a breach not a bridge' as he had said in the Supreme Court. The third White Paper came two days later and outlined Bhutto's economic policies. 'Bhutto pursued disastrous economic policies,' said the newspapers. 'Bhutto brought economy to virtual collapse.' But in reality the document was a criticism by capitalists of socialism and came at a time when the military régime was forced to admit that its own position was not very satisfactory. The fourth and final volume appeared at the end of January, a little more than a week before the verdict in the murder case was announced. Pertinently, it dealt with murders in general and pointed to numerous ones for which Bhutto was allegedly responsible, stating 'Bhutto misused power widely' — 'Murders and abductions'. It was almost as though the military régime realised it had to substantiate the frail charge of conspiracy to murder with many more alleged ones to bolster up Bhutto's image as a murderer in the eyes of the people.

Hardly anyone took any notice of the White Papers. Most of the charges had been heard before. Bhutto had no possibility of defending himself to the public. The military régime had tried to paint Bhutto as black as the Devil when everyone else posed as Snow-White. Many of the alleged misdeeds matched clearly those of the present régime. Moreover, for those who knew the inside story they were told in half-truths and presented in such a way as to give only half the picture. What pro-PPP supporters accepted as understandable government regulations were made out to be draconian measures of autocracy. The faults of the army were neatly side-stepped. But although Bhutto could not reply to all these allegations, many of them had appeared in a document called 'The Truth about the Trial and the Terror' which had been circulated in June the previous year. In answer to this pamphlet, a book entitled 'Rumour and Reality' appeared clandestinely in Pakistan at about this time, giving much of the background to the allegations and high-lighting the role of the army in many of the accusations against Bhutto himself. It took each 'rumour' of the régime and gave its own picture of the 'reality'. Naturally, the inability to circulate it openly meant that it did not receive anything like the degree of publicity of the government propaganda.

As with the charge on rigging, Bhutto was also charged with corruption and misuse of funds and these cases were pending in the Lahore court. Along with the TV series this blast of propaganda against Bhutto was also construed to be contempt of court. Hafeez Pirzada drew up a petition against the circulation of the documents but again, with characteristic procrastination, the Supreme Court maintained it would hear the petition later, or, as Bhutto put it in more blunt terms, 'after my burial'.

Yet ultimately, whatever allegations were brought against Bhutto in White Papers or elsewhere, however much his opponents said he destroyed the institutions of Pakistan, only those who were already convinced were affected. Throughout his own tenure of power, Zia ul Haq had been unable to suppress the popular support which Bhutto enjoyed. For the masses he was still their undisputed leader and the first democratically elected Prime Minister.

Just one of the reasons for Bhutto's long standing in the hearts of the people was that Zia himself had never managed to pose as a charismatic figure. Pro Zia sympathisers said that he was sincere and genuine both about his religion and his enforcement of it on other people. His opponents believed he was ruthless, ambitious and hypocritical. If they had been allowed to have political meetings and raise slogans, along with 'Long Live Bhutto' one such slogan would have been 'Death to Zia'. Those who supported Zia's *coup* said he was in an unenviable position and undoubtedly did not realise what he was undertaking when he assumed power in July 1977. They believed his only way out was indeed execution of Bhutto because otherwise he would be threatened by Bhutto's re-emergence. However Zia, characterised by his well-groomed moustache and his engaging but artificial smile, did not show any regrets about assuming power and seemed to be enjoying the pomp and circumstance of a high office of state. Whatever criticism was levelled against him, he always seemed totally convinced that he had done the right thing. 'After I have gone, by all means, hang me if I have done something wrong,' he said innocently. In view of the repressive nature of his régime many were astounded that he appeared to have such a clear con-science.

The undemocratic nature of Zia's régime, its harshness, its apparent double standards between what was meted out to the followers of Bhutto and his opponents and the harsh penalties prescribed by Islam which Zia was using as modern-day pun-ishments, did not inspire much affection or loyalty to the military régime. Zia constantly pointed out the alleged wrongs of Bhutto's régime but seemed oblivious to those in his. People detested the idea of the lash; whereas Bhutto had stood for progress many people saw Zia as standing for regression. With the verdict unannounced and elections virtually inescapable, it seemed that the military régime was setting a very dangerous precedent for itself.

In domestic affairs there seemed to be little improvement. Prices were still on the increase; people still complained of what they termed 'wasteful expenditure'; there was little incentive for foreign investors to invest long term in a country whose political future was unsure; Pakistanis were still consuming more than they were able to manufacture. Criticisms of the economy were countered by government statements that there had been increases in most areas of production. A particular improvement they chose to highlight was that rich Pakistanis abroad had shown themselves willing to launch industrial enterprises by providing foreign exchange from their own resources. However, these 'improvements' did not make peo-ple feel Pakistan was in the ascendancy. They were disgruntled and anxious for a return to normal political activity and civilian rule. They did not like their country to be ruled by the military. It was undignified and greatly reduced their self-esteem in the eyes of foreigners.

Nor did Zia have the same stature and influence as Bhutto in foreign affairs. In fact, so unsubstantial did Pakistan's position appear on the international front, vis-à-vis its neighbours, that many believed that without Bhutto Pakistan would never be able to reassert itself as a stable power in a troubled area. His supporters mooted the possibility, indeed probability, that if Bhutto were to be executed it would eventually mean the end of Pakistan. They pointed to the 'unitary effect' which Bhutto had had on the various provinces and the good relations he had maintained with Pakistan's neighbours. The military régime, however, said that this was all nonsense and no one was indispensable to the running of Pakistan.

But the question of the break-up of Pakistan, if feasible, was vital to both eastern and western power blocs. Interested parties began to look more closely at the secessionist problem in the provinces. Although during his tenure of power Bhutto had experienced grave secessionist problems in both Baluchistan and Frontier Province, it appeared that he had mastered the situation. Now it seemed that secessionist grievances, prompted possibly from outside, would once more come to the fore. Savage and inhospitable Baluchistan became a focal point because of the political crisis in Iran. Bhutto supporters said that it was a 'boiling cauldron'; government sources said it was calm. Nonetheless, with Baluchis on both sides of the border, trouble could not be ruled out if instability prevailed. Already the Baluchi leaders in Pakistan had pressed for more provincial autonomy after Bhutto withdrew power from the provincial government during the insurgency in order to retain unity within the federation of Pakistan.

Neither could the situation in Frontier Province be ignored. Ever since the pro-Russian *coup* in Afghanistan in April 1978 Pakistanis felt that for what it was worth, the Russians might as well be at the Khyber Pass— the classic invasion route from the north to the Indian sub-continent. With Russian 'experts' in Kabul the Soviet Union was in command of a modern-day invasion route to warm waters, after which many believed it still hankered. To the highly religious Moslems the spread of Soviet

Communism was abhorrent. People said that one reason why the Arabs maintained relations with the West was their intense fear of Communism, in spite of the West's association with colonialism and imperialism which was marginally less distasteful to them than Communism. Others saw the Russian link with Afghanistan as posing no real threat to Pakistan. But the possibility of Russia extending her influence still further could not be overlooked. Also, Frontier Province, with a little provocation from outside, could pick up the threads of the Pakhtoon separatism fostered by Wali Khan in the past. Pakhtoon tribesmen were still wandering back and forth across the unrecognised modern boundary line. Nor did Zia appear able to come to the agreement with the new President, Noor Mohammed Tarakki, which Bhutto was on the verge of reaching before he fell from power.

In view of Bhutto's success in dealing with these problems — his good relations with Russia and China and with other Arab Moslem States; even the esteem in which he was held as Chairman of the Islamic Summit conference — the forceful line he adopted towards India in comparison with the rather conciliatory one of Zia in full view of India's increased military capacity made even those who did not personally like Bhutto believe that he, as a strong leader, was the only one who could keep Pakistan together and, from the western point of view, in line with western thinking, if not subservient to it. Not only was there the possibility of secessionism in Frontier and Baluchistan, many also considered that if their Sindhi President were to be executed there would be little reason for Sind to keep within the federation of a united Pakistan. During the time Bhutto was in confinement no leader emerged to take his place either from the ranks of his own party or from those of the other splintered and fragmented ones.

It seemed that all the allegations, including the one of conspiracy to murder against the former Prime Minister were immaterial as compared with the greater threat of instability in Asia. Accountability seemed to be a farce when it appeared that Pakistan was about to deprive itself of the only decent leader it had thrown up since Mohammed Ali Jinnah fought for the country's existence. It was of course, questionable whether in view of the dramatic changes which had occurred since Bhutto himself was ousted, it would be too late to re-float a contented Pakistan and, of course, whether or not Bhutto would be in a position to do so, now that things had substantially altered since his departure from the political scene. Some thought he would return angry and vindictive; others that he would merely pick up where he had left off. But indicative of the sense of desperation and the limbo in which Pakistanis found themselves, they were looking to the re-emergence of a leader who would be dead within two months of the announcement of the verdict.

Bhutto himself had claimed that his future and the death of Pakistan were both at stake. Tragically, only with his death could this claim be put to the test.

12
THE FINAL ACT

The confidence which Zulfikar Ali Bhutto reposed in the Supreme Court before Christmas was swiftly shattered by the verdict given on Tuesday, 6 February 1979 at 11 a.m. By a majority decision the court dismissed the appeal of the former Prime Minister. The decision was split 4–3 in favour of dismissal. The judges who upheld the verdict of the Lahore High Court were the Chief Justice, Mr Anwarul Haq, Mr Justice Akram, Mr Justice Chauhan and Dr Naseem Hassan Shah. Their vote was just as Bhutto's supporters had predicted long ago when the other two judges disappeared one by one. Those who opposed the verdict, giving a clear acquittal, were Mr Justice Safdar Shah, Mr Dorab Patel and Mr Justice Haleem — the judge who had remarked 'all's well that ends well' at the end of the appeal.

The Chief Justice read out a fragment of the overall judgment — one page of a few lines stating that the appeals were dismissed and the sentences recorded by the High Court were 'upheld and confirmed'. It was over in less than a minute. Only the appeals of Bhutto and Mian Abbas, the man who retracted his statement and then retracted his retraction, were dismissed by a majority decision although no one knew until later which way the voting went. The appeals of the other three confessing accused were dismissed by a unanimous decision.

Journalists of the various news agencies rushed out of the packed court to get the verdict to the outside world within record time. They had come from all over the world to hear the judgment and along with a few of the regular spectators were given entry passes to the court. Before the judgment was announced the atmosphere was tense and solemn. At the beginning of the proceedings a bearded man in his early thirties got up, dressed in army uniform (as it turned out in disguise), protesting that 'If Bhutto is punished, I will not spare any general's life'. He was quickly removed. His military uniform had helped him to reach the court room despite heavy security arrangements, the authorities said.

As before, traffic was diverted by the police and the Mall leading to the Supreme Court was empty of cars except for police vehicles and jeeps. There were even more police than on the day of Bhutto's appearance in the Supreme Court. A few expectant opponents and supporters of Bhutto waited outside the closed iron gates. Some pleaded to be allowed entry. Photographers and cameramen waited to snap anything of interest. Denied important personalities like the lawyers, who went in by the back gate, they ended up taking shots of the journalists as they darted in and out.

After the speedy announcement of judgment the proceedings dragged on whilst the defence asked orally for permission to lodge a petition to review the judgment. Meanwhile outside there was confusion as all the policewomen at the court gates were quickly hustled into a van which went at top speed down the Mall. Some said that a group of women had organised a protest march in the middle of Rawalpindi, but in fact the policewomen had been summoned to return Begum Nusrat Bhutto to house arrest. Tuesday was the day she always visited her husband in jail and from early morning she had been requesting permission to see him from the jail authorities. Rather than blank refusal, excuses like 'there is no car', 'there is no escort' were given to her. Finally, regardless of whether or not a car was given to her, or an escort, she took her own car and drove to the jail. Unsuspecting, the jail authorities let her past the gate and she reached her husband, spending about twenty minutes with him until the policewomen caught up with her and took her somewhat roughly back to house arrest in Islamabad.

Some people cried at the announcement of judgment; many were incredulous that the authorities could still entertain ideas of hanging the former Prime Minister. They kept thinking of the two judges who were on the bench and who, if they had remained, might have cast their votes in favour of dismissing the appeal. Then it would have been 5–4 in favour, as anticipated at the outset. Instead, they were left with 4–3 against. It was also said that even a 4–4 split would have made the death sentence impossible.

Security measures were even more extensive than before the judgment in March the previous year. Schools and universities were closed. Supporters were swept into jail: official figures recorded hundreds; PPP supporters said it was thousands. The police worked from new lists of Bhutto's supporters, concentrating on those who had come forward to replace those already in jail. One security measure ordered by the government of Punjab was for all 7-mm rifles in the province to be handed in by 15 February. Army personnel and government servants were exempt. The weapons would be returned at an unspecified time.

Mainly on account of these stringent measures there was very little protest. A few burnt buses and a procession or two were visual signs that the judgment was not welcomed by the people. There were a few acts of sabotage and stoning incidents in Karachi. In Sind there was an unsuccessful attempt to breach the walls of an irrigation canal. But it was not the sort of movement that could overturn the verdict. Many of Bhutto's supporters were disappointed at the turn-out. Why don't they come out on the streets? they asked. Possibly the answer to this was that people felt their protest was futile against the might of the judiciary and executive combined. They were prepared to fight but they needed direction to know how to fight — they needed a call. Going out on the streets merely to get put in jail seemed to achieve nothing. They too, had their families to look after. Others also said that they feared they might jeopardise the position of their leader by such demonstrations on the streets, which would inevitably lead to violence.

The judgment document was considerably longer than that of the trial. The latter was 405 foolscap typed pages; the judgment in the appeal was 1,500. The casting vote of the Chief Justice against Bhutto brought him so near and yet so far from release. Anwarul Haq, as the main architect, wrote nearly 830 pages; the other three judges of the majority merely indicated their agreement. As there were dissenters amongst the judges,

their views were also included. 670 pages were devoted to them
— 441 written by Mr Justice Safdar Shah; 221 by Dorab Patel;
and a few supplementary pages by Haleem, who expressed his
agreement with Safdar Shah. Two very contradictory views
emerged: on the one hand those upholding the death sentence
were quite happy to accept the prosecution's case; on the other,
the dissenters believed that it was not sustainable and ordered
the appellants to be released forthwith unless they were to be
detained on some other charge. Safdar Shah wrote:

'I have not the slightest doubt in my mind that the prosecution has totally failed to prove its case against Mr Bhutto and
Mian Mohammed Abbas.'

He made it quite clear that his reasons for convicting the
other three were not because he believed the prosecution story
but because of their own confessional statements.

Refuting the charge that Mahmud could have conspired with
Bhutto to perform the murder, amongst other examples Safdar
Shah relied upon the illustration of the conspiracy of the
brothers to kill Joseph, contained both in the Bible and the
Koran, which, because of spontaneous agreement clearly was a
conspiracy. An agreement, or for that matter an agreement of
criminal conspiracy, has to be the product of 'spontaneous and
free volition', he wrote. In the murder case it clearly was not.
Safdar Shah concluded with regard to Masood Mahmud that
'he has evidently trampled on his own credibility as a witness
and so,' he said, 'how can any court believe him?' In the opinion
of the dissenting judges this applied to the whole prosecution
story.

The majority decision, however, was that Bhutto was guilty
and that he alone had the motive to want to kill Kasuri, whose
speeches in the National Assembly showed that he had 'a flair
for pungent speech'. 'There is also voluminous oral and
documentary evidence,' wrote the Chief Justice, 'to show that
after the murder Kasuri was kept under special surveillance and
reports of his activities and utterances were being submitted to
the former Prime Minister.' He maintained that the investigation was not properly conducted because of the interference
of Saeed Ahmed Khan and Abdul Hamid Bajwa, following the
prosecution case. The Chief Justice also described how efforts
were made by Bhutto to bring Kasuri back into the fold of the

PPP as opposed to Kasuri taking this action independently, and he referred to this as a 'subtle campaign' initiated by Bhutto.

He explained the mystery of the spent cartridges by saying that there were 'strong indications' that they '*might* have been replaced'. Like the prosecution, the majority judgment was only able to rely upon conjecture. In its opinion, the testimony of approvers and witnesses alike was satisfactory and sufficient to condemn the former Prime Minister.

The Chief Justice referred to the use of the FSF for 'political vendetta' as 'a diabolic misuse of the instruments of State power as the head of the administration', echoing the condemnation of the Lahore judgment. The majority judgment also said that there was 'absolutely no support' for the contention that the case against Bhutto was politically motivated because of an international conspiracy, as Bhutto had alleged. He also rejected suggestions that the Lahore High Court Trial had been biased. 'Any omissions, errors, irregularities or even illegalities that have crept in were not of such a nature as to vitiate the trial,' he wrote, conceding perceptively that it was an 'unprecedented trial'.

Politically speaking, people were not surprised at the verdict; legally they were. More so, since the authorities appeared to have no qualms about hanging the former Prime Minister on a split verdict. Whereas the defence said there was no precedent for hanging a man on a split verdict, the prosecution said there was. The majority decision was highlighted in the press and the authorities even seemed proud of the difference of opinion. General Zia said that it illustrated the independence of the judiciary.

Mr Bhutto was formally notified of the dismissal of his appeal at 2.15 p.m. on the day following the verdict, but he had already heard unofficially from various sources. The first to tell him were the prison guards who tauntingly said that his appeal had been unanimously dismissed. Thereupon they removed the table, chairs, medicines, books and the heater in his cell as if he were to be hanged at once. When it was apparent that this was not the case they were restored to him. Bhutto was as calm as if he were about to resume political office rather than be hanged for murder. But he was preparing, for the time being prematurely, for death. He refused medical treatment for his gum complaints and stopped taking the drugs prescribed for him by the government doctors when diagnosis had been made that he had chronic gastritis. To the doctors who came to visit him Bhutto said, 'I am grateful to you doctors that you came, but I hope you don't mind if I say that there is a time for everything. There was a time when I needed medical care and I demanded it but it seems that the time is now over.' It was later reported that he spent the time accorded to the doctors — ninety minutes or so — reminiscing, saying that he would leave the final judgment on himself to history.

Bhutto believed the split verdict had regional implications and even said that he would have preferred to have been convicted by a unanimous decision in the national interest rather than a split one along provincial lines. However, the fact that three judges had acquitted him proved, he believed, his innocence. 'My honour is vindicated,' he said. 'I have been found innocent by three of the judges in very clear terms.' 'And,' he declared, 'an innocent man does not ask for mercy.' Bhutto had always made it clear that he would not ask for mercy and he was abiding by that resolution. But many people thought one of his relatives might — more especially his aged uncle Nabi Baksh Bhutto, the father of his cousin Mumtaz Ali Bhutto who lived in a Shangri-la type house in Sind, nineteen miles from Larkana. For the first time in the proceedings, donning western clothes, he appeared in court when the matter of the review petition was raised.

Bhutto had seven days to file the review petition although there was argument that in fact thirty days should have been permitted. The lawyers, summoned from the various parts of the country in which they had resumed their practices, moved back to Flashmans, virtually into the same rooms they had occupied earlier. Bakhtiar stated that there were 'numerous grave and serious instances of misreading of evidence on the record, misappreciation of facts and misapplication of law, resulting in a grave miscarriage of justice' in the judgment. The task of the review petition was to pinpoint these errors. But Bakhtiar also feared the petition would be dismissed out of hand. 'I am not an expert in filibustering,' he said, 'but I need two or three months to argue these points.' Most, however, agreed that two or three months were needed for a change in the political situation rather than a change in the minds of the judges. It seemed unlikely that having accepted the arguments of the Lahore court they would concede they had made errors in their own judgment. The defence took the verdict in their stride but they were bitterly disappointed at the majority judgment.

The lawyers requested four copies of the judgment so that they might all be in a position to examine it. One was supplied. One of the secretaries of the team, Mr Peter Jilani, was despatched to photocopy it. Thereupon he and the owner of the photocopying machine were arrested. Mr Jilani was subsequently accused of having a hand in the distribution of a 'People's Party White Paper' which castigated the military régime. He was accordingly imprisoned in a jail in Rawalpindi and then transferred to Attock jail.

The lawyers worked on the review petition night and day. The day before its submission they were up until 5 a.m. Copies were also made to give to the journalists who hovered around Flashmans, anxious for the latest news.

Lest the other secretary be apprehended while photocopying, a machine was brought to one of the rooms in Flashmans. The petition was 97 pages long and the defence believed it pointed to the main errors they detected in the majority decision of the judges. However, much of it once more re-stated the defence's case. The defence believed that the judgment of the Chief Justice side-stepped the issues which they had raised and did not answer their arguments. For instance, the paragraphs relating to Bhutto being a Moslem in name only had been expunged. But the next paragraph which stated that 'the principal accused is thus liable to deterrent punishment' remained. If the foregoing paragraphs were no longer part of the judgment should not the basis on which the accused was thus liable to deterrent punishment be reconsidered? asked the defence.

The petition was presented on 13 February. The court met on the 14th. Although the court granted a stay of execution while the review petition was to be discussed, no fixed time was given. Bakhtiar requested the customary thirty days but it appeared that once the petition had been handed in, the 30-day entitlement lapsed. Bakhtiar's submissions that he needed more time to examine the judgment did not hold water with the

Chief Justice, who answered testily:

'You have filed a petition of 97 pages. All the seven judges have gone through your grounds. It shows an application of mind to almost every paragraph of the judgment so it is not correct for you to say that you have hardly studied it. You and your colleagues have examined it with a fine needle [sic].'

The date for presenting the arguments for admission of the review petition was fixed for the 24th.

This date was also given by the Supreme Court to hear a contempt petition brought against foreign journalists for highlighting the nature of the split in the verdict, with the four judges from the Punjab upholding the verdict and the three non-Punjabis calling for acquittal. The authorities were angered that the foreign press, particularly the BBC, had publicised the fact that the voting was split on provincial lines. Zia himself said that if such comments were made about judges being from England, Scotland and Wales this would not be accepted in Britain. Other newspapers which came under attack were the *Guardian*, the *Daily Telegraph*, the *Spectator* and *Newsweek*, as well as Reuters News Agency. The resident AFP (Agence France Presse) correspondent, although making identical remarks, was not attacked, probably because the lawyer who lodged the complaint did not take the trouble to have AFP's reports translated. As it was, he had not obtained copies of the articles but merely of the telexes sent from Pakistan, which the journalists complained was a breach of the privacy of the postal service. The lawyer's remarks to the journalists were most uncomplimentary, calling one a characterless mercenary and alleging that another was in the pay of the defence lawyers in a conspiracy against the judiciary.

The contempt petition also condemned the whole team of defence lawyers and the Central Executive Committee of the PPP, which had held an emergency meeting three days after the verdict. It had passed a resolution stating that a dagger had been put into the heart of the federation by the judgment, as well as criticising the campaign of vilification and character assassination against Mr Bhutto as the 'most obscene, blatant, poisonous and unconscionable campaign'.

As it happened, the foreign journalists were let off the hook. The court appeared only interested in their comments where it was stated that their information came from the defence lawyers, more especially Mr Yahya Bakhtiar. On these grounds, it was alleged that the defence lawyers had led the foreign correspondents astray by feeding them with the theme of provincial bias in the judgment. When the petition was brought up in court the Chief Justice stated that their reports were undoubtedly 'tendentious' as they put forward the idea that the verdict reached was motivated by the 'origin of domicile' of the justices concerned. They were warned as 'educated and enlightened' persons that they should respect the institutions of Pakistan as long as they remained in the country. In the original contempt petition the lawyer, Mr Habib ul Khairy — a man with a beard who looked like a priest in the black smock coat which he wore to appear in court — had even said that the foreign correspondents might attempt to leave the country, and called for their passports to be impounded, which action the court deemed unnecessary. One of the correspondents — Mark Tully of the BBC — stood up in court and said that he took great exception to the assumption that he might not be prepared to face the charge against him, and said he had come from India especially for the occasion. After the dismissal of the contempt petition, Mr Khairy appeared almost apologetic to the foreign journalists and liberally handed out copies of their contempt petitions to them. His position did not appear enviable. He was the same lawyer who had drawn attention to the publication of court material before its submission to the court, at the time Bhutto's Rejoinder was due to be presented in September of the previous year. Even the foreigners thought that his contempt petition against them was made on behalf of the Government, because of the access he had been given to use their telexes.

But the defence lawyers and members of the Central Executive Committee were sternly reprimanded and told to make a reply to the accusation within four weeks. The justices let the foreigners off, but were not prepared to be lenient towards their own people.

*

The authorities objected strongly to the flood of clemency appeals which inundated the President from all over the world.

General Zia dismissed them lightly as a 'trade union activity', stating that 'all the politicians are asking to save a politician but not many non-politicians have asked me for clemency'. Zia's attitude to mercy appeals in general appeared indifferent — in less than two years of martial law he was reported to have received 400 mercy petitions from condemned prisoners and to have rejected every one of them. He kept talking of the supremacy of law which applied to all men, high or low, rich or poor, and it was almost as though the more mercy appeals he received on behalf of Bhutto, indicating his stature as a former Head of State, the less notice he would take of them. Delegations also arrived from certain Middle East countries to plead for the former Prime Minister, but Zia appeared impervious. The Prime Minister of Turkey who had offered exile to Bhutto was apparently dissuaded from making his clemency appeal in person. A country conspicuous by its absence of appeal was Saudi Arabia. Bhutto supporters looked longingly to this influential Arab state, stating that if only it would appeal, Zia would have to take cognisance of the request from such a powerful Moslem state. Finally the appeal from Saudi Arabia came; yet automatically, people began to doubt its sincerity. People suspected that Saudi Arabia made the appeal to annoy Zia because of the number of Pakistanis who were entering Saudi Arabia illegally on the pretence of going to Mecca on pilgrimage. King Khaled had adopted a programme of repatriation when Pakistanis without the proper papers were apprehended, but apparently part of the trouble was that the Saudi Embassy in Pakistan itself had been selling visas at exorbitant rates, making a handsome profit. When the Pakistanis who were repatriated complained that they had bought what they considered were valid visas, the Pakistani Government instituted an enquiry which brought them close to exposing the Saudi Embassy. For a while it was reported that Zia would not meet the Saudi ambassador. And so in retaliation, people said Saudi Arabia decided to annoy Zia by making the mercy appeal for Bhutto.

This was all behind-the-scenes talk, difficult to verify, but it served to dampen the enthusiasm of Bhutto supporters, who believed that finally Saudi Arabia had come out in favour of Bhutto and that with such an appeal the life of the former Prime

Minister would have to be saved.

To counteract the impact of the clemency appeal, reports appeared in the newspapers that the clemency appeals were an interference in the internal affairs of Pakistan or that, worse still, they were Zionist-inspired, which was an obvious tactic to put Arabs off appealing for Bhutto's life and to detract from the *bona fide* quality of the appeals. Publicity was also given to appeals by organisations and political parties which called for the sentence to be carried out, which seemed intended to smother those in Pakistan which had asked for clemency. Notable among those who called for the verdict to be implemented was Kasuri himself.

Nonetheless, appeals continued to flood in from heads of state. President Carter of the U.S.A. said he would strongly disapprove of the sentence being carried out; China sent two appeals. Brezhnev, speaking for the Soviet Union, called for mercy. The British Prime Minister, James Callaghan, said that he believed the consequences of clemency 'and General Zia is a very wise man' would be more beneficial to Pakistan than carrying out 'the strict application of law'.

Others did not think so. One senior military man was reported as saying, 'Hanging Bhutto will be a danger. Not hanging Bhutto will be a disaster.'

Amongst those who appealed from abroad, no one appeared to be in a position to point to the injustice done to, and the innocence of the former Prime Minister. Many prefaced their appeals by pointing out that clemency was asked for on humanitarian grounds. It was a clear indication that very few abroad had followed the proceedings carefully enough to give a strong value judgment on the legal aspects — if they had, it was thought, their appeals might have been phrased somewhat differently.

An eloquent and enlightened letter came from the ex-President of Pakistan, Fazal Ellahi Chaudhry, a Bhutto appointee but kept on by Zia until he himself assumed the presidency in September 1978. The letter released to the foreign press was, however, censored by the Pakistani press. Although Zia was apparently too busy to see the former President he was obliged to read his advice. 'Executing Bhutto would threaten Pakistan's independence, integrity and sovereignty,' Chaudhry wrote. 'It would aggravate instability in the sub-continent area. Today the spectre of further catastrophe is ominously visible on the horizons,' he said, referring to the time when the country was last dismembered in 1971. 'The execution of Mr Zulfikar Ali Bhutto can provide much more than a detonation. The subdued reaction can become vocal and ultimately turn militantly violent. The resultant chaos will certainly fulfil the wishes of national enemies.' Chaudhry referred to the fact that the judges who upheld the verdict were from the majority province while those who acquitted Bhutto were from the smaller provinces as an 'unfortunate coincidence'. But he said that highlighting such a fact was 'deplorable'. However, he could not deny that the 'peculiarities in the Supreme Court judgment were too glaring and solid to be ignored'.

Chaudhry's letter reminded people that there was a time when he was President after the verdict in Lahore when he could himself have commuted the sentence outright. Many wondered, however, in view of the letter, whether with the split-verdict decision in the Supreme Court Chaudhry would have carried out the sentiments expressed if he had still been President, or whether he would have been pressurised into following Zia's unrelenting course of action. It was felt that Chaudhry's letter would bear no more weight than the appeals of other foreign heads of state. It appeared that Zia would not even pay lip-service to them.

Busy dealing with the introduction of Islamic laws which he conveniently did four days after the verdict — as it were to distract the attention of the people — Zia calmly protested that nobody was above the law, however big he happened to be. 'I may not have given anything at all to this country,' he said, 'but I have given them one thing. I have given them the rule of law.'

He did not think the review petition would come to anything. 'It can't be a matter of fact which can be brought up so Mr Bhutto's lawyers will have to think hard because the Supreme Court took what, nine months? ten months — and in ten months if they ignored a matter of law, I am afraid there must be something fundamentally wrong,' he said in yet another interview with a foreign correspondent.

Momentarily, Zia did not seem to wish to take the sole responsibility on himself and it was announced that when granting mercy came into his domain, he would submit the decision to the senior generals and his Cabinet for discussion. It also seemed clear that he would not be anxious to do the deed and then be ousted by them, which is what many people suspected might happen with yet another *coup*. Briefly, therefore, Bhutto's supporters saw a ray of hope; even if Zia was set on seeing Bhutto dead, maybe not all his Cabinet would concur. But it was shortlived. Zia soon denied ever having announced that he would consult his colleagues.

After the judgement many people predicted that the majority judgement had pronounced the death sentence on Pakistan. Benazir and her mother were secluded even more from contact with the outside world. Soon after the decision was given they were notified that they were going to be moved from the house in Islamabad to a 'rest house' in Sihala, about fifteen miles from Rawalpindi on the road to Lahore. They were told that it was not necessary to bring bedding, food or heating since all would be provided. There is a comfortable rest house at Sihala and they anticipated that this was where they were destined to go. Instead they were taken to a remote government building, perhaps once a rest house but more latterly government offices — up a winding, bumpy road difficult to reach and easy to cut off. The building was surrounded by barbed wire and police camped in the grounds. The night they were moved was very cold; none of the promised facilities were there and so servants had to be sent back to the house to procure the bare essentials. The rooms were sparsely furnished and smelt of urine. Luxury furniture like bookshelves had been locked into another room.

But both of them retained an unusual optimism. Mindful that they had possibly been brought there so that they would be inaccessible from the people if and when the death sentence was carried out, Benazir managed to say that if it had been kept up, it would probably have been very beautiful. 'A bit like Murree,' she said. She took it in her stride that it was probably also an effort to humiliate them further. 'Even if they go so far as to hang my father,' she said, 'they will never take away his genius, his place in history ...'

She spent the first day scrubbing walls and later improved her room by pasting up pictures. She had her pets with her, a dog and four cats, upon which she lavished great affection.

*

Hafeez Pirzada, once accepted as Bhutto's counsel, busied himself with independent petitions which he hoped would improve Bhutto's position. One of these was for Waheeduddin and Qaiser Khan to be allowed to hear the review petition. Without much consideration this was dismissed. In fact, Waheeduddin was more ill than Bhutto supporters previously believed. A trio of foreign correspondents went to Karachi to visit him and found that he had not even read the judgment. He showed little interest in the outcome of a case which he had heard for six months. Pirzada drew up another petition against the Chief Justice himself, stating his appointment was illegal. The petition complained about the abrupt termination of the previous Chief Justice's office at the end of September 1977, when he would not swear allegiance to the martial law authorities. But it took so long to be heard in the Supreme Court that judgment had already been given regarding the review petition, with the result that the petition became infructuous. As it was, no one believed that any judge would rule that the appointment of the Chief Justice was not in order.

Along with Pirzada's petition against Anwarul Haq holding the office of Chief Justice, Bhutto himself had something to say. In a long letter written to the Chief Justice on 3 March Bhutto gave his final blast of invective against the man whose mammoth judgment had condemned him to death. He once again enumerated all the misdemeanours of the Chief Justice which he believed had occurred throughout the appeal. Added to the acting presidency and the trip to Jakarta were Anwarul Haq's failure to give enough attention to Bhutto's complaints about his treatment in jail; the suppression of the Rejoinder amidst the wealth of government propaganda against Bhutto; Waheeduddin's departure; the insufficient time granted to him to file both his appeal and his review petition. He described as Anwarul Haq's 'masterstroke' his permission for Bhutto to appear in the Supreme Court as it were to atone for 'all the sins of omission and commission' in the trial and appeal. 'How wonderful,' he wrote. He castigated the judgment, stating that

'This earth has no place to bury the document you have drafted.' He also pointed to some background information, revealing a documented instance when Anwarul Haq back in 1972 explained to the Chief of Air Staff that Bhutto and his Government should be overthrown: an open indication of his 'pathological' hatred, as Bhutto described it. Bhutto, confident in the acquittal given him by three other judges, predicted that the Chief Justice would be 'haunted and tormented' until the last breath of his 'pitiable life'. Although Bhutto said that application would be made for the letter to be read in court, it never reached the court room.

Pirzada also met Zia. A few considered that this was Bhutto's final manoeuvre and that having claimed that the trial was politically motivated, he would accept a political solution in an effort to save his life. In fact the initiative was taken by Pirzada, not Bhutto. The press immediately tried to say this visit was a mercy appeal and consequently that Pirzada was rebuffed; they were ignorant, however, of the actual conversation which took place. Pirzada said categorically that he could not ask for mercy on behalf of the former Prime Minister but that he did want to put forward cogent arguments for not executing Bhutto. Although Zia maintained that the time for such arguments was after the matter had left the court, assuming the review petition were to be dismissed, he said channels of communication should be kept open. According to Pirzada, Zia also stated that Pirzada himself had a great future ahead of him. 'What do you mean?' asked Pirzada incredulously. 'If you execute Bhutto and I am not a coward, I shall put a bullet right here,' he said, pointing to Zia's chest. 'But if I am a coward I shall come to you, begging for you to put me in some jail to save me, otherwise the people will come and get me.'

Only a few optimistically believed that the meeting of the two men from opposing sides might in some way help to save the life of Bhutto when finally the matter left the courts.

On account of the hurried nature of the first review petition, additional grounds were furnished in an 80-page document. In all, over sixty grounds of complaint about the judgment of the majority judges were outlined, pointing out errors on the face of the record. Many of the grounds appeared to be a last-ditch effort to convince the judges that they had accepted wholly untenable evidence of the Lahore trial. Arguments were also presented with regard to the question of sentence which did not come within the scope of the review petition. Having lost the chance of acquittal which he had hoped for at the outset Bakhtiar was forced to lower his sights and accept that the former Prime Minister was now a twice convicted murderer in the eyes of the law. It was, therefore, in his client's interest to seek for a reduced sentence on the grounds that Bhutto at best could only be an abettor.

Tempers ran high; everyone was getting tired of what appeared to be the same arguments in different clothing.

'Tell us now the point you wish to make,' ordered the Chief Justice, almost shouting.

Bakhtiar received more encouraging words from Justice Safdar Shah, the judge of the minority. He urged him to point to the extenuating circumstances with regard to reduction of sentence — the fact, for instance, that the wrong man was murdered, he suggested, and that five men were to be hanged for one unintended murder. But he too, appeared to be tired of the seemingly endless submissions and was no doubt aware of the losing battle that was already lost.

'Be a little more penetrating and attentive to your argument,' he suggested. 'Kindly clarify the position.'

At times Bakhtiar asked assistance from the judges regarding what aspects he might enlarge upon.

'Some points might appeal to your Lordships,' he said, 'otherwise you will be lost in the jungle.'

Bakhtiar, often pressed for time, did not always have every point at hand. He was advised by Rehman to refer to his documents. The Chief Justice remarked approvingly that he was taking the advice of the advocate on record for the prosecution.

'Yes,' replied Bakhtiar, 'I'll take good advice from any devil — good advice is good advice.'

The Chief Justice, anxious to get in his quip, replied, 'Yes, better the devil you know.'

Rehman, unable to let the repartee at his expense go by

without his own contribution, thereupon remarked, 'Yes, he has been in the company of devils for a long time.'

Bakhtiar could not let this pass. Turning to Rehman and laughing at his own ingenuity, he replied, 'Yes, I have known you for a very long time.'

But little of the post-judgment period was coloured by the same joviality. From the defence's point of view they were grasping at the last straws offered to them by the legal mechanism before General Zia ul Haq could perform his own role and exercise his will. It was a tantalising hope to believe that the judges would reconsider their judgment. For the prosecution, it was merely tedious for them to have to hear the well-worn arguments of the defence when they knew they had won by the grace of one vote. Yet even then, they did not give time graciously. The prosecution objected to the three judges in the minority making comments, stating that it was not their judgment under review and that, therefore, they should keep quiet. However, after a bit of legal wrangling, nothing came of this objection. Bakhtiar made the observation that since the majority judgment had now been adopted as the judgment of the court, since all seven judges had signed it, which fact had been emphasised by the Chief Justice, then no judge could be barred from giving his opinion on the review petition.

Bakhtiar was also forced to admit what might have been a grave error in the defence of his client—the boycott. Regarding the death sentence he said:

'Supposing the accused person, through some bad advice boycotts the proceedings and does not produce evidence in his defence or he is made prejudiced against the court by some other person ...'

This was something which the majority judges wanted to hear.

'You should have started this case on 20 May on this point,' observed Dr Naseem Hassan Shah with a spark of interest.

Bakhtiar carried on what was obviously a painful topic for him, saying that regarding the quantum of sentence to be imposed this should be a consideration — 'that he never had a chance to make his defence for one reason or another.'

'Thank you,' said the Chief Justice. 'You have taken pains ... we will contemplate.'

Bakhtiar was given a last chance to make final submissions. They were tired. They asked for more time. Bakhtiar promised that if they were given extra time he could be more concise in his submissions. He jokingly told the story of the lover who wrote a very long letter to his girl friend with the apology that he did not have time to write a short one. 'You have to have time to be concise,' he submitted. But the Chief Justice only gave one extra day after the weekend.

Bakhtiar was so dependent on Ghulam Ali Memon that often he never bothered to check facts and law cases, trusting solely to Memon's knowledge. At times in court Memon, sitting at Bakhtiar's elbow, could be heard prompting and coaching him, passing him law books to read from and acting as an *éminence grise*. His prominence as a lawyer was recognised by both sides of the legal battle. On the weekend before Bakhtiar was due to make his last submissions, Memon was working on a final blow to be cast at the majority judgment, giving counter conclusions to those furnished by the judges. He called it his 'epitaph' to the judgment. He alone of the lawyers had read all the judgments and could see and pinpoint the contradictions voiced in the majority judgment. While dictating in the early evening he stopped at the end of a sentence, poised as if in thought. He repeated the last words he had dictated, 'the late Abdul Hamid Bajwa', as if trying to hold onto a sentence and an idea which was slowly slipping. But no more words came. He turned his head, indicating pain. 'Allah, oh Allah,' he cried. And within fifteen minutes he was dead, with those with whom he had worked for so many months standing by watching helplessly as their colleague breathed his last.

His death was a great loss, emotionally and psychologically, at a time when many believed the legal battle was already lost and the arguments they presented were an exercise in futility when the minds of the judges were already made up. Bakhtiar said that he felt 'paralysed' in the case, knowing that for Bhutto's sake they must not give up the final opportunity and must fight to the last.

The evening news on BBC informed many, including Begum Bhutto and Benazir, although Bhutto was left to read about it in the papers the next day. As soon as news of Memon's death spread, people flocked to Flashmans to pay their respects to the dead lawyer. Women came to weep and say prayers; men to offer condolences. The three prosecution lawyers, equally grieved, came to the hotel to pay their respects, emerging out of the darkness, right into the camp of the opposition. But in death there is no more battle to be fought, legal or otherwise, and Bhutto's supporters were heartened by their appearance. Only a few murmured, 'Why do the good people die? Why could it not have been one of them?' — forgetful that during the trial they had lost their Chief Prosecutor.

On the following morning Mr Justice Akram, one of the majority judgment judges, also came to pay his respects. All the lawyers went to Karachi to take the dead body back to the family and attend the funeral. Crowds came to the airport to see them off.

Memon's former master, A.K. Brohi, likewise grieved, wrote:

'To those who knew him it would be no information to say that he was a brilliant lawyer and an able advocate and above all, a gentleman par excellence. I will miss,' he said, 'that warm cordiality and enlightened help that I received from him both in my professional and personal life.'

He would not be alone. Memon's death proved how emotionally and physically demanding the appeal was.

The Chief Justice paid his respects to the lawyer who had died 'while still in harness'. 'One of Memon's greatest qualities,' he said, 'was his acute awareness that institutions far transcend the individuals who might be manning them' — a pertinent comment in view of his own controversial position. He concluded his remarks with his customary 'Yes. As life has to go on, yes, Mr Bakhtiar, let's start.'

Bakhtiar looked shaken as he stood for the first time without Memon at his side. 'I feel like a plane,' he began, 'whose engine has failed and I am just waiting to fall down. I relied so heavily upon him, I just cannot believe he has gone.'

Most of what Bakhtiar said on that final day was taken from Memon's last 'epitaph', highlighting the important contradictions made by the majority judgment, in particular with regard to weapons and ammunition. On the one hand the majority judgment agreed with the prosecution's theory that the spent cartridges *might* have been substituted; on the other, it accepted the prosecution's contradictory story that the cartridges were the same used for both attacks at Islamabad and Lahore to connect the two incidents. But, they said, there was no substitution at Islamabad. How, therefore, could the spent cartridges be the same and yet be substituted after one attack? asked Bakhtiar.

He pointed to some other errors on the face of the record: the mystery of cartridges in four places but two assassins had still not been resolved. In an attempt to do so, the majority judgment had conjectured:

'It is therefore, only natural that the two attackers inside the roundabout *might have* in their own way chased the target and fired from more than two places,' of which the accused themselves had made no mention whatsoever in their statements. It made the erroneous calculation that 10 cm equals 1 in. According to its calculations the spent cartridges were brought closer together, thus making it possible for two people to have fired the shots, but it also went contrary to the evidence and the site plans that spent cartridges were picked up from four places, making it appear they were scattered in as many as twenty-four different places.

The defence also pointed to the lack of corroboration of Masood Mahmud; the inconsistency of Ghulam Hussain; the majority judgment's claim that there was 'voluminous evidence' in the case but yet they had not come up with any evidence to show that the investigation *was* misdirected; the tainted evidence of Saeed Ahmed Khan and the inconsistency that on the one hand he was consciously interfering, on the other than he was an independent witness; the inability of Welch to corroborate. In so many instances the majority judgment gave the benefit of the doubt — the Big Benefit of the Doubt, as Bakhtiar said — to the prosecution. He continually maintained that Bhutto had not been proved guilty beyond all reasonable doubt.

He concluded his arguments with the separate issue on sentence giving the reasons for a lesser penalty to be imposed. There was no motive to kill the man who died; the appellant was not present at the occurrence; the conviction was based on the testimony of Masood Mahmud — the approver who had an advantage to be gained in deposing against the former Prime

Minister; three judges of the Supreme Court had acquitted him; the High Court awarding the maximum punishment had condemned him for not being a good ruler nor a true Moslem, which paragraphs had been deleted by the majority judgment; the Federal Security Force's role was doubted because of the ammunition; finally, he said, the law awarded two sentences for murder, death or imprisonment for life. If the lesser punishment were given, reasons must be furnished 'and there are several factors which call for lesser punishment, which read together show that this is the strongest case which calls for lesser punishment'. 'It is a question of discretion,' Bakhtiar pleaded. 'And', he added, 'according to the Islamic laws recently introduced into the country, the evidence of an accomplice is not acceptable. According to Islamic law, a witness who says a man is his enemy, or who has something to gain by giving evidence is not a competent witness.' The Chief Justice did not seem anxious to bring these new laws into the picture, since as yet they did not relate to murder. But Bakhtiar's point had been made. 'With these submissions I conclude my case,' he said, and sat down.

It was 17 March. A year ago on 18 March the death sentence had been awarded for the first time. It had taken a year to submit the appeal. Many felt it was all a wasted effort.

The learned justices of the Supreme Court only took a few days to deliberate on whether or not the review petition should be accepted or, more important still, whether reduction of sentence to life imprisonment came within its discretion.

But just before this second judgment was given, Pakistan celebrated 'Pakistan Day' — on 23 March — the day when in 1940 members of the Moslem League demanded the establishment of Pakistan. For Zia it was an occasion of pomp and pageantry with all the troops — about 1,000 men from the various provinces — lined up on the race-course at Rawalpindi, with Pakistan's weaponry in the background. Zia rolled up in a horse-drawn carriage lined with blue velvet. Addressing the troops he was once more going to speak to the nation. Finally, he made an announcement they had all been waiting to hear:

'I have accepted the recommendations of the Election Commission,' he said, 'and decided to hold the next elections insha'allah — God willing — this year on Saturday, 17 November. I hope they [the people] will be motivated by the spirit of Islam and return only virtuous persons as their representatives,' he said optimistically, in the warm sun of a March morning in Pakistan. He made it clear, however, that he intended to strike a balance before the elections between the powers of the President and the Prime Minister. As opposed to having a mere figurehead President, it was surmised that Zia would give greater power to the President and retain the office himself. Just how virtuous the representatives would be was another matter. Applauding the announcement of the date for elections, other political parties which had not joined the civilian government under Zia thought those members who had should forthwith leave. Wali Khan's party under the leadership of Mazari complained already of malpractices and irregularities in administration.

But the announcement of elections, coming the day before the judgment on Bhutto's review petition, seemed to be designed to draw the attention of the people from the fate of their former leader. As expected, the review petition was swiftly dismissed to a full but not packed court room. Yet there was an interesting change in the judgment. It was declared that it was 'unanimously' dismissed, which made many believe that the three dissenting judges had altered their opinions; in fact in a note added to the 150-page judgment, Dorab Patel made it clear that although Bakhtiar argued for nearly two weeks, 'he had failed to persuade the judges who pronounced the majority judgment of the Court, to revise the finding of guilt of the petitioner, it follows that the review petition *must* be dismissed'. Consistent with judicial dignity and the practice of the Court, Patel said it was not proper for him to make observations on Bakhtiar's submissions. This was a disappointment for those who had expected that the three dissenters would make clear their belief that the review petition should be admitted, once again indicating the 4–3 split. Safdar Shah looked angry and glum in court as Anwarul Haq announced the dismissal of the petition.

The judgment in the review petition was written by Akram. He met few of Bakhtiar's grounds, ruling that most of them would amount to re-arguing the case, which was not possible. Discrepancies over errors, like the calculation of 10 cm to 1 in., he believed did not matter because anyway the site plan was corroborated by the evidence of Ghulam Hussain, the approver whom they accepted as reliable. Likewise the ammunition question was resolved by the fact that all the seven judges had condemned three men of the FSF, thus indicating the involvement of the FSF in the attack. None of the errors pointed out by Bakhtiar were, Akram said, grave enough to have a bearing on the fate of the case.

Leaving a glimmer of hope, he concluded that 'the grounds are relevant for consideration by the executive authorities in the exercise of their prerogative of mercy'. Patel added to this, making it clear that the time for submitting that the sentence should be reduced was during the appeal, not at the review petition stage which was to deal with errors on the face of the record of the judgment delivered.

The defence maintained that it had not given sufficient coverage to the question of sentence during the appeal because they believed it was a clear case for acquittal. But it was a vital omission, although even then the four in the majority would probably still have upheld the death sentence. Now, instead of the reduction of sentence being within the discretion of the court, it was within that of the executive, which all along had maintained that it would observe the verdict given by the Supreme Court.

The time came for the agonising ticking away of the seven days allowed for the filing of a mercy petition. Bhutto, ready for death, took the dismissal of his review petition, according to Bakhtiar, 'very well'. He was not so optimistic as to believe that the recommendations given by the judgment regarding the relevant considerations for the reduction of sentence would carry any weight, unlike his defence counsel who had proclaimed that the death sentence was 'out' because of this recommendation. Soon they were all to realise that it was not 'out' at all. Bhutto stated that he had always expected to die in some revolutionary manner, fighting for justice and, he still believed, in the cause of the people.

In fact, with the dismissal of the review petition, the death of Zulfikar Ali Bhutto was a foregone conclusion. There was absolutely no indication whatsoever that the executive authorities were going to heed the advice proffered, that there were relevant considerations for mercy to be shown. However, Justice Safdar Shah, who had always been the most outspoken in his disbelief of the prosecution case, came out in the open and stated that the Supreme Court had given a clear lead to Zia to show mercy. With this statement given to some foreign journalists whom he met sauntering along a road in Islamabad, it appeared for a moment during those seven days as if the judicial suggestion were going to have some weight after all. But then the following day his remarks were virtually repudiated and Safdar Shah was severely reprimanded for making a 'statement' to the press. The people were informed that his remarks were his personal opinion and that he could in no way speak on behalf of the other judges. Whereas Safdar Shah had stated that he could not recall any instance in which the recommendation of the superior court had not been followed by the executive authority, a news item appeared contradicting this, stating that there was one such instance in the previous régime when Bhutto himself disregarded the recommendation of the court.

Bhutto's supporters believed that Safdar Shah's 'gallant' position in the cause of justice was the more remarkable since they recalled that he was the only judge who could have had a real grievance against Bhutto because of his own dismissal as Chief Justice of Peshawar High Court on account of the amendments regarding the retirement age made in Bhutto's régime. But his remarks came to nothing.

The statements which appeared in the press were also an indication of the thinking of the authorities. It seemed that if they had not been intent on carrying out the sentence there would not have been so much publicity to the effect that 'S.C. verdict supported', 'Zia urged to implement S.C. verdict', 'No clemency for Bhutto', 'Court verdict must be implemented', 'Bhutto deserves no mercy' ... Again prominence was given to the opinions of Kasuri who, through the newsprint of the press, could not hide his hatred of Bhutto. At all times through his statements emerged his criticism of Bhutto as a ruler. 'If Pakistan has to live, then Bhutto has to go,' he said. His invective was directed towards Bhutto's role in politics. To those who supported Bhutto, the items appearing daily urging that the verdict be carried out appeared indecent. They were just rubbing salt into the wounds.

In his death cell the former Prime Minister was being subjected to further discomfort. He was locked into his cell for
twenty-four hours with the commode for his toilet in the cell
with him. It was not cleaned and became odorous and infested
with flies. Visits from members of his family were reduced to
half an hour. Several relatives made the journey from Karachi,
Larkana or Hyderabad, where some of them had settled, to see
him before it might be too late. The bed was removed as well as
other personal effects including his razor, which meant that a
white beard grew on his pale face. A light bulb was left to burn
constantly, preventing him from sleeping on the mattress
which remained on the concrete floor, soaked by the recent
rains. It was surprisingly cold for April and heavy rain made the
outlook even more gloomy.

Benazir wrote a letter to the jail superintendent vehemently
objecting to the conditions. With his discretion, she said,
according to the jail manual her father could be granted certain
privileges. If they were not to be given to a former President and
Prime Minister of the country, then who were they for? she
asked angrily.

But the authorities would not budge. They issued a statement to the effect that Bhutto still enjoyed all the 'concessions'
previously granted to him. Unable to take food, with his teeth
and gum ailments untreated, Zulfikar Ali Bhutto was weak and
ill.

During the last week of his life his supporters were anxiously
exploring all methods to save his life. His senior defence was
drafting another review petition. The Central Executive Committee met for three days and issued a request for the sentence
to be commuted, describing Bhutto as one of those men who
had acquired 'institutional dimensions affecting the destinies
and aspirations of millions of human beings'. It was a polite
representation without the invective of former statements. But
many people saw it as a feeble attempt and believed they were
confirmed in their suspicions that the PPP — without the
Bhutto family — was merely a bunch of rather uninspired men.

Hafeez Pirzada also made a request for commutation,
although he and the PPP Central Executive Committee said
they did this without Bhutto's permission or knowledge. He
himself still refused to make a clemency appeal, insistent that

this was tantamount to confessing guilt. Many thought that the conditions under which he was kept were to break his spirit and make him write the few lines necessary to plead for clemency. But most realised by now that come what might, the authorities would never break the will of their former leader.

But a mercy petition did come from a close member of the family — from an elder half-sister of Bhutto — they shared the same father, Sir Shah Nawaz Bhutto — she at sixty-eight the eldest child, Bhutto at fifty-one being the youngest. She arrived from Hyderabad and virtually at the last minute, at 10.45 p.m. when the time for the filing of mercy petitions was due to expire at midnight, she handed her petition in at President Zia ul Haq's house. As an illiterate Sindhi woman she had had the petition translated into English. With amazing astuteness she raised several issues:

'His eminence emanates from him,' she wrote, 'and there had never been eminence which did not excite envy and malice. General, is it right, is it moral, is it fair to the people and the Army that such a man should be done away with?'

She concluded her representation to the President:

'You have promised to devote yourself to the great Islamic principles. Mercy and compassion are inherent in the Islamic system. I pray to Allah that in a magnificent gesture of Islamic magnanimity, you will commute the sentence against my only surviving brother.'

But it seemed at this stage that nothing would save the former Prime Minister. The drama which everyone feared was to be enacted for the past year, ever since the death sentence was first pronounced, was about to take place. More clemency appeals came as the foreign press reported that the hanging was imminent, despite official spokesmen saying that the mercy appeals were still being processed. Mr Callaghan, beset with his own electoral difficulties, sent a fresh appeal — the third he had made. Contradictory reports arrived regarding instructions given to family members: first that they were told to be present at the airport at Sukkur, 65 km from Larkana, on the morning of Wednesday, 4 April, then that they were not. But more ominous was a statement by Bhutto's cousin, Mumtaz Ali Bhutto, that the family graveyard near Larkana at Garhi Khuda Bux had been cordoned off by the police since the morning of the 3rd. He also said that his own father — Nawab Nabi Baksh Bhutto — had been told to be present at the graveyard, although again this order was withdrawn.

Begum Bhutto and Benazir, incarcerated at Sihala, awaited the fate of their 'Chairman'. Benazir was issued with another detention order as her three months' detention was up. It stated callously that because the review petition had recently been rejected 'it is apprehended that you will further resort to agitational politics as a final bid to secure the release of your father, posing a serious threat to peace and tranquillity and to the efficient conduct of martial law.' This time the order was for only fifteen days, which looked ominous. On Monday, 2 April, both she and her mother were to be taken together for their visit to the jail. Benazir was not well and so her mother said that she was willing to go alone unless, of course, it was the last visit, in which case Benazir would obviously make the effort. The authorities would not say one way or the other, merely that they would be taken some time the following day. It appeared clear to them that it would be the last visit. 'But we will be brave and not cry,' Benazir said. The expression on their faces as they emerged from the jail after an unusually long meeting indicated that this was indeed the last visit.

Even as they met, no intimation was given that it would be for the last time. It was left to Bhutto to call the jail officer and obtain the information himself; if such was the case he asked for an extended visit. The three-hour meeting in the cold, pitiful cell between the three of them was the culmination of twenty-one months of tragedy which had been visited on the family and, as many believed, on the whole people of Pakistan. Bhutto was calm and serene. He lit a cigar and talked; he kept a second cigar for the evening. They asked the jailers to be allowed to embrace him but the bars of the cell separated them and a wooden table was in front of the cell, making wife and daughter sprawl across it to hold his hand. When the time came to say goodbye, Bhutto, leaving them with a message to impart to the people when they were free, bade them farewell. With the jailers Benazir pleaded: 'Please I beg you to open the cell door so that we can kiss my darling father goodbye.'

They refused. The two women were taken back to Sihala to count each agonising hour as it passed before dawn — the time appointed for the hanging. Exhausted, at 2 a.m. they slept until 4.30 thinking that he would be hanged at dawn.

For anyone to face death it requires courage; for a man pleading his own innocence to face it in cold blood requires the strength of a giant. To his people Bhutto was a giant and it was for this reason that his enemies could not tolerate him. According to the government statement, from the time his family left him Zulfikar Ali Bhutto had almost another twelve hours of his life left until the jailers came to take him to the gallows. He wore his own clothes and the wedding ring given to him by his wife, Begum Nusrat. According to the press note, he was allowed to take a bath and shave and have his meals. The Holy Koran was recited 'loud and in chorus' by the other prisoners.

Initially, said the press note, the former Prime Minister showed some resistance but then went with the jail authorities to the gallows. It was 2 a.m. He had been hanged before dawn, contrary to jail manual regulations. To the people it seemed just one more indication that the authorities were aware that they were not dealing with an ordinary criminal, as they liked to maintain, but a former Prime Minister. Most assumed that the early hanging was to prevent crowds suspicious that the hanging was imminent from gathering outside the jail.

According to the official announcement the body was flown to Larkana on a plane which left Rawalpindi at 4 a.m. at just about the time expectant journalists were gathering outside the jail, anticipating the dawn execution. The body was taken at top speed to the airport in a large army truck which was seen backing up to the gates of the jail. The body of the former Prime Minister was taken back to the place of his birth in the heart of Sind, to be buried in the graveyard of his ancestors. Only a few of his relatives were allowed to be present, including his first wife, Begum Amir. A place was found amongst the marble tombstones near his elder brother, Imdad Ali. It was 4 April 1979, twenty-one months after the *coup d'état*, when all his troubles had begun. Now for him they were over.

EPILOGUE

News of the execution stunned and shocked the world. No one believed that the military authorities would go ahead with such unprecedented and indecent haste after the rejection of the mercy petitions. The shortest time in which a condemned prisoner has been executed after the rejection of petitions for clemency has been twenty-two days — the longest seven years. The *Guardian* leader expressed the sentiments of many: 'Death came to Bhutto not with the due panoply of justice, but like a thief in the night, a deed done shamefully, apprehensively and with desperation.'

Bhutto's lawyers were still busy drafting petitions on their client's behalf when he was abruptly removed from their jurisdiction. General Zia, amidst statements that he was still considering the countless appeals on behalf of the former Prime Minister and would not make a hasty decision, had already, with what looked to many like undeniable duplicity, given the go ahead for the secret operation to be accomplished before anyone could get wind of it. Bhutto should have had forty-eight hours' notice before his execution but was only informed of his impending death when his wife and daughter came to visit him for the last time. People even said that but for the fact that Benazir was ill the day before and could not pay her last visit, he would have been hanged the night before.

To add even more to the humiliations of the family, on the night he was hanged the three houses at Karachi, Larkana and at nearby Naudero where his first wife lived, were raided. An announcement was made the next day that 'top secret documents' had been found concealed in 'secret closets' in the bathrooms, 'inside mattresses and in hidden chambers behind large size mirrors and cupboards'. These apparently had not been found on previous raids. This confirmed suspicions that having dealt with Bhutto, the authorities could now be turning their attention to mother and daughter, to eliminate them, if not physically, then politically. Pictures of the former Prime Minister were forthwith not allowed to appear in the press; many feared it would not be long before the same happened to pictures of Begum Bhutto and Benazir, which still appeared daily in the pro-Bhutto press. Censorship became even more strict and more white paper than printed columns appeared in newspapers when an article concerned the late Prime Minister.

International reaction to the execution was hostile. 'By putting him to death at the end of a rope, General Zia and his colleagues have not only committed a far worse crime than could ever have been laid at the door of Mr Bhutto, they have surely guaranteed their exclusion from the community of civilised men,' wrote the *Evening News*. Other papers predicted the fate of the military. 'If ever the day comes when he [Zia] in turn is overthrown and faces a trumped-up charge — even perhaps the murder of Mr Bhutto — General Zia can be fairly certain of two things, first that he will be found guilty, and second that it would be a waste of breath to appeal,' said the *Daily Mirror*. Bhutto's sons in London said that they had buried a martyr. Rather than send messages of congratulations to the President, heads of State preferred to send condolences to the bereaved widow, Begum Nusrat. Still imprisoned in the police camp at Sihala, neither she nor her daughter Benazir were permitted the privacy or minimum comforts to mourn the death of Mr Bhutto until nearly two months after the execution. The French President, Monsieur Giscard d'Estaing, who had great respect for the former Prime Minister, expressed his deep emotion and sorrow over the execution. Soon afterwards a letter which Bhutto had written to Giscard d'Estaing secretly from jail the previous July was released in a French weekly magazine, *l'Express*. In it Bhutto not only expressed his gratitude for the concern of the French President over his present confinement, but also developed what the magazine termed 'certain aspects of his political thought and his vision of the world'. Amongst others, Syria paid recognition to Bhutto's services to the cause of Islam and requested the President to postpone indefinitely a visit planned for the end of the month. The authorities denied that there was any connection between the two but they were the only ones who would not accept the correlation.

To compensate for international disapproval and disgust at

the execution, the government-controlled press was obliged to churn out the statements of those of their supporters who approved of it, stating 'equality of all before law established', 'supremacy of law upheld', 'Bhutto's end a lesson for nation' and so forth. Zia disappeared from the public eye for a few days and then came out with a statement given over the telephone to a correspondent in London saying that 'he felt he had done the right thing' in allowing the execution of Bhutto. Bhutto's story was soon dropped from the papers after the appearance of a giant article entitled 'Death of a Traitor' which brazenly tried to set out how Bhutto would have been executed for treason if he had not been hanged for murder. The papers were then taken up with news about the impending elections and more about Islamisation.

In large prayer meetings — the only way the people could legally assemble in large numbers because of the political ban — stricken with grief at being deprived of their leader they offered prayers for his departed soul. The authorities appeared unable to tolerate reports that 'large numbers' attended and asserted that only a few hundred assembled. One press commentary made the pointed remark that out of 75 million people only 400 gathered to offer prayers, which most knew was a gross under-estimation. Inevitably the meetings had their political over-tones and the people shouted slogans against the military régime, calling the police 'Zia's dogs'.

The military authorities quelled this spontaneous show of support for the dead leader by the use of tear gas, lathi blows, imprisonment and very harsh penalties, including lashes. The women, who showed themselves especially militant, were shunted off to prison in trucks. Ultimately the people turned to violence, burning buses and throwing stones at the police in Rawalpindi, Lahore, Karachi and many other smaller towns in the provinces. But after a few days of firm action by the authorities it was proudly announced that calm prevailed in the main cities.

But beneath the surface the people were outraged and their anger was fed by stories which gradually emerged about what actually took place before the former Prime Minister was pro-nounced dead. Suspicions were aroused by the denial of the authorities of reports that Bhutto's last words were 'Oh God help me, I am innocent.' The authorities said that this was a figment of the imagination and Mr Khairy once again instituted legal proceedings against the two BBC correspondents who reported it. Later eye-witnesses testified in court that he made no such utterance. Other reports made people suspicious of the state Bhutto was in when he reached the gallows — some said that he walked boldly to the scaffold, others that he was carried on a stretcher. The idea that he had been severely beaten lodged in the minds of his followers to the extent that a party worker in Lahore filed a petition before the High Court for Mr Bhutto's body to be exhumed, claiming that Mr Bhutto was tortured before he was hanged and that he may have been 'murdered'. Suspicion was also aroused by the remarks of those who were permitted to see the face of the former Prime Minister in the coffin. 'He looked as innocent as a flower' said his first wife, Begum Amir, but many people felt this was not an apt description of the face of a hanged man which would inevitably have contortions of the face.

To put an end to speculation of this sort the Governor of the Punjab and a man close to Zia said in a statement to the press, 'It is rather immoral to even conceive that Mr Bhutto was tortured to death.' Nonetheless, the *Daily Telegraph* correspondent present in Islamabad said in his report: 'Senior public figures I have spoken to in the past few weeks seem persuaded that something went amiss that afternoon ... It is believed that on the eve of his hanging,' the correspondent wrote, 'Mr Bhutto was severely tortured in an attempt to extract from him a confession to the crime for which he was to be executed. It is claimed that the torture attempt failed, but that when he was taken to the gallows, Mr Bhutto was already half dead.'

The petition to have the body exhumed was dismissed; nor were the family willing to give the necessary permission, when quite obviously the authorities would not concede that there had been any torture. In London, Bhutto's elder son, Murtaza, received anonymous letters from staff at the jail and other reports from Pakistan to the effect that his father was tortured. The denial by the authorities, as the *Daily Telegraph* correspondent said, seemed certain to fuel further speculation. The way in which he died was fast becoming part of the legend of the man — hounded to the grave — who had once been their Prime

Minister. The struggle to save his life was over. But the battle to atone for his death was only just beginning.

*

It will undoubtedly be some time before a balanced appraisal of Zulfikar Ali Bhutto's place in the history of Pakistan can be given. There will be those who will obviously seek to keep alive the message and memory of Mr Bhutto, provided they are not prevented from so doing by the military authorities. Pakistan in the late 1970s has shown itself a very different place from what it was in the early 1970s. Gone is the desire to emulate the west; the whole area has seen a resurgence of the practice of the Islamic faith in its strict application, accompanied by a revulsion from western customs and habits.

It seems that one of the reasons why Zia felt himself on such safe ground was because of what was happening in neighbouring Iran, with summary executions being carried out daily. Great publicity was given in the Pakistan press to events in Iran, in particular the execution of the former Prime Minister — Amir Abbass Hoveida — and a transcript of part of his incomplete trial appeared in the newspaper. Zia's bloodless *coup* also looked mild compared with the revolutionary methods used to overthrow the Government of Afghanistan in April 1978. During his confinement Bhutto saw both the Shah of Iran and the late President Daoud of Afghanistan go: the one getting off comparatively lightly by going into exile; the other had no time for reflection, being shot on the night of the *coup*. Bhutto's fortunes lay in between the two. Right up until the moment Zia rejected the mercy appeals on his behalf there was the opportunity for his life to be saved. It was ironic that of all the Islamic laws introduced by General Zia, the ones relating to murder were not among them. As there is no death penalty for conspiracy to murder under Islamic law, Bhutto's life could well have been spared if he had been tried under these laws instead of the common law inherited from the British. He could even have been acquitted since, under Islamic law, the evidence of approvers is not acceptable.

Other people disheartened by the circumstances — in particular the lengthy appeal which lost them two judges and even the boycott which prevented defence material being brought on record — felt that his life could perhaps have been saved through the judiciary, although once his fate was in the hands of the military there was very little hope that Zia would in fact show mercy. People also looked further afield and blamed foreign powers for not exerting enough pressure to save Bhutto's life, if only to preserve a strong leader in a troubled area. In particular people felt that Saudi Arabia's role could have been far more influential. It was later said that the appeal for mercy had not come from King Khaled at all but merely from the Saudi Arabian Embassy in Pakistan. Nonetheless, the countless appeals for mercy were a tremendous boost and showed that of all the world's leaders, only General Zia did not think Bhutto should live.

Bhutto's confinement, which he was forced to undergo under immense physical and mental strain, did allow him to leave to posterity some of his thoughts in several legal documents, particularly the Rejoinder. This document shows the workings of a great mind under extreme hardship. It also supplies material in his defence. On the record, too, are the transcripts of his four-day appearance in the Supreme Court, when for the first time since the trial began, the former Prime Minister took pains to present his defence. There is also the mammoth and contradictory judgment of the seven judges of the Supreme Court. When those who support Bhutto are in a position to tell their own story, documents such as the judgment itself and Bhutto's Rejoinder will help them in their task. They will not have to look far to find those whom they consider responsible. The behind-the-scenes story is as complicated as the one revealed to the public eye: most of Bhutto's supporters are convinced that family connections and personal hostility clearly played their part. They believe that there was a great deal more to the downfall of Zulfikar Ali Bhutto than the simple conviction of the former Prime Minister for conspiracy to murder, when there were so many reasons why his life could have been saved. The fact that the other four confessing co-accused were not executed, either at the same time or soon afterwards, made the speedy execution of Bhutto appear even more suspect.*

* They were executed nearly four months later

What happens to the People's Party will greatly depend on the extent to which its members, in particular the new Chairman for Life, Begum Nusrat Bhutto, and her daughter Benazir are victimised and harassed. It is generally assumed that under their leadership the PPP would sweep into power if free and fair elections are held. The future of the PPP itself will also depend on the sincerity and loyalty of the people, high and low, to the memory of their leader. Those who believe in the greatness of Bhutto will revere him as a legend and use him as their inspiration in future conflicts in Pakistan. His faults will inevitably be balanced with his outstanding qualities. Bhutto was not a religious zealot or a fanatic; he was a modern man who wanted his country to progress, not as a subservient tool of the eastern or western power blocs, but as an independent Islamic republic which could confront east and west with a dignity of its own, without, however, having to denigrate western standards and culture, as is the tendency today. In time, the people of Pakistan — provided they are at liberty to show their true sentiments — will undoubtedly indicate which sort of government they would prefer. At any rate, the general feeling is that a repressive régime which does not have the support of the people will inevitably be overthrown.

INDEX